ELECTORAL BEHAVIOR IN THE UNITED STATES

Pat Dunham
Duquesne University

PRENTICE HALL, *Englewood Cliffs, New Jersey 07632*

#21081508

Library of Congress Cataloging-in-Publication Data

Dunham, Pat.
    Electoral behavior in the United States / Pat Dunham.
        p.   cm.
    Includes bibliographical references.
    ISBN 0-13-258559-6
    1. Elections--United States.   2. Voting--United States.   3. United
States--Politics and government--1945-   I. Title.
JK1967.D79   1991
324.973--dc20
                                                              90-31450
                                                              CIP

Editorial/production supervision and
    interior design: Shelly Kupperman
Cover design: Ray Lundgren Graphics, Ltd.
Manufacturing buyer: Bob Anderson

© 1991 by Prentice-Hall, Inc.
A Division of Simon & Schuster
Englewood Cliffs, New Jersey 07632

Printed in the United States of America
10 9 8 7 6 5 4 3 2 1

ISBN 0-13-258559-6

Prentice-Hall International (UK) Limited, *London*
Prentice-Hall of Australia Pty. Limited, *Sydney*
Prentice-Hall Canada Inc., *Toronto*
Prentice-Hall Hispanoamericana, S.A., *Mexico*
Prentice-Hall of India Private Limited, *New Delhi*
Prentice-Hall of Japan, Inc., *Tokyo*
Simon & Schuster Asia Pte.Ltd., *Singapore*
Editora Prentice-Hall do Brasil, Ltda., *Rio de Janeiro*

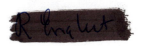

FOR   TIM

Contents

3 PARTICIPATION AND NONPARTICIPATION   40

4 POLITICAL PARTIES AND ELECTIONS   75

Preface

Elections are of vital importance in any democracy, and especially so in a nation with the broad franchise and free press of the United States. Our electoral contests nominate and elect officeholders, determine majorities in the U.S. Congress, offer opportunities for expression of public opinion, and help determine public policy.

National and state elections are incredibly important, and yet many U.S. citizens are woefully ignorant about how such elections operate. This is understandable, since the subject *is* complex. But one unnecessary reality makes things worse than they have to be—the useful information is often divided in such a way that it can rarely be gained from one source (or even from a few sources). For example, books about presidential elections may present nothing about congressional elections, or about voter attitude formation. This lack of easy accessibility to pertinent information imposes heavy costs on those who would try to be well informed.

This text addresses this problem for undergraduate students by taking a broad approach toward electoral behavior. We begin with an introduction that recognizes the changes that have occurred in national elections since 1960. The influence of the mass media, particularly television, is acknowledged. After this presentation of the subject matter's horizon, we turn to the basics of politics—beliefs, attitudes, and opinions. The development of attitudes, attitude change, influences on voting, and polling are explained. One fundamental attitude that is examined is whether or not one should care about or be involved in politics at all. Chapter 3 discusses who participates and who does not and examines the theories that attempt to explain why.

Chapter 4 describes the changing role of political parties in elections. The decline in power of political parties and their response are detailed. After this introduction to elections, Chapters 5, 6, and 7 present presidential and congressional elections from 1960 to 1988. Chapter 8 generalizes about state parties and elections. Finally, Chapter 9 addresses the topic of the classification of elections and the question of where the electoral system goes from here.

I feel that this approach ties together the topics that are essential for understanding elections and electoral behavior in this country, and I have without hesitation relied on the works of experts in these areas. Of course, no single book can be the final word on any subject, and each chapter includes a list of suggested readings for those who wish to pursue these topics further.

Finally, the issues covered in this book inevitably involve some controversy. I have included discussion questions at the end of each chapter to encourage faculty and students to address these controversies, and, I hope, to grapple with the larger question of what democracy in the television era means.

I want to express appreciation to my teachers, especially Michael Corbett of Ball State University, whose enthusiasm for political science was infectious. I thank colleagues Michelle Fistek and Charles Hanna for reading portions of this manuscript, and also students Susan Kosanovich and Christopher Reibold for reading the entire text. I also thank my former colleague William Markus for his advice. Any errors that may be found are, of course, my responsibility. I greatly appreciate the help I received from our department secretary, Janet White, from our student aides, Colleen Bradley and Christina Zigler, and from Mike Dunham. Karen S. Horton, my editor at Prentice Hall, was an immense help, and the comments of anonymous reviewers were invaluable. Thank you to Michael Corbett, Ball State University, Darrell West, Brown University, and Paul Blanchard, Eastern Kentucky University for their helpful suggestions.

I dedicate this book to my husband, Tim. Without him, it would not exist.

Pat Dunham
Pittsburgh, Pennsylvania

1

The Electoral Climate in the United States

DEMOCRATIC THEORY AND ELECTIONS

Elections have a special place in U.S. politics because of their importance in democratic theory. We do not all define democracy the same way, but our notions about democracy are greatly affected by the liberalism of thinkers such as John Locke, who argued that individuals possess rights and have claims against the government. Locke believed that government is based on a contract involving the consent of the governed.[1] He believed popular consent and involvement in government are necessary in order to check the power of government. Political authority resides in the people, even in representative democracy. Most of us have abandoned the notion that we can have a direct democracy in a country as vast and diverse as is ours, but political participation is, nevertheless, an essential feature of republican government, or representative democracy.

Revolutionary philosopher Thomas Paine also adopted the notion of government as a contract, but argued that it was a contract that only bound citizens with each other, not a contract binding citizens with the government. Citizens were free, in his view, to give the government direction through frequent elections.[2]

The following paragraphs will provide the reader with some idea of the complexity involved in defining democracy. For example, Kenneth Janda and his associates distinguish between procedural and substantive democracy. They define *procedural democracy* as involving "a set of normative principles that state how a government ought to make decisions."[3] Procedural democracy centers on the questions of who should participate in decisions, how much should each participant's preferences count, and how many votes are needed to make a decision. Janda and his colleagues maintain that according to ideal democratic theory, everyone should participate in governmental decisions, everyone's preference should count the same as anyone else's, and the majority—50 percent plus one more vote—should rule. Richard Pious adds more elements to this mix. His criteria include that each citizen vote for each elective office, that two or more candidates run for each office, that elections be scheduled at regular intervals, that the government not interfere with the campaigns of the opposition, that the government not coerce the voters into making particular choices, that those who win elections not be prevented by the government or the military from assuming office.[4]

Janda and his colleagues, argue, however, that in a representative democracy it is necessary to go beyond these principles. It is not enough to be able to vote and know that your vote counts the same as anyone else's; it also must be shown that the government is responsive to the public. They define *substantive democracy* as involving the substance of governmental policies, rather than decision-making procedures.[5] Substantive democratic theory emphasizes government guarantees of civil liberties and civil rights. (Political philosophers disagree on whether or not it is essential that government guarantee social or economic rights.) The importance of elections in substantive terms is in their impact on governmental policy.

E. E. Schattschneider argues that there are two classes of democratic ideas: those dealing with democracy as a moral system, and those treating democracy as a form of government.[6] As a moral system, democracy promotes equality, based on the belief that all human beings are of value, worthy of love:

> The love of people goes far beyond liberty, rights, equality, and justice. It is something positive, seeks the fullest possible self-realization; it contemplates *happiness*, overflows all differences, and creates the kind of *wealth* that can be produced only by people who enjoy their common participation in a community.[7]

Schattschneider writes that equality is as important for what it denies as for what it asserts. "It attacks all of the ancient structure of special privilege and says something about man himself, beyond all artificial contrived social arrangements and distinctions." Schattschneider holds that because democracy is an "attitude toward people," it is "never perfect or complete."[8] Its goals are therefore unlimited.

As a form of government, according to Schattschneider, democracy mandates a system of representation involving government by consent and by the election of candidates for fixed terms. More significant, Schattschneider believes that we begin with majority rule. Consensus, if it exists, comes later. The people who support a party or candidate may not all be supporting their choice for the same reasons. A given candidate may win an election, but not receive any kind of mandate from the voters, because their motivations are different. Schattschneider argues that to require consensus first would lead to stalemate:

> The Jeffersonian *begins with a government which governs and gets the consent of the governed* in order to continue to govern. The Jeffersonian does not wait for the people to assemble under a tree in the forest to decide to form a government. He is concerned about making an ongoing government responsible to the people.[9]

Schattschneider points out the difference between direct democracy and representative democracy, between government by the people and government by the consent of the governed. He argues that people want to leave government up to their governors, as long as they retain the power to hold their governors responsible. He is also careful to say that this goes beyond mere voting. He writes that "government can function only with the daily support and cooperation of the people." Democracy is work; in a sense "we vote every time we pay taxes, every time we stop at a traffic light, every time we listen to a TV documentary or turn off the set because we object to the commercials. . ."[10]

ELECTIONS BEFORE THE RISE OF TELEVISION

Our ways of going about the work of democracy in the United States have evolved as the country has grown and industrialized. Campaign styles that were prevalent at various stages in U.S. history have been studied by Alan R. Gitelson and his associates.[11] They found that a first "electoral party system" existed from the 1790s to 1824. This was an era when the masses deferred to economic and social elites. The franchise still was restricted (by property requirements, among other things), so mass participation in politics was limited.

From 1824 to 1860 we experienced an era of "mass politics." Under Andrew Jackson's leadership, the franchise was extended (to white males twenty-one years or older), and the masses began to identify with political parties. During the period from 1860 to 1896, campaigns were "militarist" in nature.[12] Political parties were strong organizations, analogous to armies. Voters were loyal troops. Charles Merriam and Harold Gosnell strongly relied on this analogy in their 1933 description:

> The party organization at the height of its activity consists of thousands of workers, regulars and volunteers, spreading the propaganda of the party, with its traditions, its policies and its candidates. At the center is the core of *seasoned veterans,* led by *commanders* skilled in the strategy and tactics of *political war,* the general staff in whose souls the noise and confusion and shock of *battle* raise no panic or dismay. Many of them sniff the battle from afar off and rejoice in it.

Around them are the larger numbers of the volunteers whose enthusiasm may be great, although in all probability of short duration.[13] (Emphasis added.)

Merriam and Gosnell called campaign oratory "a type of party warfare" and described the culmination of party propaganda as a "battle cry." Patronage workers were an "army of officeholders."[14] The analogy is apt. This was a time when the public took political parties and political duties seriously. Rates of turnover in office and other forms of participation (writing to politicians, signing petitions, and so forth) were high. There was no support in the political culture for independents.[15] Walter Dean Burnham wrote that

independents tended to be scorned as "traitors," "turncoats," or corrupt sellers of their votes. Thus rational party strategy and campaign tactics were overwhelmingly oriented to the "drill" and to the mobilization of the maximum possible number of known party followers at the polls.[16]

This militant style of campaigning was replaced from 1896 to 1932 by an "advertising" style, which relied heavily on the use of public relations techniques. The passionate commitment of the earlier period had died away, and voters had to be wooed by candidates. The advertising style of campaigning led subsequently into "mass media politics," which developed in 1932 and continues to the present day. This style, as its name implies, relies on television, radio, direct mail, and campaigning by telephone. Throughout these last two periods, voter loyalty to parties declined, and interest in candidates as individuals increased. Voters are no longer loyal troops; they are shoppers in the political marketplace.

The rise of television[17] certainly facilitated the advertising style, but this was not the only critical development that occurred. Political parties were weakened by many changes, some taking place as early as the 1890s. These changes include the introduction of the Australian ballot (as opposed to the party ballot), the use of direct primaries, the replacement of the partisan press with objective journalism, and the introduction of personal voter registration requirements.[18]

The Australian ballot took ballot preparation away from the parties and gave it to the relatively impartial government. Party ballots list only the candidates for that party, facilitating (if not mandating) straight-ticket voting. The Australian ballot lists candidates from all parties, according to the office for which they are running.

Direct primaries are an alternative to nomination of candidates through party caucuses. In the early years of our history, party caucuses were made up of officeholders, party leaders with experience in winning elections. Today's caucuses are open to all party members, but still are often dominated by party elites. Vote choices are often made by a show of hands, visible to all present. Primaries allow any party member (and in some states, nonparty members) to

SOURCE: Steve Lindstrom, Duluth News-Tribune. Copyright 1984. Reprinted with permission.

enter the privacy of the voting booth and help select the party's nominees. The results sometimes disappoint party leaders.

In this country, journalism was originally tied quite closely to parties. Printers made their political preferences known through the newspapers they printed, and some were rewarded with government printing contracts when their party gained office. As the population increased, however, publishers went through a "yellow journalism" period, sensationalizing reporting and sometimes even creating fictional stories in order to beat the competition. Later, as educational levels increased and as printing press technology improved to allow mass production, publishers turned toward objectivity and impartiality to reach a wide audience. Today, while the editorial columns of papers may reflect partisan biases, the news columns are virtually free of it.[19] Political parties do not find boosters in the press anymore.

Prior to personal registration, it was easier for people, especially newcomers in town, to vote. Parties capitalized on this, working hard to get every potential supporter to the polls. Today, to be eligible to vote, individuals have the responsibility to get themselves registered with the local board of elections, and in most places the deadline for doing so is well before election day. The efforts of party workers are wasted on the unregistered.

These developments robbed the parties of some important functions and helped make the electoral environment less militant. This in turn paved the way for other influences to rise up and fill the vacuum left by the decline of political parties.

ELECTIONS SINCE THE RISE OF TELEVISION

For many, the highlight of the 1960 presidential election was the series of debates between John Kennedy and Richard Nixon. These debates left an impression because they were televised, viewed by millions of people. Of interest, those who viewed the first debate on television believed Kennedy won, while those who listened to the same debate on radio believed Nixon won.[20] This was not the first presidential campaign in which the mass media played a role, but it was the first such campaign in which television may have made a difference for one candidate over another. Few voters changed their candidate preference as a result of the 1960 debates, but the election was won very narrowly, and the attractive televised image that Kennedy projected may have made the difference.

Campaigns have not been the same since the rise of television. This book is about the changes in national elections since 1960, including changes wrought by the mass media. Voters, candidates, and political parties have undergone transformations that have resulted from several causes—decline in political trust, the social upheavals of the 1960s, Vietnam, Watergate, delegate selection reform, campaign finance reform—and the media have had some role to play in each of these.

Today, well after the rise of television, political parties are weak organizations and voters are fickle, commonly splitting their tickets when they vote. Parties may be able to draw on volunteers from the interest groups they tend to join with, but often as not these interest group ties prove as troublesome as helpful to the political parties. (See Chapter 6 for a discussion of the 1984 election.) Instead of "seasoned veterans," parties are faced with the participation of amateurs—activists who care more for a particular issue or candidate than they care for the party. The "battle cry" today stems not from party propaganda but from phrases designed for 30- or 60-second television ads, phrases touting the candidate, not the party. Indeed, some scholars feel that the mass media have largely replaced political parties as the link between the governed and their governors.[21]

The increased use of presidential primaries is probably the most important change affecting the relative influence of political parties and the mass media. Prior to 1972, most delegates to the national nominating conventions were selected through mechanisms controlled by the parties such as state conventions and caucuses. Reforms promulgated by the Democrats after their disastrous 1968 national convention in Chicago changed this dramatically, and since 1972 a majority of delegates to both party national conventions have been chosen through primaries.[22] (See Chapter 4 for details.)

Primary elections impose costs on voters, and many choose to reduce those costs by relying on the media for guidance.[23] Since primaries are party elections, voters cannot use the simple cue of party identification in deciding how to vote. Sometimes there will be many candidates seeking the party's nomination, forcing conscientious voters to inform themselves on many individuals and issues. Not all voters, not even all conscientious voters, have the time or energy to educate themselves thoroughly. They rely instead on the mass media, particularly television, to help them sort out their choices. According to Richard Rubin,

> Primaries expand the nomination arena from one dominated by established party leaders to a more fluid and volatile combination of contesting political activists and ordinary party voters. They thus enable the press to serve as a crucial link between candidates seeking nomination and a party's rank and file. When all candidates run under the same party banner, the value of the party as a cue of voter information is virtually worthless. The press has moved into this vacuum to organize information, appraise candidates' qualities, and evaluate trends and outcomes, and the importance of its role in filling these functions—once the function of the party—has grown with the increase in the importance of the primaries in the nomination process.[24]

It appears, given the number of those voting split tickets (supporting both parties at different office levels), that many voters also are using the media to help them make up their minds in the general election.[25] This is not a problem for democracy if the media are capable of giving voters the information they need. Scholars disagree on the impact the mass media have in this context. Information is certainly readily available today, with our wide variety of newspapers, magazines, newsletters, and cable television channels, and with increased levels of education. Information can be instantaneously transmitted through television and radio. Television allows us to witness events thousands of miles away as they occur. It brings us candidate debates, providing us with an opportunity to hear positions on issues and to consider candidate qualities. With the rise of television and advertising style campaigns, however, the information transmitted to voters is often shallow, personality-oriented, and focused on the "horse race" aspects of the campaign (that is, events are explained merely in terms of who is winning and who is losing).[26] Included with some stories about issues, parties, and what James Fallows calls the "stakes in the game,"[27] the public gets many stories about gaffes, opinion polls, and whether or not the candidates have dyed their hair or changed the spelling of their names. Television encourages us to be spectators, not participants, and, unfortunately, most of us get most of our news from television. More important, the media in general do not perform and are not capable of performing the major function of parties: aggregating the interests of discordant groups.[28] Parties are not perfect either, but at their best they are capable of reminding us of the interests we have in common, inspiring members to join together for the good of all in the party. The media are incapable of doing any such thing (and were never intended to).

CONSEQUENCES OF THESE CHANGES

The uncertainties of the 1960s and the rise of television produced an electorate that is largely cynical and unresponsive. Only half of those eligible to vote in 1988 did.[29] Assassinations, the controlled Democratic nomination and chaotic national convention in 1968, politicians who promised peace and produced war, a reliance on opinion polls and marketing techniques to sell candidates, and the Watergate, Abscam, and Iran-contra scandals have reduced voters' feelings of political efficacy and their trust in government.[30] Continued efforts at reform, of both the nomination process and the financing of federal campaigns, seem destined to lead only to calls for still more reform. At the same time, however, interest groups of all kinds are proliferating, in part because of campaign financial reforms. These include not only corporate and labor groups, but also a host of issue-oriented groups (organized around the issues of abortion, nuclear war, the environment, neighborhoods, and so forth). Some of these groups have been instrumental in getting desired initiatives put on ballots and written into state laws. "Good government" groups such as Common Cause also thrive.

People seem more interested in televised news programs than they were twenty years ago. The news program "60 Minutes" is a ratings leader for the Columbia Broadcasting System (CBS), and "Nightline" is popular on the American Broadcasting Company (ABC). The networks also have experimented with early morning news programs. On cable, the Cable News Network (CNN) provides nothing but news, and the Cable Satellite Public Affairs Network (C-SPAN) provides viewers with the televised proceedings of the U.S. House of Representatives and Senate. Many communities have all-news format radio stations.

What is going on here? Are people turned off by politics or not? What are the implications of all this for democracy? These are not easy questions to answer because human beings are complex organisms, quite capable of holding contradictory views simultaneously. Chapter 2 will provide basic information about attitudes, beliefs, and perceptions. Campaigns, indeed all political activities, are aimed at influencing precisely these things.

SUGGESTED READINGS

ALGER, DEAN A., *The Media and Politics.* Englewood Cliffs, NJ: Prentice Hall, 1989.

ASHER, HERBERT B., *Presidential Elections and American Politics* (3rd ed.). Homewood, IL: Dorsey Press, 1984.

CROTTY, WILLIAM, *American Parties in Decline* (2nd ed.). Boston: Little, Brown, 1984.

EDELMAN, MARTIN, *Democratic Theories and the Constitution.* Albany, NY: State University of New York Press, 1984.

GRABER, DORIS, *Mass Media and American Politics* (2nd ed.). Washington, DC: Congressional Quarterly Press, 1984.

_____, *Media Power in Politics.* Washington, DC: Congressional Quarterly Press, 1984.

HARTZ, LOUIS, *The Liberal Tradition in America*. New York: Harcourt, Brace & World, 1962.
JOSLYN, RICHARD, *Mass Media and Elections*. Reading, MA: Addison-Wesley, 1984.
MCGINNIS, JOE, *The Selling of the President 1968*. New York: Pocket Books, 1970.
MILL, JOHN STUART, *Consideration on Representative Government*. New York: Bobbs-Merrill, 1958.
ROUSSEAU, JEAN JACQUES, *The Social Contract and Discourse on Inequality*. New York: Washington Square Press, 1967.
RUBIN, RICHARD, *Press, Party and Presidency*. New York: Praeger, 1980.

NOTES

1. Max J. Skidmore, *American Political Thought* (New York: St. Martin's Press, 1978), p. 13.

2. Ibid., p. 43.

3. Kenneth Janda, Jeffrey M. Berry, and Jerry Goldman, *The Challenge of Democracy: Government in America* (Boston: Houghton Mifflin, 1987), p. 37.

4. Richard M. Pious, *American Politics and Government* (New York: McGraw-Hill, 1986), p. 11.

5. Janda, et al., *The Challenge*, p. 40.

6. E. E. Schattschneider, *Two Hundred Million Americans in Search of a Government* (New York: Holt, Rinehart & Winston, 1969), p. 43.

7. Ibid., p. 43.

8. Ibid., pp. 52.

9. Ibid., p. 72.

10. Ibid., p. 77.

11. Alan R. Gitelson, M. Margaret Conway, and Frank B. Feigert, *American Political Parties: Stability and Change* (Boston: Houghton Mifflin, 1984), pp. 20–40.

12. Richard Jensen, "American Election Campaigns: A Theoretical and Historical Typology." Paper delivered at the 1968 meeting of the Midwest Political Science Association. pp. 2–10.

13. Charles E. Merriam and Harold F. Gosnell, *The American Party System,* revised ed. (New York: Macmillan, 1933), pp. 312, 313.

14. Ibid., pp. 316, 320, 333.

15. Walter Dean Burnham, *Critical Elections and the Mainspring of American Politics* (New York: W.W. Norton, 1970), p. 73.

16. Ibid., p. 73.

17. By "rise of television" I mean the increase in the number of households with television, the increase in the reliance on television for news, and the increased importance of news to television networks.

18. Burnham, *Critical Elections,* pp. 74–90.

19. Doris Graber, *Mass Media and American Politics,* 2nd ed. (Washington, DC: Congressional Quarterly Press, 1984), p. 97.

20. Richard Joslyn, *Mass Media and Elections* (Reading, MA: Addison-Wesley, 1984), pp. 1, 2.

21. William Crotty, *American Parties in Decline,* 2nd ed. (Boston: Little, Brown, 1984), p. 75.

22. Stephen Wayne, *The Road to the White House,* 2nd ed. (New York: St. Martin's Press, 1984), p. 12.

23. Thomas E. Patterson, *The Mass Media Election,* (New York: Praeger, 1980), pp. 174, 175.

24. Richard Rubin, *Press, Party and Presidency* (New York: W.W. Norton, 1981), p. 184.

25. Patterson, *The Mass Media Election.*

26. See Doris Graber, *Mass Media,* and Gary R. Owen and Nelson W. Polsby, eds., *Media Momentum: The New Hampshire Primary and Nomination Politics* (Chatham, NJ: Chatham House, 1987).

27. James Fallows, "The Presidency and the Press," in Michael Nelson, ed., *The Presidency and the Political System* (Washington, DC: Congressional Quarterly Press, 1984), pp. 264–281.

28. Patterson, *The Mass Media Election,* pp. 173–174.

29. "Dismal Turnout Trend Examined," *The Pittsburgh Press,* November 10, 1988, p. A21.

30. William H. Flanigan and Nancy H. Zingale, *Political Behavior of the American Electorate,* 5th ed. (Boston: Allyn and Bacon, 1983), pp. 171–175.

2

Opinion and Voting

INTRODUCTION

Attitudes, beliefs, and opinions are crucial components of political behavior, and are of crucial significance in a democracy. We will define these terms, discuss how attitudes and beliefs change, and examine the nature of opinions. Since polling—the measurement of opinion—is such a prominent part of national elections today, we will look at how polls are administered and analyzed, and some current political attitudes will be reviewed. Finally, we will examine the relationship between public opinion and democracy.

In many ways, this topic is at the heart of political behavior. Our perceptions largely determine our behavior—whether or not we vote. Further, our perceptions determine for whom we vote, whether or not we are partisans, whether or not we belong to an interest group, and whether we support or oppose the political system.

BELIEFS AND ATTITUDES

Beliefs are things we think are true. Beliefs may be descriptive ("the house is red"), evaluative ("red houses are good"), or prescriptive ("if you want to be happy, paint your house red"). They also can be incorrect—some of the things we believe are just not true. For example, many people are concerned about the role that political action committees (PACs) play in congressional election campaigns because they believe that the majority of contributions to those campaigns come from PACs. This is not true; the majority of contributions to congressional campaigns come from individuals. But beliefs are important because we think they are true, and we act accordingly. Beliefs originate in our own experiences and in things we have learned from others. Some of our beliefs are more *salient* than others. Salient beliefs are ones that we have actually taken into consideration in the formation of an attitude. They are particularly important beliefs, ones we are aware of and pay attention to.

These things that we believe do not necessarily exist independently of each other. *Belief systems* are "networks of beliefs that are related to one another because of their mutual perceived relevance to a larger belief or value."[1] In political terms,

> a belief system is a set of related judgments and perceptions about politics or political objects at a relatively general level that can be used by the individual who holds them to give meaning to the more specific things he or she experiences, and can be used as well by an observer. . . to describe the general characteristics of that individual's preferences.[2]

Belief systems are constrained by some organizing principle. An ideology is a good example of a belief system. Marxism, for example, is a set of related judgments and perceptions constrained by the principle that politics is defined by class struggle. There is disagreement among political scientists as to the extent to which the average American possesses an ideological belief system.[3] In classic work done by Philip E. Converse in 1964, little support was found for ideological consistency in political attitudes; that is, attitudes were not constrained along a liberal–conservative continuum.[4] In 1976 these findings were disputed by Norman H. Nie and his colleagues, who argued that people do organize their beliefs into some kind of system, but that the process fluctuates in response to stimuli from the political environment.[5] For example, it is easier for people to think in ideological terms during an election campaign if the candidates are emphasizing ideological differences.

Later, a set of researchers produced studies suggesting that people's beliefs are structured, but around multiple dimensions, not just along a liberal–conservative dimension. The "ideal" liberal or conservative is often defined in terms of economic issues, but in recent years other important issues have come to the fore, including drug use, feminism, and racial concerns. These are issues that do not lend themselves easily to the question of governmental intervention the way economic issues do. It is possible that standard measures of belief constraint are missing the logic found in the way people organize, in different ways, their beliefs on social, racial, and economic issues.[6] Also, these studies have used different research designs and different question wordings, making it difficult to compare their results.

John A. Fleishman found that, even when people lacked consistently liberal or consistently conservative positions on issues, they did show "patterns with some coherence and meaning."[7] Inconsistency did not mean absence of attitude organization. Fleishman also found that he could group the people he studied according to their positions on the issues, and these positions were strongly related to their vote for president in 1980. He wrote:

> Some groups, such as liberals, conservatives, or laissez-faire advocates, may be fairly stable in their partisan attachments and voting behavior. Other groups, however, may align themselves differently, depending on the issues made salient in a particular campaign.[8]

M. Margaret Conway shows how a belief system about politics is related to political participation. She calls *psychological involvement* the possession of a structure of attitudes, beliefs, and values about something, in this case, politics. Those who have a greater psychological involvement in politics are more active politically than those who do not. According to Conway, the components of this involvement are a sense of civic duty (perceived obligation to participate), an interest in politics, an interest in political campaigns, a sense of political efficacy (see the section entitled "Some Current Political Attitudes" for a full definition), and an identification with a political party.[9]

Our view of the world is thus greatly affected by our beliefs. Attitudes stem from our beliefs and may even constitute belief systems in their own right. Milton Rokeach defines an *attitude* as "a relatively enduring organization of beliefs around an object or situation predisposing one to respond in some preferential manner."[10] Because of attitudes, we are ready to respond to certain things in certain ways. In terms of politics, our attitudes provide a context for the things we learn and experience. Put another way, "attitudes act as a screen through which an individual's perceptions of reality must be filtered."[11] Attitudes have both cognitive (based on the intellect and on reasoning) and affective (based on emotions and on values) components, involving both belief and evaluation.

Beliefs and attitudes serve several functions for us, besides organizing our perceptions. They serve

1. a utilitarian function (attitudes can maximize our rewards and minimize our penalties)
2. a knowledge function (attitudes help supply frames of reference for understanding our world)
3. a value-expressive function (attitudes can give expression to the types of persons we perceive ourselves to be)
4. an ego-defensive function (attitudes can protect us from harsh realities about ourselves and the world; this can involve denial, misinterpretation, and rationalization)[12]

Because attitudes are so important to us, we resist efforts to change them.

ATTITUDE CHANGE

Attitudes of the public are obviously important to politicians who wish to be reelected. Politicians want to reinforce attitudes that engender support and to change or neutralize attitudes that engender opposition. During election years it also is important to activate people, to motivate supporters to work in the campaign, or, at least, to encourage voting.

Human beings, however, have defense mechanisms to protect the attitudes that serve them so well. We are capable of at least some control over our impressions through perceptual screening devices known as selective exposure, selective perception, and selective retention. If this were not true, then uniform stimuli would be followed by uniform attitude changes; shared experiences would result in shared attitudes. Obviously, this is not what takes place in life. In most communities, while a degree of conformity may exist, a wide variety of political attitudes can be found at any given time.

Selective exposure is a process through which we prevent certain kinds of messages or information from reaching us. Liberals do not routinely read *The National Review,* nor conservatives *Mother Jones.* Persons who prefer NBC's "Nightly News" may watch that network news and no other. This notion argues that we are bombarded with messages (or "message opportunities") every day, but it is impossible to pay close attention to all of them. We make choices, and expose ourselves to certain messages, while saying no to others. According to the selective exposure process, those who desire to reinforce our views or activate us need to get their information included in the media to which we choose to expose ourselves. Current research, though, tells us that in today's world, it is difficult to uphold the notion of selective exposure, at least in terms of major stories. News about the space shuttle Challenger's explosion, or about major campaign events, is so prevalent, and gets repeated so often, that it is hard to miss stories such as these.

Other defensive techniques are available to us, however. *Selective perception* is a process through which we more or less see what we want to see. Two individuals can read the same story (or watch the same story on television) and interpret it differently. One sees the president's remarks as conciliatory; the other sees them as combative. The first person probably supports the president; the second probably opposes him. Each is predisposed to perceive the president's message in a certain way. Selective perception is a roadblock in the path of those who would change our attitudes. They might get past the selective exposure problem; they might get their message included in the media to which we expose ourselves. But as we receive the message, we may perceive it in a fashion that suits our own needs.

Selective retention is a process through which we choose to remember some things and discard others. Studies have shown that many people cannot remember what stories were included in a news broadcast shortly after watching it.[13] People often choose to forget things that hurt them or contradict strongly held beliefs. It is easier to forget a news story than to reconstruct our world view once a week. This too makes it difficult for those seeking to change our minds.

Keep in mind that some beliefs can be rather easily changed—the beliefs that are not salient, that do not perform important functions for us, the beliefs in which we have no strong emotional involvement. Remember, too, that most of the messages we receive about national news come from the mass media. Most of the time the media reinforce our already held beliefs. In part this is due to our use of selective exposure, perception, and retention, and, in part, it is because the commercial networks and major periodicals reflect dominant societal values.[14] We definitely acquire information from the media, but the mainstream, commercial media are not likely to challenge our beliefs often.

Several theories attempt to describe the process through which attitudes of the masses *do* change. (Elites take politics more seriously than do the masses, and the process of attitude change may be different for them.) We will examine balance theory and functional theory first.[15]

Balance theory is more appropriate for a discussion of political attitudes, and more difficult to explain. It begins with the notion that human beings are not content when faced with contradictions, particularly contradictions among our important attitudes and behaviors.[16] When we become aware of these contradictions, we strive to alter conditions so that we may return to a state of cognitive balance and relieve ourselves of the tensions created by imbalance. For example, let us say there is an individual who is Catholic and against abortion, but is otherwise a strong liberal. This person lives in Massachusetts and is a strong supporter of Edward Kennedy. There are no cognitive imbalances so far. This individual, though, eventually discovers that Kennedy is pro-choice on the abortion issue. (The message is repeated often enough and prominently enough to get through perceptual screening devices.)

There may be pressure now to bring these cognitions back into balance. The individual may change his or her opinion about Kennedy, or about abortion, or even about politics in general. It may be decided that politics is not all that important. If the conflict among these beliefs is strong enough, the person may withdraw from politics altogether. Conversely, a pro-life advocate may be born. It is at this point, when cognitive imbalance exists, that others may be successful in influencing someone's opinion. A message sent out now may contain precisely the piece of information needed to make the individual feel comfortable again, feel in balance again.

We will suppose that the abortion issue is extremely important to our individual, and he or she votes against Kennedy in a Senate election. At this point, cognitive dissonance may rear its ugly head. This strong liberal has just voted for a Republican! Dissonance is very likely to bring with it pressure to return to a state of balance, and this can be achieved in a number of ways.[17] The individual might reinforce the choice made by concentrating on additional data. (Not only is Kennedy pro-choice, but he was involved in the accident at Chappaquiddick, and a person of such questionable judgment should not hold prominent office.) Reinforcement also can come from social groups, such as anti-abortion groups. If enough additional data are collected, it may convince the individual that the right decision was made and reduce the dissonance the individual feels.

It is important to note that issue positions do not always affect perceptions of candidates; perceptions of candidates can affect issue positions.[18] If one's admiration for the candidate is stronger than one's opinion on the issue, then it is the issue position that will change. The opinion that is least important to the person is the one that will change.

Denial also may be used to reduce dissonance. This involves attacking one or both of the attitudes that are causing disharmony. The individual might argue that a single Senator is not important or powerful, or that his or her vote for this office doesn't really matter. While some achieve balance in sophisticated ways, others attain it by projecting their own issue preferences onto candidates, or by misperceiving candidate positions.[19]

Not all contradictory attitudes will encourage such responses. Not all of our attitudes are equally prominent in our minds or equally important to us. We may hold contradictory beliefs and not even know it, simply because we have not thought our feelings through well, have not organized them into a belief system. Balance theory argues that when political issues and actors are important to us, these reactions can occur.

The last of Hennessy's approaches to attitude change, the *functional theory,* focuses on those previously discussed functions that attitudes perform for us. Attempts to change attitudes may be more successful if the new attitude can be shown to serve the individual's needs better than the old attitude. Attitudes that are important to one's self-concept are particularly difficult to change.

Carol Barner-Barry and Robert Rosenwein would add to this list the *group dynamics theory,* which argues that groups exert pressures on members to conform. If our attitudes differ from those of a group we value, we will probably want to adjust those attitudes, rather than risk being ostracized.[20]

It is important to note again that these are theories; some provide better explanations for particular attitude changes than others. The functional theory probably has the most utility for explaining routine attitude changes. That aside, what all these theories suggest is that those who would change our attitudes must first penetrate our perceptual screens and defenses. Repeating messages to the point of saturation, timing them well, using attractive and trusted vehicles for transmitting the messages, and lacing the messages within a thematic context are tools that can help would-be persuaders when we are in a state to be persuaded.[21] In the end, our attitudes are usually quite stable.

OPINIONS

We know that beliefs and attitudes have important electoral consequences and that leads to the subject of public opinion. To start at the beginning, what is an opinion? How does it relate to an attitude? One definition calls an *opinion,* a normative and/or pragmatic judgment about an object. Opinions are more specific than attitudes. Opinions are usually consistent with the attitude or attitudes to which they are related in the perception of the opinion holder. Opinions refer to single objects, or to a set of objects taken singularly, whereas attitudes are more generalized and diffused with respect to their objects. . . . Attitudes. . . are predispositions to respond; opinions are responses.[22]

A variety of theories attempt to describe opinion formation.[23] Certainly our beliefs and attitudes provide the grounding for our opinions. But what happens after that? The *rationalist approach* argues that opinions are the result of the reasoning processes. People deduce opinions from facts or laws. (We hold different opinions because we do not all understand these facts and laws equally well.) The *Freudian or psychoanalytic approach* encompasses a number of theories which, to oversimplify, emphasize the effects of experiences in infancy and childhood on opinions. This approach argues that these early experiences shape self-image, which helps determine what kinds of opinions we possess. *Sociological approaches* hold that opinions are formed by cultural traditions, social institutions, and societal norms. Still another approach emphasizes *economic determinism,* arguing that our opinions are the result of economic factors impinging on our lives. Owners and workers view politics from different positions, and their opinions reflect that.

Another theory approaches the process from the perspective of interpersonal relations. Paul Lazarsfeld and his associates formulated the notion of the *two-step flow* in their classic 1948 study *The People's Choice.*[24] This hypothesis speculated that some people in society are opinion leaders, while the rest of us are opinion followers. The leaders are particularly attentive to the news and help shape it. They come into contact with others, and, in discussions of the issue or issues that they are interested in and informed about, they instruct others. This theory has been controversial, and is especially so today. Television, radio, and newspapers are so prevalent that most of us are capable of hearing news more or less simultaneously. It follows that we might form our opinions before opinion leaders have a chance to get at us. Or perhaps, as Joan S. Black suggests, those identified as leaders simply respond to the media more quickly than those identified as followers.[25] The two-step flow may indeed operate in some instances, but caution must be exercised in using this theory to explain opinion formation in general.

Some believe that *the mass media* themselves have a large influence on our opinions, but others argue that media influence is exaggerated. Benjamin I. Page and his colleagues found that television news may play a role in changing opinions. They discovered that television news variables accounted for over 90 percent of the variance in public opinion on various issues. They argue that new information provided to viewers through television news can change opinions if five conditions are met: The information must be (1) actually received, (2) understood, (3) relevant to evaluating policies, (4) different from past beliefs, and (5) credible.[26]

The media, especially television, are certainly readily available (too available if one listens to critics decrying the amount of hours a day the average child spends in front of the TV), but again one has to question whether or not the messages being transmitted are being received. The media are not monolithic, either. While the media do tend to reflect the values of our culture, it is rare that a single message on an issue or candidate is pounded into our unsuspecting brains. A variety of messages exist, and we often filter these messages through mechanisms such as selective attention and perception. The mass media have, at least, helped make society better informed than it used to be, and being informed is related to opinion formation. (Those who are better educated are more likely to remember what they saw on the news and are less likely to answer "don't know" to survey questions.) The media also help to set the public agenda. It is commonly noted that the media may not tell us what to think, but they do tell us what to think about.[27] The Gallup organization regularly asks survey respondents what they think is the most important problem facing the country. G. Ray Funkhouser found that the amount of media attention given to an issue is related to the likelihood that issue will be included in responses to this question.[28]

But the media often are criticized for not giving enough attention to issues in political campaigns. They do cover candidates' issue positions, but after their initial discussion such stories are old news to journalists. And in nomination campaigns, it often is difficult to separate candidates from the same party on the basis of issues. Since the candidates share their party's basic beliefs, journalists tend to focus instead on campaign issues (controversies arising out of campaign events) and stories about character.

Researchers have discovered, though, subtle differences between the effect television has and the effect that newspapers have. Joseph Wagner found that "even after education, class, interest in public affairs, and like factors are taken into account, reading a newspaper, in contrast to watching television, increases the ability to discriminate between the candidates in a presidential election."[29]

Public opinion obviously involves some expression of privately held opinions, but it is more than merely that. According to Hennessy, it is "the complex of preferences expressed by a significant number of persons on an issue of general importance."[30] We speak of a "complex" of preferences because there will be many opinions on the issue, not just one. There is no set number at which a group of persons becomes "significant"; effectiveness is considered more important than raw numbers. An "issue" is something around which publics— those affected by an action or policy—form. There is the "newspaper-reading public," or the "library-using public," or the "church-going public." The issue must be capable of provoking disagreement or conflict.[31] This definition allows us to distinguish the opinions of, say, the "Podunk Tuesday Study Club" from those that have the potential to affect public policy. Public opinions vary in stability, direction, intensity, degree of polarization, how they are expressed, and impact on voting and policy.

We attempt to discover, describe, and interpret public opinion through the use of polls. Polls have been the object of much attention and criticism in recent years because they are used increasingly by politicians, private organizations, and journalists. During presidential election years there seems to be a new poll every day. The effects of the continual reporting of poll results are difficult to assess, but it is safe to say that their impact is probably greater in primary elections (where voters cannot use a simple party cue to help them vote) than in general elections. Campaign polling and general polling are discussed in separate sections.

CAMPAIGN POLLING

Polls are used by politicians throughout campaigns. Even before a candidacy is announced, *benchmark polls* are used to "test the waters," to discover how people feel about current officeholders and issues, and how they feel about the potential candidate. A good showing in such polls can help the candidate raise money, using the poll as proof of support in the electorate. For the 1984 election, pollster Patrick Caddell even went so far as to create a fictional model presidential candidate—"Senator Smith"—based on his public opinion research. According to a memo circulated by Caddell, Smith is

> a moderate liberal in his early forties who has served in the Senate for a decade. He has bold solutions for the future; he doesn't support the past policies of either party. He calls for a new generation of leadership that will restore shared sacrifice and will put the national interest above particular interests.[32]

Caddell envisioned people like Senators Dale Bumpers or Joseph Biden stepping into Senator Smith's shoes and making a run for the Democratic nomination in 1984. When they did not, he ended up working with Gary Hart. The idea of starting with public opinion data and working from there to find a candidate, rather than starting with a candidate, is rather novel to say the least. But it is not surprising, given the current prominence of polls.

Professional pollsters and campaign management consultants use the results of polling to shape campaign strategy. The first part of adviser Harry Treleaven's strategy for Richard Nixon's 1968 presidential campaign discussed public opinion and the public mood. Treleaven noted how campaign themes could be used to shape public perceptions. Strategy memos written for Jimmy Carter by advisers Gerald Rafshoon and Hamilton Jordan dealt with popular perceptions of their candidate as early as three years prior to the election.[33]

Polls that are used to detect quick changes in public opinion are called *tracking polls*. These polls can be used to determine the effectiveness of televised advertising. If the polling is done quickly enough, and if the money is there for production, weak ads can be replaced with stronger ones. Some campaign pollsters make use of *focus groups*. These are small gatherings of less than twenty. Candidates, campaigns, and issues are discussed with a moderator. The discussions allow pollsters to find out in more detail about voters' reactions and beliefs. Voters' statements can be probed to draw out their deeper feelings, and give the pollsters a more accurate response than can be provided with questionnaire items that allow only yes or no answers. Focus groups can help campaigners find out what kinds of campaign themes will be effective. Sometimes these groups are used before a survey is drawn up, to help improve the questions.[34]

In 1987 it was reported that the Reverend Pat Robertson, Republican candidate for the 1988 presidential nomination, altered his campaign because of polls that showed many people had a negative view of Robertson and could not distinguish him from other television evangelists. His advisers sought to repackage him as a Christian businessman.[35] Dotty Lynch, who worked in the Democratic presidential races of 1976, 1980, and 1984, stopped doing political polling because of disillusionment that resulted from "politicians waiting to look at a poll to formulate an opinion on basic—not minor—issues."[36]

Of course, candidates do not always follow the poll-based advice they receive, but there is no doubt that a great deal of attention is being paid to public opinion. In addition to shaping campaign strategies, polls also help to set campaign agendas for the politicians, the press, and the public.

In 1960, television ad campaigns were drawn up, the commercials produced and aired relatively close to election day. With today's technology, ad campaigns can be drawn up, produced, aired, scrapped, and the process begun all over again several times during the campaign. According to Democratic media consultant Robert D. Squier,

> What we're trying to do is have a conversation with the voters. Before, it was like trench warfare in World War I. You'd get the guns ready, and three weeks before the election, you would fire off your stuff, and then on Election Night, you'd count the bodies. Today, you listen [to the electorate] and talk back and listen again and talk back.[37]

In political campaigns the mass media agenda is usually dominated by "horse race" stories.[38] These stories, often based on poll results, tell us who is ahead in the campaign and who is falling behind, where the "momentum" seems to be going. Statements, events, and issues are examined not in light of their own merits but in terms of how they affect candidate rankings. This type of reporting is particularly important during primary election campaigns. The media's power in this regard is particularly strong during the first caucuses and primaries, which get a disproportionate share of attention.[39] The media, using their own standards, may decide that an underdog who does better than expected (Eugene McCarthy in New Hampshire in 1968; Jimmy Carter in Iowa in 1976; Gary Hart in Iowa in 1984) deserves to be treated like a winner, and that the winner deserves to be virtually ignored. Front-runners often receive harsh treatment. Upon what do journalists base their expectations? They are based upon discussions with candidates, voters, party officials, and polls. Major news organizations now regularly pay for polls to be used for the express purpose of writing or televising stories about them.

Critics argue that in doing this the media come close to creating news rather than reporting it. However, James Glen Stovall and Jacqueline H. Solomon found that, while opinion polls make up an important part of the coverage of presidential campaigns and while horse race polls dominate the poll stories, they do not dominate the coverage. They even found that editors are "less likely to play a poll story as prominently as other campaign stories."[40]

Election day *exit polling* creates another controversy. These polls were pioneered by the television networks, and involve surveying voters as they leave the polls after casting their ballots. The networks sample precincts or election districts from a list that usually includes all the precincts in a given state (or all voting districts nationwide for a general election). Interviewers are then sent to the selected precincts on election day. The results achieved are usually quite accurate; they do an excellent job of predicting who is going to win the election.[41] That is where the problem comes in. Once the networks have enough responses in from enough precincts to predict the outcome, they want to broadcast that news. Some feel that such announcements, made while the polls are still open, can affect turnout and voter choices. This is a particular problem, of course, in presidential elections, where the polls in the East close much earlier than those in the West. Because of the dictates of Electoral College rules (and the technology of exit polls), it is possible to announce a projected winner while much of the West Coast is still voting. A variety of studies have tried to measure the impact of early announcements on voting behavior (particularly in 1980, when President Carter conceded victory to Ronald Reagan while polls in the West were still open), but they give us contradictory findings. This subject will be pursued in Chapter 3.

GENERAL POLLING

Not all polls are conducted during campaigns, nor do all polls include questions about campaign events. General polls usually involve asking people their positions on various issues or policies. Individuals are asked to comment about a wide variety of items—how they feel about political parties, about the federal budget, about social issues. While government officials often pay heed to poll results, there is a body of evidence to show that this is not always how it works. David L. Paletz and Robert M. Entman put a spin on the two-step flow theory and argue that

> elites crystallize and define issues, provide supporting information; they substantially influence, if they do not establish, public opinion. Because of the way news is defined, gathered, and reported, the mass media are often the unwitting handmaidens of the powerful. When elites agree, media depictions tend to be onesided, to relay and transform elite consensus into public affirmation. But when

elites conflict, the mass media may influence public opinion in ways that favor one elite position over another, thereby redistributing power.[42]

If opinion flows down from the top, then it is political and media elites who have power, not the public. This was shown to be true even during the Watergate scandal. Was Richard Nixon driven to resignation by public opinion? The answer is no according to Gladys Engel Lang and Kurt Lang, who write that

> the public never was an active participant in the campaign against Richard Nixon. It did not direct the course of events, except when the reaction to [Archibald] Cox's dismissal signaled those in power that the time had come to do something. The impression of public support made it easier to move against Nixon simply because the bystander public withheld the vote of confidence the President had so eagerly sought in order to defeat impeachment politically. Only in this sense, and in this sense alone, was Nixon "driven" from office by his loss of public support.[43]

The Langs credit Nixon's downfall to "political insiders," not to public opinion.

Even if public opinion is molded by elites or ignored by them, it receives a great deal of attention in the media. It behooves anyone who reads or hears stories about polls to have some familiarity with how survey work is done.

POLLING: THE RIGHT WAY AND THE WRONG WAY

The science of polling has come a long way since its early years. Most of us are familiar with the famous photograph of Harry Truman holding up a 1948 *Chicago Daily Tribune* newspaper with the headline "Dewey Defeats Truman." There was, of course, no President Dewey. Like most enterprises, polling got better with practice. The problem in 1948 was that most pollsters stopped polling in early October. Many people were undecided in October, though, and their last-minute tilt toward Truman was not detected. (Another problem was that the sampling was partially based on the 1940 census, and a variety of changes had occurred in the population in the intervening eight years.) Today, major polls such as those done by the Gallup and Harris organizations are accurate because they are administered in a precise, scientific manner. Unfortunately, not everyone who does a poll is as precise. Anyone studying political behavior, or anyone reading about a particular poll, needs to be able to distinguish between polls that are done correctly and those that are done incorrectly.

Question Wording

First of all, the wording of the questions is extremely important. Many of the people who respond to polls have not spent a great deal of time thinking about the subject of the questions. A slight alteration in how the question is phrased can change the response. Also, it would be very helpful if pollsters would word questions that are used routinely in exactly the same way so that responses to the question over time could be studied. Since 1945, the Gallup organization has asked, "Do you approve or disapprove of the way [the incumbent] is handling his job as president?" changing only the president's name. This has resulted in a body of useful data about presidential support.

On other items, though, Gallup and other pollsters are not so consistent. An example comes from two Gallup polls taken a month apart during the Korean War. The first asked, "If the Chinese Communists continue to send hundreds of thousands of troops into Korea, far outnumbering our forces there, what do you think we should do?" The other question provided specific options: "Now that Communist China has entered the fighting in Korea with forces far outnumbering the United Nations troops there, which one of these courses would you, yourself, prefer that we follow—A. Pull our troops out of Korea as fast as possible, or B. Keep our troops there to fight these larger forces?"[44] Not only are the questions phrased differently, but the first allows respondents to set their own frame of reference, to choose their own options without limitation, whereas the second allows only two possible responses. We can, therefore, compare responses to these questions only with great difficulty.

The second major consideration with survey questions is that they be free of bias, that no "leading" questions be asked. If people are asked how they feel about the Panama Canal Treaty, one set of responses will result. If they are asked about the *president's* Panama Canal Treaty, a different set of responses will result, with a higher percentage in favor of the treaty. Admiration for the president—whoever he or she is, of whatever party—will skew the responses.

Other things that can affect responses include the placement of the question (it helps to ask personal questions last because by then the respondent is used to answering and may want to get the whole thing over with), ambiguity, and the asking of two questions instead of one. Posing questions about issues prior to questions that ask for an evaluation of candidates can alter the results. If the issues chosen are issues that are associated favorably with one candidate, then the responses to questions about that candidate will be more positive than if the survey asked about candidate preference alone. "Do you favor or oppose foreign aid to Nicaragua?" really asks two questions—are we talking about military or economic aid? Some respondents would favor one but oppose the other. Open-ended questions ("Tell me about your voting habits") will encourage a variety of responses, while fixed-alternative questions ("How often do you vote in presidential elections? A. Always, B. Sometimes, C. Never") will encourage respondents to check off an answer, even if it does not represent their views exactly. Pretesting survey questions can help pinpoint errors, but the writing of good survey questions remains an art.

Academic as well as commercial pollsters take surveys. The Survey Research Center/Center for Political Studies at the University of Michigan has provided a wealth of data for those interested in survey data on political behavior.

... PAID FOR BY THE COMMITTEE TO UNDERMINE THE OPPOSING CANDIDATE.

SOURCE: Rob Rogers, The Pittsburgh Press. Copyright 1986. Reprinted with permission.

Sampling

With most surveys, the aim is to get responses that reflect the opinion of the general public. It is impractical (and impossible) to question all citizens, and so we take samples instead. A *sample* is a smaller group that is representative of the general population in all relevant ways. Getting such a sample is imperative if the survey is to be of much use, and it is at this stage that some pollsters make disastrous mistakes.

The kind of survey that will allow us to generalize from the sample to the population is one where the sampling procedure is based on probability theory. We get such a sample when its design guarantees that "each person in the population has a fair chance of being selected and we can know the arithmetic value of that chance."[45] This is based on mathematical laws of chance, not on personal judgments. Since human biases are eliminated, only random errors should affect the selection of the sample. (Random errors have no pattern and tend to cancel each other out; they do not bias the results.) Probability theory allows us to measure the amount of this random error in samples.[46] National surveys can adequately get by with samples of less than 2,000 people, because it is how the sample is chosen that is critical, not how large it is.

An example from 1936 illustrates the point. A magazine called the *Literary Digest* conducted an election poll and used a huge sample—over 2 million voters. The poll results predicted a big win for Alfred M. Landon, but Franklin D. Roosevelt was reelected by one of the largest popular vote margins in history. How could they fail to make the correct prediction with such a big sample? They were not the *right* 2 million people. The sample was drawn from lists of those who owned telephones and automobiles. In 1936 this measured only the more affluent. And this election, in the midst of the Depression, attracted unprecedented numbers of poor people to the polls. The *Digest* sample, large as it was, was not representative of those voting.[47]

Even with a proper sample, problems still can arise. In 1980, all the major pollsters predicted a close election between Jimmy Carter and Ronald Reagan, but Reagan ended up winning in a landslide. How did the pollsters miss it? Were their samples inadequate? No. The problem for pollsters in 1980 was that many people were undecided until the last day of the campaign. Those who knew whom they were going to vote for were evenly split between Carter and Reagan, but the majority of the undecided voters went for Reagan. Organizations that continued polling until the last moments of the campaign saw this trend, but by the time this could be communicated to the press, the election was over.

When examining preelection polls, readers must pay attention to the description of the sample. Samples of the general public are not very useful, since so many people do not vote in elections. Samples of registered voters are better. Better still are samples where likely voters—those who are registered, who have a history of voting, who are interested in the current campaign, and who intend to vote in the current election—are included. Samples of likely voters will allow more precise predictions about the outcome of the election than will samples of registered voters or citizens in general.[48]

When a local television station or newspaper sends a reporter to a downtown street corner and the reporter asks people questions as they go by, the principles of probability are violated. Many people will not go downtown that day, or will not pass that particular corner. Everyone, therefore, does not have a fair chance to be included. Such a survey describes only the views of those few interviewed; it tells us nothing about citywide opinion. Equally suspect are telephone polls promoted by television shows. Viewers are asked to call a number to express their preference on an issue or for a candidate. The call costs money (usually fifty cents). Viewers themselves decide whether or not to call, so such a "sample" is self-selected. Self-selected samples do not follow the rules of probability theory, and are likely to be quite unrepresentative of the general population.

When a survey *is* done the right way, with a probability-based sample, the next step is equally important—careful recording of the responses. This means checking and double checking to ensure accuracy.

Interpretation of Results

The final step is also critical—interpreting the results. It is commonly observed that it is easy to mislead the uninitiated with statistics. You do not have to be a statistician, though, to know when to be suspicious. The following are a few of the things to look for:

Degree of Precision. This term refers to how closely the sample results resemble the true characteristic in the population, and largely depends on sample size.[49] If the degree of precision is set at plus or minus 3 percent, for example, and our sample results tell us that 40 percent of the respondents consider themselves to be Democrats, the actual percentage of the population that calls itself Democrat may be as low as 37 percent or as high as 43 percent (although the *most likely* result will measure 40 percent Democrat). Researchers determine the degree of precision they want and can afford for their study (based on costs, available resources, and degree of exactness needed for the purpose of the study) and adjust the sample size accordingly. Obviously, if the degree of precision is set too high, the sample results are not going to be very helpful. The *Des Moines Register* ran a story in 1984 about a poll of those likely to participate in the state caucus. The survey's degree of precision was plus or minus 12 percent![50]

Also important, but rarely divulged, is the *confidence level.* As researchers set the degree of precision, they also set the level of confidence they will have that they will reach their target of precision. For example, a common confidence level is 0.95. If the degree of precision is set at plus or minus 3 percent, and the confidence level at 0.95, it means that 95 times out of 100 the results the researchers discover will be within their target of plus or minus 3 percent.

Something else needs to be kept in mind here. Sometimes those reporting survey results divide the sample into subgroups—black and white, male and female and so forth. The degree of precision is based on the number of people in the *entire* sample, however, so comparisons between or among subgroups will have higher error rates.

In preparing this chapter, the author discovered that information on degrees of precision is not always readily available. The degrees of precision used in the surveys discussed in this book are not always included because this statistic was not discussed in the sources used. The data were used in spite of this lapse because they came from sources (such as the Gallup organization) that normally use small margins of error.

Statistical Significance. Sometimes survey data are used to create crosstabulation tables, two-way classifications of the data aimed at discovering whether or not two factors (variables) are related to each other. Two kinds of statistics should be provided with these tables: a measure of association (which reveals how strongly the variables are related in the sample) and a measure of statistical significance (which provides the odds that the relationship discovered in the sample could have occurred by chance alone). The significance figure tells us how safe it is to generalize from the sample to the population. If a relationship is not statistically significant, then the measure of association is meaningless. It applies only to the sample.

Causation.   Scholars are very careful in how they use the word "cause," but commercial pollsters and journalists are less so. Be skeptical. Two variables may very well be related to each other (occur at the same time), but that does not necessarily mean that one causes the other. Criteria for causality include (1) the cause must precede the effect in time, (2) the two variables must be empirically correlated with each other, that is, there must be demonstrative real-world connection between the two variables, (3) the correlation between the two variables must not be due to the influence of a third variable that causes both of them.[51]

Level of analysis.   There is an important difference between *individual data* and *aggregate data*. Information gathered on individuals is just that, but once it is collected with data on other individuals, it becomes data about an aggregate, or group. Generalizations based on aggregate data can be applied only to that group, not to individuals. For example, you might find that redheads in Cleveland tend to vote Republican, but that does not mean that any particular redhead from Cleveland votes Republican.

In any poll, it is best to pay close attention to the precise meaning of the words used. Greg Schneiders wrote that

> the *New York Times,* on January 29, 1984, attempted to settle the debate over whether Iowa "is a fair and representative testing ground for beginning the presidential race." They surveyed voters in Iowa and across the nation and determined that "on no political issues did the surveys uncover dramatic differences, and similarities generally outweigh differences." There is only one problem. Only 85,000 people participated in the Iowa caucuses in 1984—slightly more than one-sixth the 500,000 Democrats who normally vote in a general election in Iowa, from whom, presumably, the *New York Times* sample was drawn. The caucus participants are more politically active and more liberal, *and* less nationally representative.[52]

None of this is meant to imply that the mass media are particularly careless in their handling of surveys. Scholars do not always get it right, and journalists do not always get it wrong. It merely points out that consumers of reports about surveys need to watch and read carefully. With the advances in the science of sampling that have occurred in the past forty years, scientifically conducted polls are extremely accurate in measuring where public opinion stands at a certain point in time. The error in election predictions made by the Gallup poll in 1984 was only 0.3 percent.[53] Wise consumers of news, however, will pay attention to what the consensus is among a variety of polls, rather than relying on just one.

SOME CURRENT POLITICAL ATTITUDES

What follows are some examples of information we have discovered through the use of opinion polls and academic surveys, information that can be very useful to campaigners, and helpful in explaining voting choices. One subject consistently addressed by pollsters is the amount of confidence felt about society and government. Surveys taken by both Time/Yankelovich, and Skelly and White show that positive feelings about "how things are going" increased greatly between the end of 1980 and the end of 1983. The question posed was "How do you feel that things are going in the country these days—very well, fairly well, pretty badly, or very badly?" In October of 1980, only 31 percent of those surveyed said things were going fairly well or very well. In December of 1981, that figure was up to 43 percent. The next December, only 35 percent felt things were going fairly well or very well, but by December of 1983 a whopping 60 percent were in these categories.[54] Answers to this question are often related to election returns; when most people feel things are going well, they are likely to retain incumbent officials.

Another question consistently asked is "How much of the time do you think you can trust the government in Washington to do what is right—just about always, most of the time, or only some of the time?" (See Table 2-1.) The Michigan Survey Research Center/Center for Political Studies combines this question with three others to form a trust in government index. The other questions are the following: "Do you think that people in the government waste a lot of money we pay in taxes, waste some of it, or don't waste very much of it?" "Do you think that quite a few of the people running the government are a little crooked, not very many are, or do you think hardly any of them are crooked at all?" and "Would you say the government is pretty much run by a few big interests looking our for themselves or that it is run for the benefit of all

TABLE 2-1   Trust in Government, 1958-1983

TRUST GOVERNMENT TO DO WHAT'S RIGHT:

YEAR	ALWAYS	MOST OF THE TIME	ONLY SOME/NONE OF THE TIME
1958	16%	59%	25%
1964	14	63	22
1970	6	48	45
1974	2	35	63
1980	2	23	74
1983	6	40	54

SOURCE: Surveys by the Center for Political Studies of the Institute for Social Research, University of Michigan National Election Studies, 1958 through 1980; and *The New York Times*, November 18-22, 1983, as reported in *Public Opinion* 7 (February/March, 1984), p. 29. Rows do not always add up to 100 percent due to "don't know" answers and lack of response. Copyright 1983-1984 by The New York Times Company. Reprinted with permission.

the people?"[55] (See Table 2-2.) Trust in government changed hardly at all between 1958 and 1964, but from 1964 to 1970 there was an "explosion" of mistrust in government, according to Seymour Martin Lipset and William Schneider.

> According to the Michigan index, trust in government fell from +42 in 1964 (i.e., a net trusting attitude) to +2 in 1970 and 1972. The drop between 1972 and 1974 was again severe, from +2 to −26 (net mistrusting). After 1974, things did not get much worse, but they did not get any better either; the Michigan index was −31 in 1976 and −33 in 1978.[56]

There is some evidence that citizens have become more trusting in the 1980s. A 1986 CBS/*New York Times* poll (with a sampling error margin of plus or minus 3 percentage points) found that 49 percent said they trusted the government in Washington to do what is right "all or most of the time."[57]

Belief that government is run for the big interests was high in the 1970s, but eased off in the early 1980s, as Table 2-2 shows. The turmoil of the 1960s and 1970s is long gone, and the cynicism that took root then is receding, as the data for 1984 show. Ronald Reagan's leadership revived trust in government for many. Some would blame the mass media for the decline in trust that occurred in the 1960s and 1970s, arguing that the media take a negative, cynical approach to stories, emphasizing the bad news and casting doubt on official government statements. Certainly the media, particularly television, gave plenty of coverage to disruptive events—the assassinations of the 1960s, the violent race riots and antiwar protests, the Vietnam war, and the Watergate scandal. It is unfair, though, to hold the media solely responsible for changes that took place throughout the socialization process. There is no conspiracy on

TABLE 2-2   For Whom Government is Run, 1964–1984

GOVERNMENT IS RUN FOR:

YEAR	BENEFIT OF ALL	A FEW BIG INTERESTS
1964	69%	31%
1970	45	55
1974	27	73
1980	23	77
1983	34	66
1984	40	49

SOURCE: Surveys by the Center for Political Studies of the Institute for Social Research, University of Michigan National Election Studies, 1964 through 1980; and *The New York Times*, November 18-22, 1983, as reported in *Public Opinion* 7 (February/March, 1984), p. 29. Reprinted with permission. Data for 1984 are from Adam Clymer, "Americans in Poll View Government More Confidently," *The New York Times*, November 19, 1984, p. B10. This poll has a margin of error of plus or minus 2 percent. Rows do not always add up to 100 percent due to "don't know" answers and lack of response. Copyright 1983-1984 by The New York Times Company. Reprinted with permission.

the part of the media to rob citizens of their trust in government. As Hennessy points out:

> Why do newspapers, TV and radio stations, movies, journals, and mass-circulation books exist? For one thing, they make money for their owners and producers. . . .From the perspective of the consumer, however, the mass media serve three main functions: they provide (a) entertainment; (b) guidance and orientation for daily living; and (c) information and opinion about public events. It is undeniable that the third is least important for the majority of media consumers. Much of the intellectual's criticism of the mass media misses this point: *most mass-media consumers neither want nor appreciate the subtleties of political discourse.* Moreover, for those who are politically aware and active, the mass media provide only a part of the environment of influence.[58]

Whatever the cause of this decline in trust, it seems to be connected to declining electoral turnout rates.

Related to trust in government is the concept of political efficacy. *Internal political efficacy* refers to a person's "estimation of their own personal capacity to comprehend and influence political events."[59] It is measured with the following items (respondents are asked whether they agree or disagree): "Voting is the only way that people like me can have any say about how the government runs things." "Sometimes politics and government seem so complicated that a person like me can't really understand what's going on." "People like me don't have any say about what the government does." Levels of agreement with these statements have remained fairly stable since 1968. However, a different questionnaire item—"I don't think public officials care much what people like me think"—elicited increasing agreement, from 36 percent agreement in 1964 to 47 percent in 1970. Why the discrepancy in responses? According to Lipset and Schneider,

> The political efficacy items seem to be, in [Philip E.] Converse's terms, both "cognitive" and "affective." They involve a perception and an evaluation of both the *self* and the *system.* Thus, when respondents are offered the statement "People like me don't have any say about what the government does," their answers reflect the respondent's opinions of (a) people like themselves and (b) what the government does. It is the cognitive component that rises with education. The evaluative one is mostly a response to events and conditions. If "what the government does" seems to bear no relation to how people feel, then more and more people will agree that they have no say.[60]

In response to this discovery, scholars devised the notion of *external political efficacy,* using measures that test attitudes toward the system. These measures include the following: "I don't think public officials care much what people like me think." "Generally speaking, those we elect to Congress in Washington lose touch with the people pretty quickly." "Parties are only interested in people's votes, but not in their opinions."[61] Agreement with these items has increased steadily. (The last two questions were added to surveys starting in 1968.) In other words, levels of internal efficacy have not changed much, but external efficacy has declined in much the same way as has trust in government.

These developments may have an impact on voting behavior. Lipset and Schneider report that those who desired change wanted reforms that

> were mostly changes in leadership and in the way the system is run, not changes in the underlying institutional structure. It appears that the trend of declining trust in government is focused on the performance of government and the behavior of public officials, and not on the system itself or the institutions and norms associated with it.[62]

If these disaffected citizens decide to act on their feelings, they are apt to put different kinds of people in office; they are not apt to plot revolution.

Polls also inform us of the public's views on foreign policy. A CBS/*New York Times* survey taken in April of 1983 showed that 61 percent of those questioned believed that El Salvador and other Central American countries are very important to U.S. defense interests.[63] A different poll conducted in 1983 (for the Garth Analysis) showed that 85 percent felt it would be of very or somewhat serious concern to the United States if El Salvador were to be taken over by Communist forces.[64] Incumbents and challengers will notice such figures when outlining their positions on U.S. involvement in the region.

At the same time, though, a *Los Angeles Times* poll showed only 21 percent approving a proposal for Congress to spend $110 million in military aid to the El Salvador government (in addition to the $26 million granted for 1983).[65] The question was posed differently by the CBS/*New York Times* survey, and received a different response. In this poll, the question was "If the communists were about to overthrow the government of El Salvador, would you support giving the present government three times as much U.S. military aid to try to stop the rebels?" Out of those responding, 49 percent said yes.[66]

Differences among various subgroups in the population have been revealed by surveys. We know that blacks, for instance, are strong supporters of the Democratic party, and 70 percent were Democratic identifiers, according to a 1984 survey.[67] The same poll showed that 56 percent of the Hispanics questioned also were Democrats, while only 30 percent of those with English, Scottish, and Welsh backgrounds were Democrats. Furthermore, 48 percent of those with East European or Soviet Union backgrounds were Democrats.[68] There also were differences in response to the question, "Taken all together, how would you say things are these days—would you say that you are very happy, pretty happy, or not too happy?" The answer "not too happy" was given by 22 percent of the black respondents, by 19 percent of the Hispanic respondents, by only 10 percent of those with English, Scottish, and Welsh backgrounds, and by 12 percent of those with East European or Soviet Union backgrounds.[69]

Other data show that while 45 percent of the respondents in a national survey said most people could be trusted, only 18 percent of the black respondents were so positive. Among Hispanic respondents, 31 percent said that most people can be trusted. Further, 56 percent of those of English, Scottish, and Welsh backgrounds agreed, as did 49 percent of those with East European and Soviet Union backgrounds.[70] Again, it is likely that the positions of various subgroups on these kinds of questions affects their voting behavior, and this affects how candidates court them for their votes.

An examination of opinion polls since 1948 in *Public Opinion* magazine traced the similarities and differences between the political attitudes of men and women. Between 1948 and 1952 there were few differences between men and women on issue positions, although women were less likely than men to approve of the use of force.[71] Significant differences were found on "expressed levels of political information and interest."[72] Women were not as knowledgeable or as interested in politics as were men. An identical pattern describes data examined from 1960 to 1964 and data from the early 1970s. It was not until the late 1970s, when women's educational levels began to match men's, that changes developed. Women were still less supportive than men of the use of force, but differences between the sexes also came to the fore on the dimensions of compassion, risk, and confidence in the system. Overall, women were more compassionate than men, and were less likely to take risks with the environment by relaxing regulations. Finally, while women often showed personal confidence, they were less likely than men to exhibit confidence in the system.[73]

Of interest, one area where men and women consistently showed agreement was on so-called women's issues. Differences between the sexes on the issues of abortion, voting for a woman for president, the Equal Rights Amendment, and other such issues, were small in all the time periods studied.[74]

The "gender gap" was much ballyhooed in the 1982 and 1984 elections, but it is difficult to translate the differences that exist into electoral results. Even if women like Candidate A less than men do, the majority of women still may prefer A to Candidate B. This is what happened in 1980, when 53 percent of the women voting for candidates from the two major parties cast votes for Reagan, while 61 percent of the men did.[75] One study suggests that the gender gap concept has been confusing because we have been misinterpreting it. Daniel Wirls points out that the gap usually has been attributed to women possessing more liberal values than men. But, Wirls argues, what has happened is simply

a general movement by the electorate toward Reagan, the Republicans, and more conservative values. While both men and women have been defecting from the Democratic party and moving away from liberal values, rates of defection among men have been greater than rates among women. . . Rather than reflecting an increase in Democratic and liberal sentiments among women, the gender gap resulted from more rapid and widespread movement among men than women to conservative values and the Republican party. Consequently, Reagan and the Republicans were never the potential victims, but the potential and actual beneficiaries of the gender gap in 1984.[76]

If Wirls is correct, his study contains bad news for the Democratic party. It has not been gaining among women so much as losing among men, particularly white men. Examination of recent voting trends suggests that those in the Democratic party who vote in presidential elections are, more and more, women and blacks. This would not be a heavy blow to the Democrats if *most* women were voting for their candidates, but that is not what is happening. It is *some* women and blacks. And it is very difficult to get a majority out of that.

Survey data also inform us about partisan preferences and differences. We know, for example, that Democrats tend to favor government action while Republicans tend to oppose it. Polls taken in 1983 indicated that 34 percent of the Democrats responding said yes, the government should do more to solve the country's problems, whereas only 13 percent of the Republicans agreed. Further, 42 percent of the Democrats believed that government should improve the poor's living standard, whereas 19 percent of the Republicans agreed. On aid for education, the two parties were somewhat closer, with 79 percent of the Democrats and 68 percent of the Republicans agreeing that they would support increased funds for education.[77]

General evaluations of the parties also are provided by polls. A 1984 survey showed that 47 percent of those polled had a favorable opinion of the Democratic party, but 60 percent had a favorable opinion of the Republican party. (And 42 percent had an unfavorable image of the Democratic party, but only 31 percent had an unfavorable image of the Republicans.)[78] Respondents also were asked, "Thinking back, do you have a better or worse opinion of the (Democratic/Republican) party than you had five years ago, or is it about the same?" The results are shown in Table 2–3.

With this distribution of responses, it is no wonder that Republican incumbent Ronald Reagan won reelection with such a comfortable margin.

Despite evidence saying that party identification is acquired at a young age and is resistant to change, Charles H. Franklin found that party identification can change in response to policy preferences. According to Franklin, young adults (by the time they are twenty-five) are capable of adjusting their partisanship to coincide with the party they prefer on issues. Such behavior need not lead to instability in partisanship if the parties themselves are stable in their issue positions.[79] Richard J. Trilling found that party images interact with party

TABLE 2–3   Party Evaluations

	BETTER OPINION	WORSE	SAME
Democratic Party	7%	24%	69%
Republican Party	31	11	58

SOURCE: Survey by CBS/*New York Times,* November 8–14, 1984, as reported in *Public Opinion*7 (December/January 1985), p. 38. The margin of error was plus or minus 2 percent. Copyright 1983–1984 by The New York Times Company. Reprinted with permission.

identification. When party images are consistent with past party identifications, then identifications are likely to be stable. When parties change their stands, or when individuals change their positions, then party identifications are likely to be changed. Trilling argues that party images help explain why some issues are related to voting and some are not; issues that are seen as defining the parties are more meaningful to the voters.[80]

Analysts have paid a great deal of attention to the question of the stability of public opinions. If opinions are fickle, then obviously public officials will have a difficult time trying to turn those opinions into coherent policies. On the other hand, if public opinions are basically stable, then officials who wish to follow the instruction of their constituents are better able to do so. Benjamin I. Page and Robert Y. Shapiro used survey data spanning 1935 to 1979 to investigate this question. They found considerable stability in policy preferences.[81] When changes in opinion did occur, they were usually gradual and related to "important changes in citizens' lives and in their social and economic environments."[82] In other words, people do not change their attitudes in a fickle, arbitrary manner that would be difficult for public leaders to fathom. (Page and Shapiro point out that the consistency they find might be the result of elite leadership or outright manipulation of mass opinion.)

Gregory B. Markus approached the question from a different direction. He used a panel survey containing members of two generations, and examined opinions across a nine-year time span.[83] Subjects were asked for their opinions on particular issues at time A, again at time B, and they were also asked at time B to recall their position on the issue at time A. Markus found that, in instances where people had changed their position on an issue, they mistakenly assumed that their position at time A was the same as their position at time B. The research showed that

> policy orientations generally do not have strong internal cognitive representations, are eminently changeable, and. . . once those orientations are changed, an individual's cognitive autobiography is rewritten so as to render the changes invisible.[84]

Not only did Markus find shifts in attitudes, but many of his respondents were not aware of the change. (Specifically, Markus found a conservative shift between 1973 and 1982 for the baby boom generation, and a weaker conservative trend for the parents of the baby boomers.)

These are just two examples of the efforts to determine the stability of opinions. Different research designs and measuring instruments make it difficult to compare study results or to come to a conclusion about the question. It is safe to say, at least, that some of our opinions—the ones we value the most—are more stable than others.

As can be seen from these examples, polls help us define the political environment. The data are used in different ways by politicians, the media, scholars, and the public. Some will use them to describe, some to explain, and some to predict the future. All three of these efforts can be successful if the data are collected and evaluated properly.

PUBLIC OPINION AND DEMOCRACY

Public opinion is obviously important in a direct democracy, but it is equally or more important in a republic. Since not all citizens are decision makers in a republic, it is vital that their representatives know and vote their interests. That, after all, is the meaning of representative democracy. For it to operate, there must be a link between public opinion and public policy.

The working of this linkage is not as simple in life as it may read on paper. Hennessy lays out the questions well:

> In what sense can it be said—or should it be said—that the people really rule in a democracy? Does the majority principle demand that the opinions of 50 percent plus one of the people on each particular issue be turned into policy? Who *are* the people? What methods are available to make certain that their opinions are properly known? Are sheer numbers enough, or ought one to consider, as many have suggested, quality of opinion as well?[85]

While today we associate public opinion with controversy, Hennessy points out that sometimes public opinion may be used to pressure people into conformity, into abiding by established norms. The freedom of thought and expression (vital elements of democracy) that we normally associate with public opinion may not always be there.

Opinion polls, while providing interesting and useful data, are usually not equipped to provide policy direction to politicians. Polls often oversimplify policy problems and alternative solutions. New technology, however, may change the way we view the role of public opinion. Some communities possess interactive cable television capabilities. Theoretically, a city council might televise debate on a proposal and then ask the viewing audience to vote on the bill. If the council felt obliged to take instruction from the viewers, the city would be moving away from representative democracy toward direct democracy. But what if few people are viewing, or if many are watching, but few vote? What if the family's three-year-old is given the controls? What if this vote measures only the initial reactions of people, and they change their minds once they have had a chance to think about it? These questions aside, such a development is not necessarily wise; our Constitution does not provide for direct democracy, and any move toward it could drastically change our system of government.

This brings up a dilemma faced by legislators—which role to play in pursuit of their tasks. Some feel obligated to vote as their constituents direct (acting as "delegates"). Others feel they should be trusted to make their own judgments (acting as "trustees"). More typically, legislators adopt an adaptive style, acting as trustees on issues that are not salient to their constituents, and as delegates on issues that are (acting as "politicos"). The point is that even representatives are divided on exactly how representative they should be. Most would probably agree that it is not necessary to mirror exactly each district opinion, as long as basic attitudes and values are shared.

Perhaps public opinion is best characterized as setting the boundaries within which public debate takes place. Officials can deduce from public opinion how far they can go before an idea stretches the tolerance of the people.

Does public opinion affect public policy? One view holds that affirmative examples abound. High levels of public support for Social Security have protected that program from budget cuts for years. Public reluctance to see U.S. troops in Nicaragua has limited U.S. government activity there. Tax reform and government funds for AIDS research are further examples of responsiveness to public opinion. Public opinion affects the platforms of political parties.[86] Our government does not always directly and quickly respond to the wishes of the people, but when citizens are united on an issue and express their feelings strongly, government usually reacts. The other view holds that special interests dominate the political agenda and public policy. Laws that benefit particular industries and regulatory agencies that fail to regulate are examples that reflect this view. A thorough treatment of this question is beyond the scope of this book, but of one thing we can be sure: When the public is informed on an issue, has a strong opinion, and articulates that opinion to public officials, public opinion is more likely to be influential on that issue.

Finally, there is an irony to our democracy. Many of us are ill informed or do not care about issues. This allows the opinions of elites—who are often well informed and usually *do* care—to influence policy instead of those of the masses. Studies have shown that elites exhibit far more support for civil rights and civil liberties than do the masses,[87] and this elite support affects policies in these areas.

SUMMARY

In this chapter we have examined the building blocks of political behavior—beliefs, attitudes, and opinions. What we believe is important, even if it is incorrect, because we act on our beliefs. Our attitudes and opinions largely determine what level of political activity we will pursue; whether or not we will join a party, and if so, which one; whether or not we will vote. We have presented a variety of theories that help explain how attitudes and opinions form and change. Our attitudes and opinions perform various functions for us that help us deal with ourselves and our world, and they are difficult to change (especially our attitudes). Scientific polls based on probability theory have done much to inform us about what people think and when our thoughts change (if they do at all).

It is important to remember, in all of this, that most people do not spend a great deal of time thinking about politics and political issues. They are busy working, raising families, and engaging in the recreational opportunities afforded them by life in twentieth century America. Before we deride the masses for their inattention, note that it may be a sign that people are satisfied with things as they are. We will see in the next chapter that the federal system in the United States makes many demands on citizens. The masses are capable of expressing their views on issues that affect them directly. Perhaps we should not be quick to blame them if, in other cases, they do not express themselves.

At any rate, measures of public opinion now abound for public officials who wish to consider and abide by public opinion. Such polls have significantly altered the way we elect officials because of their uses by candidates and the mass media. In fact, in an era of single-issue voting, some feel that constituent pressures occasionally go too far. Public opinion may be all in a direct democracy, but exactly what is its role in a republic? Our political system is still working out the answer to that question. The next chapter will examine a related subject of crucial importance in democracies and republics—who participates and who does not.

SUGGESTED READINGS

ASHER, HERBERT, *Polling and the Public, What Every Citizen Should Know.* Washington, DC: Congressional Quarterly Press, 1988.

BARNER-BARRY, CAROL, and ROBERT ROSENWEIN, *Psychological Perspectives on Politics.* Englewood Cliffs, NJ: Prentice-Hall, 1985.

CARPINI, MICHAEL X. DELLI, *Stability and Change in American Politics: The Coming of Age of the Generation of the 1960s.* New York: New York University Press, 1986.

CORBETT, MICHAEL, *Political Tolerance in America: Freedom and Equality in Public Attitudes.* New York: Longman, 1982.

HOLLOWAY, HARRY, with JOHN GEORGE, *Public Opinion, Coalitions, Elites, and Masses* (2nd ed.). New York: St. Martin's Press, 1986.

LIPSET, SEYMOUR MARTIN, "The Decline of Confidence in American Institutions," *Political Science Quarterly* 98 (Fall 1983), pp. 379–402.

MILLER, WARREN E., ARTHUR H. MILLER, and EDWARD J. SCHNEIDER, *American National Election Studies Sourcebook, 1952–1978.* Cambridge, MA: Harvard University Press, 1980.

NEUMAN, W. RUSSELL, *The Paradox of Mass Politics, Knowledge and Opinion in the American Electorate.* Cambridge, MA: Harvard University Press, 1986.

POOLE, KEITH T. and L. HARMON ZEIGLER, *Women, Public Opinion, and Politics.* New York: Longman, 1985.

DISCUSSION QUESTIONS

1. Where did *your* political attitudes come from? (Family, mass media, school, life experiences, or elsewhere?) Be specific.
2. Can you think of times when you have used perceptual screening devices (selective exposure, perception, and retention)?
3. How do you feel about the heavy reliance on polls during campaigns?
4. Bring to class a newspaper or magazine story reporting poll results. Does this story include the kind of information you need to evaluate the poll?

5. What is the significance for the political system of the decline of trust in government?

6. How democratic *should* our government be? How seriously should politicians take public opinion? What kinds of limitations, if any, should be placed on the influence of public opinion?

NOTES

1. Bernard Hennessy, *Public Opinion,* 5th ed. (Monterey, CA: Brooks/Cole, 1985), p. 3.

2. Jarol B. Manheim, *The Politics Within: A Primer in Political Attitudes and Behavior,* 2nd ed. (New York: Longman, 1982), p. 17.

3. See Norman H. Nie and James N. Rabjohn, "Revisiting Mass Beliefs Systems Revisited: Or, Doing Research is Like Watching a Tennis Game," *American Journal of Political Science* 23 (February 1979), pp. 139–175; see also the rejoinders in the same issue, pp. 176–193. Also pertinent is "Exchange: Has Attitudinal Constraint Increased Since the 1950s?" *American Journal of Political Science* 22 (May 1978), pp. 227–269.

4. Philip E. Converse, "The Nature of Belief Systems in Mass Publics," in David E. Apter, ed., *Ideology and Discontent* (New York: The Free Press, 1964), pp. 202–261.

5. Norman H. Nie, Sidney Verba, and John R. Petrocik, *The Changing American Voter* (Cambridge, MA: Harvard University Press, 1976).

6. John A. Fleishman, "Types of Political Attitude Structure: Results of a Cluster Analysis," *Public Opinion Quarterly* 50 (Fall 1986), pp. 371–386.

7. Ibid., p. 382.

8. Ibid., p. 383.

9. Conway, *Political Participation in the United States* (Washington, DC: Congressional Quarterly Press, 1985), p. 36.

10. Milton Rokeach, *Beliefs, Attitudes, and Values* (San Francisco: Jossey-Bass, 1968), p. 112.

11. Manheim, *The Politics Within,* p. 10.

12. Daniel Katz, "The Functional Approach to the Study of Attitudes," *Public Opinion Quarterly* 24 (Summer 1960), pp. 167, 170–175.

13. Thomas E. Patterson, *The Mass Media and Elections, How Americans Choose Their President* (New York: Praeger, 1980), pp. 62, 63.

14. Manheim, *The Politics Within,* p. 87.

15. Hennessy, *Public Opinion,* pp. 319–323.

16. See Leon Festinger, *A Theory of Cognitive Dissonance* (Evanston, IL: Row, Peterson, 1957) for a full treatment of this theory.

17. This section draws on an article by Robert P. Abelson, "Modes of Resolution of Belief Dilemmas," *The Journal of Conflict Resolution* 3 (December 1959), p. 343.

18. Stephen D. Shaffer, "Balance Theory and Political Cognitions," *American Politics Quarterly* 9 (July 1981), p. 298. See also Susan E. Howell, "Candidates and Issues in Local Elections," *American Politics Quarterly* 16 (January 1988), p. 27.

19. Ibid., p. 315.

20. Carol Barner-Barry and Robert Rosenwein, *Psychological Perspectives on Politics* (Englewood Cliffs, NJ: Prentice-Hall, 1985), p. 151.

21. Manheim, *The Politics Within,* pp. 110, 111.

22. Hennessy, *Public Opinion,* p. 4.

23. Ibid., Chapter 7.

24. Paul Lazarsfeld, Bernard Berelson, and Hazel Gaudet, *The People's Choice* (New York: Columbia University Press, 1948).

25. Joan S. Black, "Opinion Leaders: Is Anyone Following?" *Public Opinion Quarterly* 46 (Summer 1982), p. 175.

26. Benjamin I. Page, Robery Y. Shapiro, and Glenn R. Dempsey, "What Moves Public Opinion?" *American Political Science Review* 81 (March 1987), pp. 23–43.

27. See Lutz Erbring and Edie Goldenberg, "Front-Page News and Real-World Cues: A New Look at Agenda-Setting by the Media," *American Journal of Political Science* 24 (February 1980), pp. 16–49; Maxwell E. McCombs and Donald L. Shaw, "The Agenda-Setting Function of Mass Media," *Public Opinion Quarterly* 36 (Summer 1972), pp. 176–187; Jack M. McLeod, Lee B. Becker, and James E.

Byrnes, "Another Look at the Agenda-Setting Function of the Press," *Communication Research* 1 (April 1974), pp. 131–166; and David H. Weaver, Maxwell E. McCombs, and Charles Spellman, "Watergate and the Media: A Case Study of Agenda-Setting," *American Politics Quarterly* 3 (October 1975), pp. 458–472.

28. G. Ray Funkhouser, "The Issues of the Sixties: An Exploratory Study in the Dynamics of Public Opinion," *Public Opinion Quarterly* 37 (Spring 1973), p. 67.

29. Joseph Wagner, "Media Do Make a Difference: The Differential Impact of Mass Media in the 1976 Presidential Race," *American Journal of Political Science* 27 (August 1983), pp. 407–430. The quotation is from p. 426. See also Thomas E. Patterson, *The Mass Media Election: How Americans Choose Their President* (New York: Praeger, 1980).

30. Hennessy, *Public Opinion,* pp. 8–13.

31. Black, "Opinion Leaders," p. 8.

32. Sidney Blumenthal, "Mr. Smith Goes to Washington," *The New Republic* 190 (February 6, 1984), p. 17.

33. Richard Joslyn, *Mass Media and Elections* (Reading, MA: Addison-Wesley, 1984), pp. 22, 27.

34. Jerry Hagstrom and Robert Guskind, "Calling the Races," *National Journal* 20 (July 30, 1988), pp. 1972–1976.

35. Wayne E. King, "Presidential Polls Prompt 'Repackaging' of Robertson," *The New York Times,* June 13, 1987, p. 12.

36. Hagstrom and Guskind, "Calling the Races," p. 1973.

37. Ibid.

38. Joslyn, *Mass Media and Elections,* p. 109. Joslyn was writing about general election campaigns. See also Doris Graber, *Mass Media and American Politics,* 2nd ed. (Washington, DC: Congressional Quarterly Press, 1984), p. 189; and James Glen Stovall and Jacqueline H. Solomon, "The Poll as a News Event in the 1980 Presidential Campaign," *Public Opinion Quarterly* 48 (Fall 1984), pp. 615–623.

39. William Crotty and John S. Jackson III, *Presidential Primaries and Nominations* (Washington, DC: Congressional Quarterly Press, 1985), pp. 74–76.

40. Stovall and Solomon, "The Poll as a News Event," p. 622.

41. Mark R. Levy, "The Methodology and Performance of Election Day Polls," *Public Opinion Quarterly* 47 (Spring 1983), pp. 54–67.

42. David L. Paletz and Robert M. Entman, *Media Power Politics* (New York: The Free Press, 1981), p. 184.

43. Gladys Engel Lang and Kurt Lang, *The Battle for Public Opinion: the President, the Press, and the Polls During Watergate* (New York: Columbia University Press, 1983), pp. 307, 308.

44. Gallup Poll questions as described in John Mueller, *War, Presidents and Public Opinion* (New York: John Wiley, 1973), p. 68.

45. Charles H. Backstrum and Gerald Hursh-Cesar, *Survey Research,* 2nd ed. (New York: John Wiley, 1981), p. 53.

46. Ibid.

47. Earl R. Babbie, *Survey Research Methods* (Belmont, CA: Wadsworth, 1973).

48. Michael R. Kagay, "In Judging Polls, What Counts Is When and How Who Is Asked What," *The New York Times,* September 12, 1988, p. 10.

49. Backstrom and Hursh-Cesar, *Survey Research,* p. 71.

50. Greg Schneiders, "Sorry Wrong Numbers," *Washington Journalism Review* 6 (September 1984), p. 48.

51. Earl Babbie, *The Practice of Social Research,* 3rd ed. (Belmont, CA: Wadsworth, 1983), p. 57.

52. Schneiders, "Sorry," p. 50.

53. Hennessy, *Public Opinion,* p. 250.

54. "State of the Nation," *Public Opinion* 7 (February/March 1984), p. 21.

55. Seymour M. Lipset and William Schneider, "The Decline of Confidence in American Institutions," *Political Science Quarterly* 98 (Fall 1983), pp. 379–402.

56. Ibid., p. 383.

57. E. J. Dionne, Jr., "Government Trust: Less in West Europe than U.S.," *The New York Times,* February 16, 1986, p. 6.

58. Hennessy, *Public Opinion,* p. 250.

59. Lipset and Schneider, "The Decline of Confidence," p. 383.

60. Ibid., p. 386.

61. Ibid.

62. Ibid., p. 391.

63. *Public Opinion* 6 (August/September 1983), p. 22.

64. Ibid., p. 23.

65. Ibid., p. 26.

66. Ibid.

67. *Public Opinion* 7 (October/November 1984), p. 22.

68. Ibid.

69. Ibid., p. 23.

70. Ibid., p. 25. The question was, "Generally speaking, would you say that most people can be trusted, or that you can't be too careful in dealing with people?"

71. "Women and Men: Is a Realignment Underway?" *Public Opinion* 5 (April/May 1982), p. 21.

72. Ibid.

73. Ibid., p. 27. See also Robert Y. Shapiro and Harpeet Mahajan, "Gender Differences in Policy Preferences: A Summary of Trends from the 1960s to the 1980s," *Public Opinion Quarterly* 50 (Spring 1986), pp. 42–61.

74. "Women and Men," p. 21.

75. Daniel Wirls, "Reinterpreting the Gender Gap," *Public Opinion Quarterly* 50 (Fall 1986), p. 323.

76. Ibid., p. 317.

77. *Public Opinion* 6 (October/November 1983), p. 27.

78. *Public Opinion* 7 (December/January 1985), p. 38.

79. Charles H. Franklin, "Issue Preferences, Socialization, and the Evolution of Party Identification," *American Journal of Political Science* 28 (August 1984), pp. 459–478. See also John E. Jackson, "Issues, Party Choices, and Presidential Votes," *American Journal of Political Science* 19 (May 1975), pp. 161–185.

80. Richard J. Trilling, *Party Image and Electoral Behavior* (New York: John Wiley, 1976).

81. Benjamin I. Page and Robert Y. Shapiro, "Changes in Americans' Policy Preferences, 1935–1979," *Public Opinion Quarterly* 46 (Spring 1982), p. 39.

82. Ibid., p. 40.

83. Gregory B. Markus, "Stability and Change in Political Attitudes: Observed, Recalled, and 'Explained'," *Political Behavior* 8 (1986), pp. 21–43.

84. Ibid., pp. 40, 41.

85. Hennessy, *Public Opinion,* p. 16.

86. Alan D. Monroe, "American Party Platforms and Public Opinion," *American Journal of Political Science* 27 (February 1983), pp. 27–42.

87. See Herbert McCloskey and Alida Brill, *Dimensions of Tolerance, What Americans Believe About Civil Liberties* (New York: Russell Sage, 1983) and Thomas R. Dye and L. Harmon Zeigler, *The Irony of Democracy: An Uncommon Introduction to American Politics,* 6th ed. (Monterey, CA: Brooks/Cole, 1984).

3

Participation and Nonparticipation

The question of who participates in a political system and who does not is of vital importance for many reasons in a democratic republic. Free governments derive their legitimacy from open elections. Participation can teach citizens responsibility and other civic virtues. Those who participate are far more likely to be represented than those who do not. At this country's inception, the franchise (the right to vote) was limited to white men over twenty-one years of age who owned property. Our history has been one of slowly expanding this franchise, to the point where citizens over eighteen, of all races, male or female, are eligible to vote.

Yet, as we have expanded the pool of eligible voters, turnout has decreased. Why is it that some people care so much about politics and some could not care less? Why do some profess to care about politics but refuse to participate in the process? The answers to these questions are unique for individual citizens. We know enough about people and their voting habits, though, to develop some generalizations and theories about political behavior. Our analysis will start at the beginning, with the process of socialization. Then we will examine theories about voter turnout, theories about the characteristics of those who are politically active and those who are not, theories about vote choice, theories about the impact of the mass media on participation, and theories about the impact of participation on the political system.

POLITICAL SOCIALIZATION

Political socialization is the process by which society passes information and attitudes about politics from one generation to another. Just as parents show children how to behave as human beings, so also do they show children how to behave as political beings. Their own actions communicate messages to their children about whether politics is important or not, whether voting is important or not, which political party is worthy of their loyalty, whether politics is a private matter or something to be openly debated. The transfer of this information may be casually subtle or blatantly obvious.

The family, like many other social and political institutions, went through a rough period in the 1960s and 1970s. Divorce, remarriage, working parents, and drug abuse are just a few of the problems that have plagued modern families. But the family is not moribund; it still performs a socialization function, although some of the values being transmitted are different from the values passed on by prior generations. One enduring value that is usually communicated to children early in their lives is identification with and acceptance of the nation as a political community.[1] This identification is important for engendering loyalty and support for the political system.

While the socialization process varies somewhat among subcultures, we can say in general that children develop an emotional attachment to the term "democracy" early on, although it takes longer for them to develop a true understanding of the term.[2] Also, an attachment to the notion of "rule by the people" develops "long before there is much knowledge of what it means."[3] Children also tend to personalize the government, to see the president as constituting the U.S. government, and to see him as a good person. Young children also see the law (embodied in the form of police officers) as helpful and protective.[4] Of course, these initial attachments are altered as children grow and learn, but for most of us the process results in a predisposition to support the system in at least a very general way.

Until the mid-1960s, children tended to follow their parents' lead in choosing a political party. Once established, party identification proved quite durable. Fifty years ago parties and party affiliation were very important to people; party identification was changed about as easily as religious affiliation, which is to say not easily at all. Table 3–1 displays the distribution of party identification from 1956 to 1986. The table illustrates that the socialization process did not work as well in the late 1960s and 1970s as it had earlier. The percentage of independents has risen steadily since 1964, with small drops in 1980 and 1986. Table 3–2 lists the age groups that are most and least affiliated with the Democratic and Republican parties, and it shows that the category with the highest percentage of independents is the one with the youngest people in it.

Researchers have asked independents if they lean toward one party or the other, and they have found that independents who are Democratic leaners are not much different from those classifying themselves as weak Democrats. In

TABLE 3-1 Party Identification in the Nation

	1956	1960	1964	1968	1972	1976	1980	1984	19
Strong Democrats	21%	20%	27%	20%	15%	15%	18%	17%	
Weak Democrats	23	24	25	25	26	25	23	20	
Independents	23	22	22	29	35	36	34	34	
Weak Republicans	14	14	13	14	13	14	14	15	
Strong Republicans	15	15	11	10	10	9	8	13	
Apolitical, Other	4	5	2	2	2	2	2	2	
	100%	100%	100%	100%	100%	101%	99%	101%	
	n = 1762	1954	1571	1557	2705	2872	1614	1989	21

SOURCE: For 1956 to 1984, Survey Research Center/Center for Political Studies National Elec Studies as presented in William H. Flanigan and Nancy H. Zingale, *Political Behavior of the Ameri Electorate*, 6th ed. (Boston: Allyn and Bacon, 1987), p. 31. Reprinted with permission. Totals do not eq 100 percent due to rounding. Data for 1986 are from Harold W. Stanley and Richard E. Niemi, eds., *Statistics on American Politics* (Washington, DC: Congressional Quarterly Press, 1988), p. 124. Reprir with permission.

addition, independents who are Republican leaners are not much different from weak Republicans. The important point, though, is not that independent leaners are similar to weak partisans; it is that fewer people consider themselves to be strong partisans. But the 1960s and 1970s were years of turbulence and upheaval, and the socialization process may return to a high level of effectiveness with a return to quieter times.

Charles H. Franklin discovered that party identification can change according to policy preferences.[5] If the issue preferences of the young adult

TABLE 3-2 Party Identification According to Age Groups

	DEMOCRAT	REPUBLICAN	INDEPENDENT
All ages	39%	25%	36%
Ages 78 and older	31	43	26
Ages 62–65	48	22	30
Ages 30–33	43	18	39
Ages 22–25	31	27	42

SOURCE: General Social Surveys, National Opinion Research Center: A composite of surveys conducted in 1983 and 1984 as presented in Everett Carll Ladd, "As the Realignment Turns: A Drama in Many Acts," *Public Opinion* 7 (December/January 1985), p. 6. Reprinted with permission.

remain the same as those of the parents, and if the relative positions of the parties on these issues remain the same, then the young adult may continue to identify with the parents' party. If there is divergence, however, then the young adult is likely to depart from the parents' party. Simply put, in the 1990s young adults are more likely to be independent from their parents as far as party identification is concerned.

An important 1968 study of the political socialization of children by Robert Hess and Judith Torney found differences relating to intelligence and social class. A high IQ was associated with acceleration of the socialization process and greater interest in politics. The impact of social class was found to be more limited. Differences due to class were greatly reduced when intelligence was held constant. Lower-class children were, though, markedly less efficacious politically than upper-class children.[6] But Harry Holloway and John George also found that "social class differences in the U.S. have declined over time and by the 1980s were not a major source of variations in political attitudes."[7]

Parents expose children to their religion (or lack of it), and this can affect political beliefs. The idea that it is right and good to have a religious affiliation permeates the United States. Our money is inscribed with "In God we trust"; sessions of Congress open with a prayer; religious beliefs have affected laws on divorce and child abuse. Further, we prefer our presidential candidates to profess faith in a religion, but only up to a point; some voters were wary of Jimmy Carter's "born again" status. Religion also may affect one's stand on particular issues such as abortion, the death penalty, and U.S. aid to the contras in Nicaragua. Catholics and Jews have made up a significant portion of the New Deal Democratic coalition, the group put together by Franklin Roosevelt in 1932, although Catholic support for the Democratic party is not as strong as it once was.[8]

In the past, girls often were socialized differently from boys. There was a time when females were not expected or encouraged to express opinions about politics. While family attitudes toward sex roles have evolved considerably, evidently some of this previous behavior remains. A 1981 study showed that girls retain an immature view of the president and police officers longer than boys do, and girls were not as well informed about politics as boys.[9] For all that, the lag that used to exist in voter turnout between men and women has disappeared, and female candidates for political office abound. Women holding state and local offices totaled 7,089 in 1975, increasing to 16,881 in 1982.[10]

Racial differences in socialization exist as well, although these usually turn out to be differences due to educational level more than race per se. Black children tend to be more cynical about politics and less efficacious politically than white children, and blacks tend to vote overwhelmingly for the Democratic party.[11]

Many of our political attitudes have already taken root by the time we begin school. In general, public schools reinforce what we have already learned; that is, they reinforce the positive images of politics with which we begin life. But Hess and Torney assign more importance to school than mere reinforcement. They argue that the school is the "central, salient and dominant force in the political socialization of the young child" because "while it may be argued that the family contributes much to the socialization that goes into basic loyalty to the country, the school gives content, information, and concepts which expand and elaborate these early feelings of attachment."[12] Holloway and George agree that "education indoctrinates the young in the basic values of the system."[13] (For example, we learn that it is our duty as citizens to vote.) They point out that many of us have relatively democratic experiences in school—we are able to take part in discussions, to complain, to disagree with the teacher. Exposure to democratic procedures in school helps teach democratic values to students through example.[14]

Socialization does not end with adulthood. Other groups—professional societies, peer groups, labor unions, the PTA—continue to teach and reinforce community values. It has become more difficult to generalize about party identification, but poorer people, the less educated, union workers, blacks, Mexican-Americans, Jews, and liberals tend to be Democrats. Wealthier people, the better-educated, white-collar workers, Cuban-Americans, and conservatives tend to be Republicans. (Keep in mind that these groups are interrelated.)

Why, then, with all this positive reinforcement, are partisanship and voter turnout down and levels of cynicism about politics up? As we become adults, we expand our capacity to reason and evaluate. We go beyond family and school. We interact with other adults in the workplace. We are exposed more and more to criticisms of the government and its policies in the mass media (which also, of course, present the government's arguments defending governmental policy). We may grow up during a period when events alter the standard way of looking at politics, as did the 1960s generation. We have life experiences of our own which may alter our initial beliefs. Some of us will not move very far from where we started. Some of us will.

THEORIES ABOUT VOTER TURNOUT

Nonvoting is getting a lot of attention these days. The voter turnout rate rose in the 1984 general election, but only slightly, then dropped again in 1988. (See Table 3-3 on page 53.) Turnout is even lower in primary elections and caucuses. A variety of theories have been put forward in attempts to account for voting and nonvoting behavior; some of them are interrelated. We will examine the role played by laws and institutions, the cost/benefit (or economic) model, Maslow's needs theory, and the cross-pressure hypothesis.

Laws and Institutions

One theory approaches nonvoting from a broad perspective—the laws and institutions of society.[15] According to this theory, much of the blame for nonvoting can be placed on the system itself. Examined here are the franchise, registration, absentee ballots, plurality elections, federalism, the Electoral College, and party competition. While laws pertaining to federal elections apply nationwide, states are free to set their own rules regarding state and local elections, and wide variety exists among the states.

The Franchise. The early requirements that voters own property (or show evidence of having paid taxes) gradually disappeared. Black males were given the Constitutional right to vote with the Fifteenth Amendment in 1870, although it was many years before this right became a reality. Among the procedures and means used to keep blacks from voting were literacy tests, poll taxes, grandfather clauses, white primaries, and intimidation and violence. Literacy tests were not applied equally to blacks and whites. Blacks often were asked to interpret documents, such as state constitutions, the meaning of which lawyers might fight over. Poll taxes were just that: a tax levied on voting. These taxes discriminated against all poor people, but had a disproportionate impact on blacks. Poll taxes were outlawed by the Twenty-fourth Amendment in 1963. The grandfather clause exempted from literacy tests citizens who were eligible to vote before a specified date, and it also exempted their sons and grandsons. Since slaves had not been allowed to vote, these rules benefited whites more than blacks. "White primaries" were primary elections held by the Democratic party in the South. The party decided to keep blacks from effectively voting by declaring itself to be a private club and by then not accepting blacks as members. Blacks could vote in the general election (if they could surmount the other hurdles), but since the South was a one-party area, the only election that really counted was the primary. White primaries were declared unconstitutional by the Supreme Court in 1944 in *Smith* v. *Allwright* (321 U.S. 659). Finally, violence was a common tactic used by the Ku Klux Klan and others to intimidate blacks.[16]

The Civil Rights Act of 1964 and the Voting Rights Act of 1965 were the major tools for ending the discrimination at the polls that had existed in spite of the Thirteenth Amendment. The first of these laws required uniform standards for literacy tests; the second made it a federal crime to threaten or intimidate people to prevent them from voting. Significantly, the Voting Rights Act of 1965 allowed the appointment of federal examiners to step in and register eligible citizens. This act was extended in 1982 for an additional twenty-five years.[17]

Women were inspired by their participation in the abolitionist movement to fight for their own rights. It was a long struggle. The birth of the movement is considered to be a convention on women's rights held in Seneca Falls, New York, in 1848, but women did not win suffrage until 1920 with the ratification of the Nineteenth Amendment. (Some states did give women the right to vote prior to this amendment. Wyoming was the first, in 1871. It was still a territory, and it was anxious to attract women and families in order to reach the population level necessary for statehood.)

Eighteen-year-olds received the right to vote with the Twenty-sixth Amendment in 1971. Thus, restrictions based on race, gender, and age have all but disappeared, but minor residency requirements (thirty days for federal elections, and no more than fifty days for state elections) and registration requirements remain.

Registration.   Most of those who are registered do vote,[18] so it is useful to consider whether or not registration procedures are still preventing some people from voting. Some feel that voter turnout would increase if the government had the responsibility for drawing up voter lists, as it does in England. A few states require that voters re-register periodically; some citizens forget to do so and lose their right to vote. (States requiring periodic registration have been decreasing.)[19]

About twenty states provide for mail registration. Forms are available at various public places, and citizens merely fill them out and mail them in. There is no need to visit in person the courthouse or county election board. Minnesota and Maine provide for election-day registration. Voters who might have been bored by a campaign or distracted up until the last week before the election still can register and vote. Laws like these appear to increase voter turnout, but they may be more susceptible to fraud, and long lines could occur on election day if many people decide to register then.[20]

As stated, in most states the residency requirement for registration is thirty days or less, much shorter than the waiting periods of old. However, even thirty days can be too short for some people, especially those who have recently moved. Peverill Squire, Raymond E. Wolfinger, and David P. Glass studied the impact of registration laws on recent movers to new voting districts and came to some interesting conclusions. They found that nearly one-third of the nation moves every two years, and that half of all moves take place between June and September. Summer movers, it would seem, are particularly affected by registration requirements. Recent movers are preoccupied with many tasks; registering to vote is not usually at the top of their lists.

> People in a new home have all sorts of arranging and adjusting to do, from redecorating to mastering innumerable details of domestic administration: where to shop, how to get to work, how to spend recreational time. Registering to vote is drab and boring, a weak claimant for attention.[21]

The researchers found that movers are the "biggest light-voting group in the country," but, other than their age, they possess characteristics that are very similar to nonmovers. (Movers tend to be younger than "stayers.")

> Movers are just as likely as stayers to talk about the campaign, pay attention to political items in the news, think they have a say in politics, deny that politics is too complicated to understand, and assert that public officials care what people like themselves think. They are almost as likely to care which party wins the presidential election, to be interested in the campaign, and to follow politics most or some of the time. They are equally likely to engage in political activities other than voting. These findings would lead us to expect movers to vote as much as stayers,

but only 48 percent of them voted in 1980, compared with 65 percent of the stayers.[22]

In 1980, movers made up 29 percent of voting-age citizens.[23] It is true of the population in general that those who are registered are more likely to vote than those who are not; the same thing is true of movers. Among movers in 1980, 87 percent of those registered voted.[24] Squire and his associates have a proposal that would maintain the registration of those who have moved. They suggest that the Postal Service forms that residents file to change their addresses be modified to allow movers to ask that a change of voting address be included. Multiple forms could be made using carbon copies, and the Postal Service could send one copy to the election official in the state where the move originates, that is, the state of the old address. According to the authors, in 83 percent of the cases, this would also be the destination state, the state of the new address. (Most moves are in-state moves.) The old address registration would then be canceled on receipt of this form, a procedure the authors call "an efficient and inexpensive way of removing deadwood from the registration rolls."[25] Squire and his associates maintain that this reform might increase turnout as much as 9 percent, and that it would have an effect on the Democrats about as much as on the Republicans.

Raymond E. Wolfinger and Steven J. Rosenstone found that laws allowing regular weekday office hours, registration on evenings and Saturdays, and late closing dates for registration could help increase turnout.[26] They also addressed the question of how the electorate might change if registration and turnout were increased. They found that an increase would have little advantage for one political party over another:

> Although making it easier for people to register would increase turnout, it would have a very small impact on the demographic characteristics of voters. Voters in the aggregate would be marginally less educated, poorer, blacker, and younger. These changes would be somewhat greater in the South.[27]

The main reason for registration laws, of course, is to decrease fraudulent voting. These laws, and mechanical balloting, have reduced vote fraud considerably, but it still occurs in some parts of the country, particularly in Chicago, New York City, Philadelphia, and portions of the South.[28] Big cities are where registration of persons who do not exist or fail to meet voter qualifications often occurs. Some voters register in more than one precinct; a 1982 investigation found more than 1,000 people who were registered both in Chicago and in nearby areas of Indiana. When vote buying occurs, it is usually in poor areas.[29]

Vote fraud frequently happens in areas dominated by one party, where there is no effective opposition to expose it. Robert Goldberg notes that it is difficult to determine which came first: Is it fraud that keeps the area under one party's control, or is it one-party control that allows fraud? Goldberg points out that some areas have had one-party systems for years without a fraudulent vote problem.[30]

Absentee Ballots.   Communities allow citizens who will be away on election day to vote with absentee ballots. Unfortunately, it is often difficult to obtain these ballots in time to fill them out and return them before the due date. Fraud involving absentee ballots can take the form of applying for ballots using the names of others, purchasing them from legitimate voters, and altering the ballots before they are counted.

Plurality Elections.   Another legal aspect of participation arises because most U.S. elections are plurality elections, that is, whoever receives the most votes wins (even if that candidate receives less than 50 percent of the vote). Majority elections, on the other hand, require that a candidate win 50 percent of the votes plus one vote in order to win. Also, most elections involve single-district representation, in which there can be only one winner for each office. Under this system, a vote cast for a party nominee with low levels of support is a wasted vote; such a candidate cannot win. Or a party may win by a huge margin—say, 80 percent—but since the winner needs only to win one vote more than the loser, some of these votes are wasted because the votes are "extra," not counted in a sense. On the other side of the coin, a party may keep losing seats in individual districts by a very small margin. There is obviously much support for this party, but none of it gets translated into offices held, so these votes for the losing party in a sense do not count either. But this system is not the only way to count votes. Under *proportional representation,* parties are represented in government in proportion to the number of votes they win. Thus, if a party receives 30 percent of the vote, it will get 30 percent of, for example, the seats in the legislature. Proportional representation (adopted by the Democrats for most of their presidential primaries) thus offers an incentive to vote, since votes are not wasted.

Federalism.   Another structural problem is, ironically, that we have so many elections in this country. Because we have a federal system, voters are asked to participate in local, state, and national elections. Because of current nomination procedures, voters are also asked to vote in primary and general elections as well. We are also asked to make judgments about ballot proposals, and many states have separate elections for judges. (See Chapter 8.) Such a system is quite democratic, but it also is quite exhausting to keep up with. Some people do not try. The type of election affects turnout. It is highest when presidential candidates are on the ballot. It declines as elections become more local in orientation. This is a curious phenomenon, since local elections select the politicians who have the most direct impact on our daily lives. Perhaps some people are more interested in national politics because, no matter where they live or how many times they move, they can easily watch national politicians on network television. Another factor is that, while decisions about where to build roads or put stop signs are significant in our daily lives, questions of war and peace—national issues—are even more significant.

The Electoral College. Many people, voters and nonvoters, complain about the role of the Electoral College in presidential elections. Voters do not actually vote for presidential candidates; they vote for electors who are pledged to candidates. On rare occasions, electors have gone against the wishes of the voters and supported a different candidate, one to whom they had not been pledged. Also, the mathematics of the Electoral College system overemphasizes both small and large states. Critics feel that this institution renders many votes meaningless, and many prefer direct election. (See Chapter 5 for a description of how the Electoral College operates.)

Party Competition. Other scholars, such as Walter Dean Burnham, examine the role that parties and party competition play in turnout. One-party areas have traditionally been associated with low turnout. Campaign intensity and the amount of campaign spending also influence turnout.[31] Burnham emphasizes the class structure of the electoral system. The major parties are dominated by the middle class, while no meaningful socialist party, which might appeal to the working class, has developed. Turnout might increase if the system included greater representation of the interests of the working class.[32]

Aside from these factors, we know that strong partisans are more likely to vote than weak partisans or independents, and the number of strong partisans has been declining.[33] At the same time, the number of independents has been rising. As previously mentioned, since the 1960s parents have been less successful in passing down party affiliation to their children than they were in past generations. Voters are increasingly apt to split their tickets rather than to vote a straight party ticket. People want to be individuals when they vote, as opposed to party automatons, but such individualism exacts a high price in terms of researching candidates and issues. Holloway and George account for this individualism by citing that society is increasingly middle class; more and more people work with their brains, not their hands; and communication and media use have expanded.[34] Finally, turnout is higher among Republicans than Democrats.

The Cost/Benefit Model

One theory used to explain nonvoting is based on cost/benefit analysis. This theory sees voters as rational human beings who weigh the costs of voting (in terms of time, transportation, and gathering information) against the benefits of voting (being able to support a party, candidate, or issue; the possibility of having an impact on government; a feeling of fulfillment from doing one's civic duty). It follows that, for some, the costs outweigh the benefits. Anthony Downs wrote:

When voting is costless, any return whatsoever makes abstention irrational, so everyone who has even a slight party preference votes. On the other hand, abstention does not harm those who are indifferent because (1) democracy works even if they do not vote and (2) parties still cater to their interests so as to get their votes next time. Thus there is no return from voting *per se,* and all indifferent citizens abstain.

When voting is costly, its costs may outweigh its returns, so abstention can be rational even for citizens with party preferences. In fact, the returns from voting are usually so low that even small costs can sharply reduce political power.[35]

Recall the discussion of the increasing use of primary elections in Chapter 1. Most primaries do not allow voters to rely on the simple cue of party identification when they vote; all the candidates are members of the same party. Voters must either research the candidates and issues, or base their votes on superficial images. Either choice involves more work than merely voting by party identification. It is thus no surprise that turnout in primary elections is lower than for general elections.

Closely associated to the cost/benefit theory is that of the rational voter, developed by V. O. Key, Jr., in his 1966 classic, *The Responsible Electorate.*[36] Key wrote that most voters stay with the same party, the "standpatters," some are "switchers," and some are, of course, new voters. Most voters in any election are standpatters, but the switchers can be the ones who determine the election outcome. Key argued that both standpatters and switchers can be considered rational voters. If a particular party makes a voter happy, it is rational to stick with it election after election. Switchers can also be rational. Perhaps they are unhappy with what the government or the incumbent has done to them in the years since the previous election. Perhaps a major event, such as the Great Depression, has occurred and has altered their perceptions of the parties.[37]

Maslow's Needs Theory

We can gain insight into the question of why some people participate and some do not by examining Abraham Maslow's needs theory. Maslow argues that human beings have a hierarchy of five types of needs: physical (food and shelter); security; affection, love, and belongingness; self-esteem; and self-actualization.[38] One concentrates on the most immediate needs (physical and security needs) before attempting to fulfill the higher-order needs. Belonging to a political group may help us attempt to actualize ourselves, but if the day's main concern must be getting food on the table, the political group will be ignored. Some people may have a greater need for belongingness than others, and they may join a political group out of that need. Other theories stress the role of power needs; the political world obviously offers many opportunities to those who seek power.[39]

Decline-of-Community Model

Sidney Verba and Norman H. Nie bring up another factor that may affect participation—the nature of the community. They discuss the "decline-of-community model," which

> predicts the decline of participation as one moves from the smallness and intimacy of town or village to the massive impersonality of the city. In the small town, the community is a manageable size. Citizens can know the ropes of politics, know whom to contact, know each other so that they can form political groups. In the larger units, politics is more complicated, impersonal, and distant. In addition, "modernization" shatters political units. What were once relatively independent communities—providing the individual with the social, economic, political, and cultural services that he needs—become small towns in a mass society. Such communities no longer have clear economic borders as citizens begin to commute to work. They have more permeable social boundaries as recreational and educational facilities move out of the community, and they cease to be well-bounded political units as local services become more dependent on outside governmental authorities.[40]

Verba and Nie are writing about participation in general, but voting is included in that. They found, though, that of the modes of participation, community participation is particularly affected by this model (not surprisingly).[41] The problem, of course, is that so few of us live in the ideal, well-defined smaller community.

The Cross-Pressure Hypothesis

The cross-pressure hypothesis is a controversial notion that addresses both voter turnout and vote choice. We know that a northern, black, blue-collar worker will typically vote for the Democratic candidate. But what about a northern, black, corporate attorney with an income in six figures? The *cross-pressure hypothesis* argues that people under "consistent pressure" act differently from those under "cross-pressure" (those with some factors pointing in, say, a Republican direction and some in a Democratic direction). The cross-pressured person is predicted to be more likely to split tickets, to postpone the decision on whom to vote for, and to be less interested in politics than those under consistent pressure. Cross-pressures are felt to produce anxiety. The cross-pressured person responds with avoidance reactions—attempts to lessen exposure to situations, such as politics, emphasizing the cross-pressures.[42]

Assuming that people with consistently Democratic cues vote for the Democratic candidates and that those with consistently Republican cues vote for the Republican candidates, it is the cross-pressured who must be wooed in order to win elections. Empirical data, however, do not show strong support for the cross-pressure hypothesis, at least not when it is based on social cross-pressures. Attitudinal cross-pressures, though, have been documented with at least some survey data. The phrase *attitudinal cross-pressures* refers to possession of some attitudes that favor one party and other attitudes that favor the other party. (See the discussion of cognitive balance in Chapter 2.) Studies from the Survey Research Center in 1952 and 1956 showed that conflicting attitudes *were* associated with nonvoting, indecision, and lack of interest in the election.[43]

These, then, are the theories that have been used to explain differences in voter turnout. Parts of these theories have been embraced more wholeheartedly by political scientists than others. Some theories seem to apply better to a particular election than to others. It is useful to keep these theories in mind as we turn to data on who actually votes and who does not.

WHO IS ACTIVE AND WHO IS NOT?

Demographic Factors

Turnout in recent U.S. elections has been low, as shown in Table 3–3. What types of people bother to register and vote? Research has identified a number of important factors, but bear in mind that their effect on individuals is not uniform. *Education* is one important factor; turnout is highest among those spending the longest time in the formal educational system. Since the better-educated voters tend to find good jobs and earn good salaries, *income* is also related to voting. *Age* is another important consideration. For a variety of reasons, young people often do not vote, and the same is true of the elderly. (Persons eighteen to thirty years of age often have not settled down, either geographically or socially, while the elderly are sometimes sick or infirm.) Those between forty and sixty-nine have the highest turnout rate.[44] Studies have shown, though, that the decline in later years is erased when other factors are held constant.[45] The level of *external political efficacy* is important; those who feel the government is responsive to citizens are more likely to vote than those who feel otherwise.[46]

Other factors are at work as well. *Married* people are more likely to vote than single, divorced or widowed people.[47] *Partisanship* also plays a role; strong partisans are more likely to vote than weak partisans or independents. Among all these factors, education has a special place. M. Margaret Conway explains why: The better-educated people know more about how the political system works and are more aware of the consequences of governmental action; education provides people with the bureaucratic and cognitive skills that facilitate political activity; education may increase interest in politics; the better-educated people are more likely to have political opinions; and the better-educated people are more likely to monitor the mass media, especially newspapers and magazines.[48] Education is also related to a sense of civic duty. Essentially, education reduces the costs involved in voting.[49]

The remaining indicators of participation tend to be related to these critical factors. *Race* has historically been related to turnout, with blacks voting

TABLE 3-3   Turnout in Presidential Elections, 1948-1988

YEAR	ESTIMATED POPULATION OF VOTING AGE (IN MILLIONS)	NUMBER OF VOTES CAST (IN MILLIONS)	PERCENTAGE OF VOTES CAST
1948	95.6	48.8	51.1
1952	99.9	61.6	61.6
1956	104.5	62.0	59.3
1960	109.7	68.8	62.8
1964	114.1	70.6	61.9
1968	120.3	73.2	60.9
1972	140.8	77.7	55.2
1976	152.3	81.6	53.5
1980	164.4	86.6	52.6
1984	173.9	92.6	53.3
1988	183.0	89.0	50.0

SOURCE: *Statistical Abstract of the United States*, 106th ed. (Washington, DC: U.S. Bureau of the Census, 1985), p. 255. Reprinted with permission. Data for 1988 are from "Dismal Turnout Trend Examined," *The Pittsburgh Press*, November 10, 1988, p. A21. Reprinted with permission.

less than whites, and Hispanic-Americans tending to vote at lower rates than blacks, with some variation.[50] (Cuban-Americans are very active in some areas.) As levels of education have increased among blacks, and with enforcement of the Voting Rights Act of 1965, the voter turnout gap between the races has narrowed considerably. In 1982, the gap was about 7 percent, down from 12 percent in 1964.[51] Some contests, of course, are particularly salient to blacks and turnout increases as a result. In the South, more and more blacks are winning elective posts, and, in 1983, more than 60 percent of Chicago voting-age blacks turned out to vote and help elect Harold Washington as Chicago's first black mayor.[52]

Wolfinger and Rosenstone point out that, since blacks as a group are younger and less educated than whites, lower turnout among that group is not surprising. Yet they found that, when socioeconomic factors are held constant, blacks voted at a slightly *higher* rate than whites.[53] Blacks often possess a sense of racial identity and community consciousness that motivates them to be politically active.

Women once had lower turnout rates than men; the South once had lower turnout rates than the rest of the country. Differences in turnout based on sex and region have diminished in recent years. Lower educational levels associated with women and the South largely explain the differences that previously existed. (Disenfranchisement of blacks and restrictive registration laws also help to explain low southern voter turnout. Disenfranchisement is a thing of the past; but relatively restrictive registration laws remain.) Women are somewhat less likely than men to participate in campaign activity. Women have been found to pay less attention to politics than men, and to exhibit lower levels of internal political efficacy.[54] Such differences may be due to childhood socialization patterns.

Interest in Election

One might assume that those interested in the election are more likely to vote than those who are not, but this is not necessarily the case. About half of those who say they do not have much interest in the campaign do vote in presidential elections.[55] The socialization process imbues most of us with the notion that we should not ignore this opportunity to participate in the democratic process, that it is our civic duty to vote. Also, some individuals may be manipulated into voting. Coercive voting in this country is probably quite rare, but citizens can be manipulated by emotional, inflammatory rhetoric.[56]

Comparisons With Other Nations

Our discussion of political participation, particularly voter turnout, must be placed in a broader context. U.S. voter turnout figures look quite poor when we compare them to turnout in other Western industrialized democracies. Average turnout in presidential elections from 1972 to 1980 was 54 percent; in twenty other industrialized democracies the average was 80 percent.[57] But we must keep in mind that these countries possess political cultures and laws that are very different from ours. Some of these countries make it a crime to not vote; a person not voting may be subject to fine. Such a law would no doubt increase turnout here, but our political culture, with its stress on individualism, discourages such legislation. Other countries usually base their turnout figures on registered voters, not on the eligible population, as does the United States. However, according to G. Bingham Powell, Jr., average voter turnout in nations that do not require voting was 77 percent of the voting age population. The United States still comes up short. Powell also writes that "the United States is unique in the low registration rate of its population of voting age."[58] (He attributes these differences to institutional factors, particularly the burden of self-registration in the United States.)

Behavior Other Than Voting

Voting is the most common political activity, but there are, of course, other kinds of political behavior. Table 3–4 shows the results of one effort to categorize these various activities.[59] The table shows only 8 percent reporting membership in a political club or organization. As with voting, those of higher socioeconomic status are the ones who tend to engage in all of these activities. Only 30 percent of the public take advantage of the checkoff on federal income tax forms that sends $1.00 to the presidential campaign fund.[60]

Verba and Nie point out that different forms of participation vary in what they can get for the citizen and what they can get the citizen into.[61] Some activities merely provide a sense of having fulfilled one's civic duty; some provide more

TABLE 3–4   Percentage Engaging in Selected Acts of Political Participation

TYPE OF ACTIVITY	PERCENTAGE
1. Report regularly voting in presidential elections	72
2. Report always voting in local elections	47
3. Active in at least one organization involved in community problems	32
4. Have worked with others in trying to solve some community problems	30
5. Have attempted to persuade others to vote as they planned to vote	28
6. Have ever actively worked for a party or candidate during an election	26
7. Have ever contacted a local government official about some issue or problem	20
8. Have attended at least one political meeting or rally in last three years	19
9. Have ever contacted a state or national government official about some issue or problem	18
10. Have ever formed a group or organization to attempt to solve some local community problem	14
11. Have ever given money to a party or candidate during an election campaign	13
12. Presently a member of a political club or organization	8

SOURCE:: Sidney Verba and Norman H. Nie, *Participation in America: Political Democracy and Social Equality*, (NY: Harper & Row, 1972), p. 31. Reprinted with permission.

tangible benefits. Some activities involve open conflict; some do not. Activities also differ in terms of what they require of people. Some require special skills or initiative; others do not. These factors help explain why some individuals engage in certain kinds of activities but not in others. People, in effect, match their goals, skills, and preferences to the kinds of activities best suited to them. Someone who enjoys conflict is more likely to run for political office than someone who finds conflict distasteful. Verba and Nie developed a typology of political activities, based on the amount of conflict involved, the scope of the outcome sought, and the initiative required. They argue that these different "modes" of activity foster different conditions that lead to participation.[62]

Empirical investigation by Verba and Nie discovered that people specialize in certain kinds of political activity. In their 1972 study they found that 22 percent of those studied were *inactives,* people who take "almost no part in political life."[63] These individuals either do not vote at all or vote only occasionally. Citizens of lower socioeconomic status were overrepresented in this group, and those of higher status were underrepresented. It was found that 21 percent were *voting specialists.* They vote with regularity but do not try to influence the government in other ways. Of those studied, 4 percent were declared to be *parochial participants,* people who are average voters and make contacts with government officials in a variety of ways. Such contacts are limited to activity that has a direct effect on their lives. In addition, 20 percent were *communalists,* people exhibiting high levels of community activity, but low levels of campaign activity. Another 15 percent were *campaigners,* engaging in little community activity, but very active in political campaigns and 11 percent were *complete activists,* engaging in all modes of activity with high degrees of frequency.

Their empirical analysis supported Verba and Nie's hypothesis that different activities possess different conditions for participation. Certainly we cannot expect all citizens to be complete activists all of the time. This important research reveals there might be a kind of division of labor of the "burden" of participation in society, a division of labor that, one hopes, gets the necessary job of democracy done without requiring that all citizens be constantly active. Verba and Nie's findings might be a partial result of the time in which their study was conducted, but the notion of a division of labor is still intriguing.

While many choose to remain inactive, there nevertheless exist great varieties of organizations and interest groups to serve the needs of those who want to participate in some way. There are groups representing professional concerns (the American Trial Lawyers Association), larger business interests (the Business Roundtable), ideological groups (the Committee for the Survival of a Free Congress), civil rights groups, welfare rights organizations, and citizen lobbies. The list is endless. Communities also have witnessed the development of active neighborhood groups, formed to perform an array of activities from crime prevention to boosting business. For example, there is the Association of Community Organizations for Reform Now (ACORN), which calls itself a grassroots community organization that, among other things, mounts voter registration drives among the poor and unemployed. There are fundamentalist Christian groups, court-watching groups, and police advisory councils. Many argue that interest groups have gained power as the parties have weakened.

For all the variety that exists in these organizations, it is still true that, as E. E. Schattschneider wrote in 1960, "the pressure system has an upper-class bias."[64] Participation in groups is much higher among those who are better educated and better off, and the groups that do try to represent the interests of the poor usually lack the resources of groups representing the middle class. Even the middle-class groups are vulnerable to charges that their leaders fail to represent adequately the interests of the membership. The wealthier have advantages because they have been socialized to believe that politics is important, because they have leisure time to spare for political activity, and because money is so important in U.S. politics. Verba and Nie see a different kind of potential for organizational activity and argue that it does not have to be this way:

> Organizations remain an important "potential" source for reducing the participation gap between the socially advantaged and disadvantaged. As our data show, the latter gain more in their political participation through organizations than do the more advantaged groups. If rates of membership among the disadvantaged were to increase, the net effect would be to reduce the political-participation disparity.[65]

Some political activity is unconventional, such as protest demonstrations and riots. A 1985 study by T. David Mason and Jerry A. Murtagh studied participants in racial disorders and discovered that "willingness to participate in civil violence is fairly evenly distributed across income, educational, and occupational strata."[66] They also found that the propensity to use violence is related to age (the young are more likely to be violent), and that the propensity to engage in nonviolent protests is associated with higher socioeconomic status. These finding are interesting because they suggest that two standard notions of riot behavior are false: Rioters are not necessarily the disadvantaged, who may feel that they have been forgotten by society; neither are they necessarily those of higher socioeconomic status who have had some success, but who are frustrated by a sense that they have not been allowed to reach their full potential. According to Mason and Murtagh rioters include people from both categories, and those in between as well. Certainly many who participate in antiwar, antinuclear power, and antiapartheid demonstrations are middle class.

Why Some Are Inactive

There are a wealth of reasons why people choose not to involve themselves in politics. H. Mark Roelofs and Gerald L. Houseman, wary of the oversimplification that generalization can bring, nonetheless have divided such individuals into four categories: the apathetic, the cynical, the alienated, and the anomic. The *apathetic* are people who may be quite active in other pursuits, but

> the contradictions they see and experience in the political system are so severe that they feel demoralized. Apathetics do not actively reject the system, but they are not able to speak or act out of any positive political attachments.[67]

SOURCE: Jerry Fearing, St. Paul Pioneer Press and Dispatch. Copyright 1980. Reprinted with permission.

Such individuals rarely vote, and tend to prefer private solutions to problems.

Cynics are seen as feeling a disaffection with politics that "lies beyond apathy."[68] Cynics reject the political values that the masses embrace, but accept the "principles of personal endeavor and success."[69] Cynics attempt to exploit the system for their personal advantage.

The *alienated* are estranged from politics. They "reject the ideological side of politics,"[70] but they accept the values rejected by the cynics. Alienated individuals are repelled by the compromise and negotiation that are crucial to practical politics. Ada W. Finifter believes that political alienation may be expressed in four ways: political powerlessness (having the inability to affect the actions of government); political meaninglessness (feeling that political events are unpredictable); normlessness (feeling that societal norms are not being followed); and political isolation (feeling that no legitimate norms govern the political system).[71]

The *anomic* have never been "socialized into citizenship."[72] They cannot follow the norms of politics "because they hardly know what the norms are."[73] This category can include the unemployed and unemployable, the homeless, and those suffering the cruelties of poverty.

Other Considerations

Other considerations affecting voting participation turn on our past history. We often compare presidential election turnout rates to 1960, a peak year for voter turnout (62.8 percent). If we go back to 1948, when turnout was 51.1 percent, the current figure looks better. Also, the Twenty-sixth Amendment, granting the vote to eighteen-year-olds, expanded the pool of eligible voters by including a group (young people) notorious for low rates of participation.

THEORIES ABOUT VOTE CHOICE

We move now from voter turnout to an examination of why voters choose the candidate or party to whom they grant their allegiance. Examined are the sociological model, the funnel of causality, and retrospective voting.

The Sociological Model

An initial assumption was that voting was similar to buying a product. Political parties were viewed as presenting products that they advertised, and the public was seen as evaluating these products during the campaign, making their choice on election day. Reality, however, did not support this assumption. The first major study of U.S. voting behavior, conducted out of Columbia University in 1940, discovered that most people knew who they were going to vote for as soon as they knew who the candidates were, without paying attention to the campaign.[74] A sociological model was adopted by the scholars at Columbia to explain voting. They discovered that three factors were strongly related to vote choice: socioeconomic status (educational level, income, and class), religion, and place of residence (rural or urban).

Knowing that these factors explained most of the differences in voter choice added a great deal to voting research, but scholars did not stop here. Richard Niemi and Herbert Weisberg explain why:

> This model doesn't try to explain *why* more Protestants voted Republican than did Catholics. It doesn't consider the political aspects of an election. And it is not useful in explaining change across elections, since different parties are elected in different years even if these social characteristics don't change much. Moreover, it doesn't always work.[75]

The three sociological factors were not forgotten by researchers, but were put into perspective by later studies. The Survey Research Center at the University of Michigan used a social-psychological model to study the 1952 election. Here the focus was on three psychological factors—attachment to a political party, orientation toward issues, and orientation toward the candidates.[76] These psychological factors focused on matters purely political and provided some needed balance to the sociological variables in the earlier model.

The Funnel of Causality

It was in *The American Voter,* the Michigan study of the 1952 and 1956 elections, that the interrelationships among these variables were detailed. The authors pictured the voting process in terms of a *funnel of causality*. The act of voting is at the tip of the funnel, and the axis of the funnel is time. At the mouth of the funnel are basic characteristics such as ethnicity, race, religion, education, occupation, class, parental class, and partisanship. These characteristics are long-term influences that help determine party identification, which helps determine evaluations of candidates, issues, and media campaign reports. Closest to the vote itself are conversations about the election with family and friends. Evaluations of candidates, issues, media reports, and conversations with others are considered short-term influences, and, as such, they vary considerably from election to election. While all of these factors were considered to be influential, the Michigan researchers emphasized the political variables of party identification, candidates, and issues.[77] This has remained the basic model for the Michigan voting studies, which now are now done every two years.

Retrospective Voting

The notion that voters make judgments based on the past behavior of politicians (and parties) is called retrospective voting. Morris P. Fiorina wrote that making judgments about past behavior is easier to do than attempting to predict what politicians will do in the future.[78] Much of the research on retrospective voting has involved voter evaluations of how parties or incumbents have handled the economy. It appears that economic evaluations are more important in presidential elections than in congressional ones.[79] A debate has raged in political science journals as to whether citizens are basing economic evaluations on the economy in general or on their personal financial situation.[80] Stanley Feldman addresses the problem by asking under what conditions people's economic well-being is affected by the government, and under what conditions will people connect their financial situation to the government? He argues:

> Despite protests to the contrary, the accumulated evidence very strongly suggests that vote choice and presidential evaluations are at best modestly influenced by *personal* economic considerations. This is not because people are incapable of acting in their own self-interest. When government policies have a direct impact on them *and* they attribute responsibility to the government, people do alter their evaluations accordingly. Much evidence now shows that these conditions are often not met. The result is that personal self-interest is typically not a major element in studies of political behavior.[81]

The growing independence of politicians from their parties makes retrospective voting problematic. It is easier to have an opinion on how a party has performed than it is to follow the individual actions of politicians. When parties are strong, voters can assume that party members generally support party programs, and they can hold party members responsible for those programs. But when parties are weak, as they now are, voters cannot assume that a particular candidate voted for party programs. Nonetheless, when times are good, candidates from the incumbent president's party will tend to benefit.

As candidates have become more important, parties have become less so. It is time to turn to the technological marvel that has largely taken the place of parties in our lives, the mass media.

MEDIA IMPACT ON PARTICIPATION

The mass media pervade our lives. Most of what we know of politics we know through the media. How does this affect political participation? It appears true that frequency of reading about a campaign in a newspaper is positively related to voter turnout. Decreased readership is estimated to account for about 20 percent of the recent decline in turnout, but radio listenership and television viewership do not seem to affect turnout.[82]

Critique of the Media's Role

Television has stepped into the vacuum left by weak political parties. In the past, parties were the connecting link between people and the government. According to Herbert B. Asher,

> If previously the political party via the machine, patronage, and constituent services served as a major link between citizens and government, today television provides that link by being the major source of information about the activities of government, particularly at the national level. The tenor of the news and informa-

tion conveyed by television, however, tends to be negative, focusing on the short-comings and failures of governmental actors. Thus, while serving as a link between citizens and government, television may serve to increase the distance between the two. The political party, on the other hand, may have served to bring government closer to the people since it was often a dispenser of direct rewards to the citizenry.[83]

While researchers have not been able to prove it, some observers of U.S. politics think that television is the cause of much of the nonvoting that exists. They argue that television teaches us to be spectators, not participants.[84] Why bother to vote in an election when you can stay home and have it all explained to you by a Dan Rather? Jarol B. Manheim developed a set of propositions that outline how this process works. He argued that a majority of Americans are uninterested and uninvolved in politics, and a plurality rely on television for political information. Television is a medium of low psychological involvement; all you have to do is sit and watch, as opposed to the effort required to read a newspaper or book. Persons receiving political information through television are, therefore, more easily manipulated than are readers.

As the flow of complex political information declines apace with the increasing reliance on television as a source of political information, first the perceived need, and later the ability, to perform sophisticated intellectual operations on such information, as well as an appreciation for the complexity of politics itself, also will decline.

The result will be a continuing qualitative reduction of the intellectual content of political discourse among the mass of American citizens which may enable an elite which preserves the requisite knowledge, skills, and resources more effectively to manipulate the polity.[85]

Manheim's solution? Read more, watch less. Shanto Iyengar and Donald R. Kinder seem to share Manheim's sentiments. They wrote:

With its authoritative trappings, television news seems to be saying that ordinary people cannot manage politics and should not try, that politics is for and about elites, not for and about the viewer. In this respect, television news is profoundly antidemocratic.[86]

In the same vein, Michael J. Robinson argues that television newscasts create "videomalaise," a feeling of cynicism, frustration, and detachment from the system.[87]

Henry E. Brady and Richard Johnston wrote that the media overemphasize "viability," the ability of candidates to keep their campaigns going throughout the long nomination process, the ability to gain enough support to translate into convention delegates. They argued that citizens learn about candidates, but they

learn too slowly about every aspect of the candidates except their viability. And one of the major reasons that citizens learn quickly about viability is the enormous emphasis placed on the horse race by the media, especially right after the Iowa caucuses and the New Hampshire primary.[88]

An emphasis on viability serves to justify voter decisions to ignore all but a few candidates.

Lewis W. Wolfson noted that reporters "tend to treat elections as narrow tests of imagery and footwork: Can the candidates get the voters' attention and make it through the campaign without shooting himself or herself in the foot?"[89] He further contended that the issues reporters emphasize are the kind that disappear after the election.

According to David L. Paletz and Robert M. Entman, the media provide us with conflicting signals about presidential elections. All the attention given these elections, all the reporters sent out, and all the money spent imply that these are critically important events. But another message is conveyed as well:

> For many people, a presidential campaign is experienced through the media as a bombardment of disparate and incompatible claims. Although coverage has a narrative thrust climaxing on election night, daily campaign events appear disjointed, confusing, and conflicting. In part this is accurate: candidates contradict each other, and the meanings of events are sometimes hard to discern. But the way the media report the campaigns adds to the confusion, leading to a "plague on all the candidates" attitude among many members of the electorate.[90]

Paletz and Entman discuss the lack of attention the media give to informing the public on nonelectoral kinds of political behavior. People are not routinely told how they might influence political decisions, where they should go, or who they should see. Take public service announcements, for instance. Instead of using such announcements for transmitting the kind of information just listed, the media provide innocuous announcements that admonish us against starting forest fires, or encourage us to donate money to worthy organizations.[91]

Campaign events during the nomination contests are not aimed at the citizens of Kentucky or Florida or Ohio so much as at the national television audience. Speeches and rallies are planned early in the day in order to make the network evening news programs. It is commonplace for candidates to make quick appearances at airports in one state and then go on to the next stop in another state. The airport appearances get a few minutes on television, and the candidate is free to move on to the next media market. In a positive vein, the campaigns reach far more people today than they used to. Critics would argue, however, that, with the emphasis on image, the content of these campaigns leaves much to be desired.

Defense of the Media's Role

On the other side of coin, defenders of television argue that it transmits much useful information to citizens. In fact, viewers may be better informed than they would be otherwise, because so much of the political information they pick up is inadvertent. A "newsbreak" interrupts the prime-time show they are watching, and they learn information they otherwise would not seek out. W. Russell Neuman writes that political learning is likely to be fragmentary and haphazard:

> The citizen does not "study" the candidates but rather picks up bits and pieces of information over time, gradually accumulating a composite picture of the prominent issues and candidates. This is a process of low-salience learning.[92]

Media suggestions that an election is going to be a close race may stimulate interest in the campaign, and thus increase voter turnout. In terms of cost/benefit analysis, a close contest means that the value of voting is greater.

Voters' Use of the Media

As voters rely less and less on party identification as a voting cue, they rely more and more on evaluations of candidates and issues.[93] The information on which they base these evaluations comes, for the most part, from the mass media. We evaluate candidates on the basis of all sorts of criteria: likeability, leadership, honesty, intelligence, competence, and the ability to handle foreign affairs. Those who wish can submerge themselves in news reports and arrive at rational, intelligent judgments about the candidates; an unknown number of citizens rely on hasty impressions derived from television news broadcasts and "spots" purchased by the candidates.[94] Candidates themselves spend small fortunes purchasing professional advice on how to come across well on television.[95]

What about media impact on candidate preference? Given the importance of issues in general elections, the degree to which voters can be affected by the media is limited. In primary elections, however, the media are crucial in providing (or not providing) candidates with needed visibility and name recognition. (Vote choices sometimes do fluctuate in primary election campaigns, especially when a variety of candidates are entering and leaving the field.) Candidates find that fund-raising becomes much easier once they are taken seriously by the media.[96] In general, research has shown that few vote choices or issue positions are changed by a general election campaign or media coverage of it. This is consistent with our discussion in Chapter 2, which cited the difficulties involved in changing attitudes and opinions.

Coverage given to candidates by the media is not equal, and this may affect levels of interest in a campaign and in voter turnout. Third-party candidates, or long shots, such as Jesse Jackson in 1984 or John Anderson (who was both a long-shot Republican candidate and a third-party candidate), tend to get less coverage from the major media, and stories that do appear about them often mention the fact that their candidacies are doomed. This lack of coverage can have a circular effect: The candidate is not in the news, therefore citizens are unaware of his or her campaign, therefore the media are justified in arguing that the candidate does not have a chance, and therefore they run few stories about the campaign. Candidates who do not receive media coverage have a hard time raising money, and candidates who raise less money receive less coverage.

Doris A. Graber has found that the effects of television coverage of President Reagan were complicated. She discovered that much of the television coverage of the 1984 presidential campaign was negative for Reagan in terms of the verbal messages transmitted. But the pictures that went with those verbal messages, the visually conveyed messages, were usually highly flattering. Reporters' critical words were countered by pictures of Reagan acting presidential, or being surrounded by happy Republicans. Graber found that the correlation between the public's images of Reagan and the televised images of Reagan was much better when the combined audiovisual message is studied than when just the verbal messages are considered. Graber's research suggests that in analyzing the role of television in campaigns, it is important to include both the words and the pictures.[97]

Voter images of the political parties tend to be stable, since they are seen through the screen of party identification, but some changes do occur. The public's perception of which party is better at keeping the country out of war, of which party is the party of prosperity, of which party is corrupt, have all fluctuated in recent years.[98] Media coverage of the Vietnam war, economic recessions, inflation, and Watergate did not create these changes, but it may have facilitated them.

In the absence of strong party ties, voters also look to issue positions in deciding how they will vote. Again, their knowledge of and interest in issues can be spurred by the mass media. And, of course, the media let people know where the candidates stand on the issues (to the extent that the candidates are clear on where they do stand).

Candidate images and issues are short-term influences on voting. Voters who rely on them as voting cues are more susceptible to media influence than are those who rely on long-term influences. As party identification (a long-term influence) has declined as a voting cue, the electorate has become more volatile. The influence of short-term forces has made it difficult to predict electoral outcomes.

Newspapers and television may have distinct impacts on voters' perceptions of candidates. In a study of the 1976 presidential election, Joseph Wagner found that

> for persons who are alike in sex, age, education, social class, income, partisanship, time of [voting] decision, and interest in politics, those who rely upon television as the principal means of acquiring information come away perceiving fewer differences between the candidates than do their counterparts who read newspapers. In fact, indications are that the perceptual gap is actually greatest among the most attentive, among those who (according to the uses-gratification model) go to the medium seeking information.[99]

Agenda-Setting

It already has been established that the media (both print and electronic) help to shape the political agenda. This was dramatized in 1987 when it was revealed that Democratic presidential candidate Gary Hart might have spent a night in his Washington townhouse with a woman who was not his wife on a night when his wife was not present. Reporters from the *Miami Herald,* on receipt of a tip, staked out the townhouse. Unfortunately, their stakeout was incomplete; the back door was not watched for a time. Hart said the woman did not spend the night, but he was so hounded by questions about his behavior that he decided to drop out of the campaign. (It should be noted that his past behavior had raised similar questions about his actions and judgment.) For days, discussion of Hart's alleged infidelity dominated the news. In this case, the behavior affected was the candidate's, not the voters'. No doubt many of Hart's supporters switched to other candidates, but some chose to sit out the race.

One of the many questions raised by this episode is whether or not this story was important enough to dominate the news for over a week. Did the public really need to know so much about a candidate's private life? And this leads to another question: Possessing this kind of knowledge, are citizens going to base their voting decisions on such criteria? It remains to be seen whether or not the press will apply similar standards now to all candidates, or whether or not such scrutiny will be confined to candidates who, like Gary Hart, spawn rumors of infidelity.

Iyengar and Shanto developed, tested, and found support for what they call the "priming hypothesis." They argued that television, through its agenda-setting powers, can alter the standards that people use to make political evaluations.[100] An example is instructive. Thomas E. Patterson found little initial public reaction in 1976 to President Ford's gaffe in his debate with Jimmy Carter. (Ford made an inaccurate statement about Eastern Europe and communist domination of that region.) But after forty-eight hours of media emphasis on the mistake, Ford's rating went from 53 percent in his favor to 35 percent.[101] On their own voters had failed to focus on Ford's gaffe, but after repeated discussion of it in the media, the mistake made an impact.

The implications of this are serious; by priming some issues and ignoring others, "television news can shift the grounds on which campaigns are contested." The effectiveness of priming, like agenda-setting, depends upon both the news and the audience. Unlike agenda-setting, priming affects both those with limited political skills and those who are partisans and activists.[102]

Early Predictions of Election Results

As mentioned in Chapter 2, various scholars have examined the impact on voters of the use of exit polls and the early projection of winners by network television on election day. The results are mixed: Some studies show early projections have a depressing effect on voter turnout, and some show such projections have little or no relationship to turnout. Laurily K. Epstein and Gerald Strom, for example, concluded that early projections did *not* have an impact on West Coast voter turnout in 1980 (an election year exhibiting both early calls by the networks and an early concession speech by President Carter). They argued that the decision to vote is based on a variety of factors (age, education, and income) that are not related to information received on election day.[103] These results were confirmed by William Adams. Adams surveyed 1,256 people in a congressional district in Oregon and found only a few nonvoters who said they chose not to vote because of the early projection of Reagan's victory.[104] On the other hand, John E. Jackson found that turnout in both the East and the West was lower than predicted due to the early call and concession speech. His work showed that Republicans were more likely to stay home than Democrats.[105] In any case, this is not an easy subject to research. As Richard Joslyn writes,

> Asking nonvoters to analyze the reasons for their own behavior is not a particularly valid strategy, and the number of respondents who can be interviewed in such cases is usually not large enough to provide an accurate estimate of the behavior of all eligible west coast voters.[106]

Media Variation

We have been discussing the media almost as if news coverage was monolithic. William H. Flanigan and Nancy H. Zingale point out that it is useful to remember several ways in which the media differ.[107] First, the impact that information has on us can differ depending on the type of media used. Difficult topics are often better understood by reading articles than by watching a television news story. Second, "the media differ in what they offer."[108] Television specializes in presenting visual material and action. Newspapers, on the other hand, are better at providing information. Third, political advertising (or "paid media") should be treated differently from the media in general. Unlike regular news stories, political advertising is designed to put the candidate in the best of lights, and to get across a certain message or theme (often specific in content). Advertisements on television have been shown to increase voter awareness of the issue positions of candidates.[109] Fourth, the effect (if any) of editorial endorsements and news commentary should be considered separately from the effect of news stories. Although newspaper editorial endorsements do not seem to have much impact on voters at the presidential level, they may sway voters in state or local races.

Research on the effects of the mass media on voters is in an embryonic stage; studies often contradict each other, and scholars argue about proper methods of study. One thing is certain: Growing numbers of people rely on television for news, and smaller numbers rely on political parties.

THE IMPACT OF PARTICIPATION

What consequences stem from political participation? One can approach this question from two perspectives: indirect (or symbolic) effects versus direct effects.[110] The *direct effects* approach argues that, in order for elections and participation to be effective, we must be able to show that voters and candidates have specific goals, and that those goals are implemented as a result of electoral victory. This is a high standard for elections to meet. Candidates are not always clear on their issue positions, and voters are not always endorsing platforms when they vote. (Sometimes they are merely rejecting the other party's platform.) This leads some to argue an elitist position on voting, encouraging only the well-informed voters and the politically skilled to vote.[111]

The *indirect effects* approach proposes that democracy is well served if voters attain a certain degree of protection of their interests by voting. It is not necessary to show that specific goals were sought and achieved; it is enough to show that elections provide the consent of the governed and a check on power. Proponents of this approach argue that wide participation is essential to the legitimacy of government. They would also argue that participation helps contribute to personal development and has an educational effect, and that this is important above and beyond the setting and achievement of policy goals.[112]

Gerald M. Pomper and Susan S. Lederman present a "protective meddler" model of voting that is compatible with the indirect effects approach. They argue that people cannot be expected to fulfill the ideal model: knowing the candidates, the issues, the party stands; comparing these factors with their own interests; and casting a logical vote. This ideal model makes heavy demands on voters, especially in a federal system. The protective meddler model proposes, instead, that voters, while not always informed and concerned about each election, do get involved when they see that their interests are threatened. They rely on party identification much of the time, and their party affiliation helps shape their perceptions. But they are not slaves to their party when they see a divergence between it and their interests.[113] Pomper and Lederman use black suffrage to illustrate their point. They write that, throughout U.S. history, acquiring the vote was related to the relative protection of black interests, particularly in the South.[114]

The protective meddler theory is in line with Schattschneider's position on voters. He wrote that the public tends to be permissive toward politicians, and that this was generally a good thing:

> The reluctance of the public to press its opinions on the government concerning a great multitude of issues is really not as bad a thing as we may have been led to think; it is a mark of reasonableness and common sense. The public is far too sensible to attempt to play the preposterous role assigned to it by the theorists.[115]

Schattschneider stressed that the effectiveness of the public in a democracy depends on the importance of the decisions the voters make, not on the number of decisions they make.[116] He argued that the political system must be organized so that citizens *can* make the important decisions. In doing so he also redefined democracy:

> Democracy is a competitive political system in which competing leaders and organizations define the alternatives of public policy in such a way that the public can participate in the decision-making process.[117]

There is another, more pessimistic way to look at this question, as Benjamin Ginsberg does in *The Consequences of Consent: Elections, Citizen Control and Popular Acquiescence.*[118] Ginsberg points out that, because the United States allows and encourages political participation, the populace ends up accepting conditions they might reject if forced upon them from without. Ginsberg writes:

> Electoral participation in the United States and other Western democracies has been a key factor in persuading citizens to accept the taxation, labor, and military service associated with the construction of the modern state, as well as to reconcile them to the loss of individual liberties that sometimes results. Elections, moreover, have helped to create public support for enlargement of the state's role vis-à-vis that of other social and political institutions, as well as to sustain the popular impression that ordinary citizens may somehow affect the behavior of the vast bureaucracies that this substitution brings into being.[119]

Verba and Nie are more optimistic in their assessment, arguing that participation matters. They discovered that different issues are salient for participators than are salient for nonparticipators, and also that the preferences of the two groups on these issues differ.[120] This is not surprising, given the different socioeconomic characteristics of the two groups. The issue differences between the groups mark the important reality that nonparticipators tend to be unrepresented by public officials. Officials will respond to the desires of those who vote and contact them,[121] and these are not likely to be the same as the desires of those who do not vote.

This raises the question of what is meant by "representation." Conway points out that this term can be interpreted in a variety of ways.[122] The first interpretation involves a sharing of the characteristics of those who are represented with those who represent them. If there are no female or black officeholders, women and blacks may feel unrepresented. The second interpretation refers to the representation of political attitudes and policy preferences. Do politicians vote the way their constituents wish? The third interpretation addresses "the congruence between the distribution of policy preferences among the electorate and in the representative body as a whole."[123] Your views may not be defended by your representative, but perhaps they are put forth by someone's representative. The fourth interpretation approaches representation in terms of acting on the behalf of others. For example, it is possible for the interests of women and blacks to be articulated by white males.

To sum up, an evaluation of the effectiveness of political participation depends largely on initial assumptions. If the standard is going to be goal-oriented, well-informed, logical, and constantly active voters, then our system is open to criticism. If the standard is going to be unevenly informed, retrospectively-oriented, sporadically active voters, then our system is in good shape.

SUMMARY

In the 1950s and 1960s people began organizing in unprecedented ways. Civil rights activists, antiwar protesters, the National Organization for Women, the Eagle Forum, the Mexican-American Legal Defense and Education Fund, and the Moral Majority are just a few examples of the movements and groups that resulted from these new organizing trends. New technology helped to empower people by making communication easier. Some activists used their skills to change the political parties; but the activists no longer have to work through parties to achieve their goals. The political system has been profoundly affected by this; parties are not as important to us as they once were, and voters would not be content today to allow a handful of party professionals determine the party's nominee, in a smoke-filled room or otherwise. Television gives them ready access to information, and, regardless of the quality of that information's content, people feel qualified to have their say on the subject.

During the 1984 election, groups of all stripes mounted voter registration drives. Republicans, Democrats, Hispanics, women, blacks—name the group and someone somewhere was trying to get them registered. Registration rolls increased by almost 12 million names, 4 to 5 million of which were estimated to be due to the registration drives.[124] Yet, despite all the thousands of the newly registered, many did not vote and many others must have dropped out, because voter turnout increased by only a fraction of a percent. Obviously, it is not enough just to register voters. People must be made to see, somehow, that they have an ongoing stake in the system, so they will continue to vote in future elections.

How much nonparticipation can a democratic republic stand? Some think that nonvoters are happy with the status quo. Others are concerned that these millions of nonparticipants are not happy, and that their possible sudden entry into the system, en masse, could have disruptive results. The next chapter will detail how the two major parties are responding to this state of affairs, and how they are capitalizing on the political action committees that have mushroomed in the past few years.

SUGGESTED READINGS

ABRAMSON, PAUL A., and JOHN H. ALDRICH, "The Decline of Participation in America," *American Political Science Review* 72 (1982), pp. 502–521.
DOWNS, ANTHONY, *An Economic Theory of Democracy*. New York: Harper & Row, 1957.

FLANIGAN, WILLIAM H., and NANCY H. ZINGALE, *Political Behavior of the American Electorate* (6th ed.). Boston: Allyn and Bacon, 1987.

HADLEY, ARTHUR T., *The Empty Polling Booth.* Englewood Cliffs, NJ: Prentice-Hall, 1978.

HILL, DAVID B., and NORMAN R. LUTTBEG, *Trends in American Electoral Behavior* (2nd ed.). Itasca, IL: F.E. Peacock, 1983.

NIE, NORMAN H., SIDNEY VERBA, and JOHN PETROCIK, *The Changing American Voter* (revised ed.). Cambridge, MA: Harvard University Press, 1979.

NIEMI, RICHARD, and HERBERT F. WEISBERG, *Controversies in Voting Behavior* (2nd ed.). Washington, DC: Congressional Quarterly Press, 1984.

VERBA, SIDNEY, and NORMAN H. NIE, *Participation in America.* New York: Harper & Row, 1972.

WOLFINGER, RAYMOND E., and STEVEN J. ROSENSTONE, *Who Votes?* New Haven, CT: Yale University Press, 1980.

DISCUSSION QUESTIONS

1. What was your own political socialization like? What is your family's attitude toward politics, and how has it affected your own?

2. Do you know any "cross-pressured" individuals? How do they feel about politics?

3. How serious a problem is low voter turnout in the United States, in your opinion? What influences on turnout do you think are most important?

4. Should we institute reforms in an attempt to increase voter turnout? If yes, what kinds of reforms would you prefer?

5. Do you think Gary Hart was treated fairly by the press after the incident with the woman at the townhouse? If no, how should it have been handled?

6. What is your opinion on network predictions of presidential election results?

NOTES

1. Harry Holloway with John George, *Public Opinion, Coalitions, Elites, and Masses,* 2nd ed. (New York: St. Martin's Press, 1986), pp. 36, 37.

2. Robert D. Hess and Judith V. Torney, *The Development of Political Attitudes in Children* (New York: Anchor Books, 1968), p. 75.

3. Holloway and George, *Public Opinion,* pp. 38, 39.

4. Hess and Torney, *Development of Political Attitudes,* pp. 56, 59.

5. Charles H. Franklin, "Issue Preferences, Socialization, and the Evolution of Party Identification," *American Journal of Political Science* 28 (August 1984), pp. 459–478.

6. Hess and Torney, *Development of Political Attitudes,* pp. 255, 256.

7. Holloway and George, *Public Opinion,* p. 42.

8. Ibid., p. 89.

9. Richard E. Dawson, Kenneth Prewitt, and Karen S. Dawson, *Political Socialization, An Analytic Study,* 2nd ed. (Boston: Little, Brown, 1981), pp. 43, 44.

10. *Statistical Abstract of the United States,* 106th ed. (Washington, DC: U.S. Bureau of the Census, 1985), p. 253.

11. Holloway and George, *Public Opinion,* pp. 50, 108.

12. Hess and Torney, *Development of Political Attitudes,* pp. 250, 248.

13. Holloway and George, *Public Opinion,* p. 58.

14. Ibid., p. 59.

15. See Robert W. Jackman, "Political Institutions and Voter Turnout in the Industrial Democracies," *American Political Science Review* 81 (June 1987), pp. 405–423.

16. M. Margaret Conway, *Political Participation in the United States* (Washington, DC: Congressional Quarterly Press, 1985), p. 89.

17. Ibid., pp. 89–91.

18. Robert Erikson, "Why Do People Vote? Because They Are Registered," *American Politics Quarterly* 9 (July 1981), pp. 259–276.

19. Conway, *Political Participation,* p. 93.

20. Ibid., p. 94.

21. Peverill Squire, Raymond E. Wolfinger, and David P. Glass, "Residential Mobility and Voter Turnout," *American Political Science Review* 81 (March 1987), pp. 45–65. This quotation is from p. 50.*Review* 81 (March 1987), pp. 45–65. This quotation is from p. 50.

22. Ibid.

23. Ibid., p. 46.

24. Ibid., p. 52.

25. Ibid., p. 57.

26. Raymond E. Wolfinger and Steven J. Rosenstone, *Who Votes?* (New Haven, CT: Yale University Press, 1980), pp. 77, 78.

27. Ibid., p. 83.

28. Robert Goldberg, "Election Fraud: An American Vice," in A. James Reichley, ed., *Elections American Style* (Washington, DC: The Brookings Institution, 1987), pp. 180–192.

29. Ibid., pp. 186, 187.

30. Ibid., pp. 188, 189.

31. John F. Bibby, *Politics, Parties, and Elections in America* (Chicago: Nelson-Hall, 1987), p. 254.

32. Walter Dean Burnham, "The Changing Shape of the American Political Universe," in *The Current Crisis in American Politics* (New York: Oxford University Press, 1982), pp. 25–57.

33. Flanigan and Zingale, *Political Behavior,* pp. 48, 51.

34. Holloway and George, *Public Opinion,* pp. 215, 216.

35. Anthony Downs, *An Economic Theory of Democracy* (New York: Harper & Row, 1957). For a discussion of the relative importance of costs versus benefits, see Lee Sigelman and William D. Berry, "Cost and the Calculus of Voting," *Political Behavior* 4 (1982), pp. 421–428.

36. V. O. Key, Jr., *The Responsible Electorate* (Cambridge, MA: Belknap Press of Harvard University, 1966).

37. Ibid.

38. Abraham Maslow, "A Theory of Human Motivation," *Psychological Review* 50 (July 1943), pp. 370–396, and *Motivation and Personality* (New York: Harper & Row, 1954).

39. David C. McClelland, *The Achieving Society* (New York: The Free Press, 1961).

40. Sidney Verba and Norman H. Nie, *Participation in America: Political Democracy and Social Equality* (New York: Harper & Row, 1972), p. 231.

41. Ibid., p. 247.

42. William H. Flanigan and Nancy H. Zingale, *Political Behavior of the American Electorate,* 5th ed. (Boston: Allyn and Bacon, 1983), p. 86.

43. Ibid., p. 87.

44. Flanigan and Zingale, *Political Behavior,* pp. 17–18.

45. Verba and Nie, *Participation in America,* and Wolfinger and Rosenstone, *Who Votes?* p. 47.

46. Stephen D. Shaffer, "A Multivariate Explanation of Decreasing Turnout in Presidential Elections, 1960–1976," *American Journal of Political Science* 25 (February 1981), pp. 68–95.

47. Conway, *Political Participation,* p. 17.

48. Ibid., pp. 20–22.

49. Wolfinger and Rosenstone, *Who Votes?* p. 8.

50. Bibby, *Politics, Parties and Elections,* p. 252.

51. David B. Hill and Norman R. Luttbeg, *Trends in American Electoral Behavior,* 2nd ed. (Itasca, IL: F.E. Peacock, 1983), p. 90.

52. Ibid., p. 91.

53. Wolfinger and Rosenstone, *Who Votes?* p. 90.

54. Conway, *Political Participation,* pp. 27, 28.

55. Flanigan and Zingale, *Political Behavior,* p. 16.

56. Ibid., p. 18.

57. G. Bingham Powell, Jr., "American Voter Turnout in Comparative Perspective," *American Political Science Review* 80 (March 1986), pp. 17–44. This quotation is from p. 23.

58. Ibid., p. 24.

59. Note that 72 percent report voting regularly in presidential elections. This figure is an example of how people "overreport" their voting behavior. However, the table does a good job of illustrating the relative level of activity for the various political pursuits.

60. W. Russell Neuman, *The Paradox of Mass Politics* (Cambridge, MA: Harvard University Press, 1986), p. 100.

61. Verba and Nie, *Participation in America,* p. 45.

62. Ibid., p. 54.

63. Ibid., p. 79.

64. E. E. Schattschneider, *The Semisovereign People* (Hinsdale, IL: The Dryden Press, 1975), p. 32.

65. Verba and Nie, *Participation in America,* p. 208.

66. T. David Mason and Jerry A. Murtagh, "Who Riots? An Empirical Examination of the 'New Urban Black' versus the Social Marginality Hypothesis," *Political Behavior* 7 (1985), pp. 352–373. This quotation is from p. 252.

67. H. Mark Roelofs and Gerald L. Houseman, *The American Political System* (New York: Macmillan, 1983), p. 422.

68. Ibid.

69. Ibid., p. 423.

70. Ibid.

71. Ada W. Finifter, "Dimensions of Political Alienation," *American Political Science Review* 64 (June 1970), pp. 390–391.

72. Roelofs and Houseman, *American Political,* p. 423.

73. Ibid., p. 424.

74. Paul Lazarsfeld, Bernard Berelson, and Hazel Gaudet, *The People's Choice,* 2nd ed. (New York: Columbia University Press, 1984).

75. Richard Niemi and Herbert Weisberg, "The Study of Voting and Elections," in *Controversies in Voting Behavior,* 2nd ed. (Washington, DC: Congressional Quarterly Press, 1984), p. 12.

76. Angus Campbell, Gerald Gurin, and Warren Miller, *The Voter Decides* (New York: Harper & Row, 1954).

77. Angus Campbell, Philip E. Converse, Warren E. Miller, and Donald E. Stokes, *The American Voter* (New York: John Wiley, 1960).

78. Morris P. Fiorina, *Retrospective Voting in American National Elections* (New Haven, CT: Yale University Press, 1981).

79. D. Roderick Kiewiet and Douglas Rivers, "A Retrospective on Retrospective Voting," *Political Behavior* 6 (1984), pp. 369–393.

80. See the following: Stanley Feldman, "Economic Self-Interest and Political Behavior," *American Journal of Political Science* 26 (August 1982), pp. 446–466; Donald R. Kinder and D. Roderick Kiewiet, "Economic Grievances and Political Behavior: The Role of Personal Discontents and Collective Judgments in Congressional Voting," *American Journal of Political Science* 23 (August 1979), pp. 495–527; Ricardo Klorman, "Trends in Personal Finances and the Vote," *Public Opinion Quarterly* 42 (Spring 1978), pp. 31–48; Lee Sigelman and Yung-mei Tsai, "A Reanalysis of the Linkage Between Personal Finances and Voting Behavior," *American Politics Quarterly* 9 (October 1981), pp. 371–399.

81. Stanley Feldman, "Economic Self-Interest and the Vote: Evidence and Meaning," *Political Behavior* 6 (1984), pp. 229–251. This quotation is from p. 248.

82. Shaffer, "A Multivariate Explanation." See also discussion in Chapter 8 of Richard Joslyn, *Mass Media and Elections* (Reading, MA: Addison-Wesley, 1984).

83. Herbert B. Asher, *Presidential Elections and American Politics* (Chicago: The Dorsey Press, 1988), p. 258.

84. See Thomas E. Patterson, *The Mass Media Election, How Americans Choose Their Presidents* (New York: Praeger, 1980), p. 105, and Joseph Wagner, "Media Do Make a Difference: The Differential Impact of Mass Media in the 1976 Presidential Race," *American Journal of Political Science* 27 (August 1983), pp. 407–430.

85. Jarol B. Manheim, "Can Democracy Survive Television?" in Doris A. Graber, ed., *Media Power in Politics* (Washington, DC: Congressional Quarterly Press, 1984), pp. 131–137.

86. Shanto Iyengar and Donald R. Kinder, *News That Matters* (Chicago: University of Chicago Press, 1987), p. 127.

87. Michael J. Robinson, "Public Affairs Broadcasting and the Growth of Political Malaise: The Case of 'The Selling of the Pentagon'," *American Political Science Review* 70 (June 1976), pp. 409–432.

88. Henry E. Brady and Richard Johnston, "What's the Primary Message: Horse Race or Issue Journalism?" in Gary R. Orren and Nelson W. Polsby, eds., *Media and Momentum: The New Hampshire Primary and Nomination Politics* (Chatham, NJ: Chatham House, 1987), p. 184.

89. Lewis W. Wolfson, *The Untapped Power of the Press, Explaining Government to the People* (New York: Praeger, 1985), p. 99.

90. David L. Paletz and Robert M. Entman, *Media Power Politics* (New York: The Free Press, 1981), p. 237.

91. Ibid., pp. 243–246.

92. Neuman, *The Paradox,* p. 148.

93. See Susan E. Howell, "Chasing an Elusive Concept: Ideological Identifications and Candidate Choice," *Political Behavior* 7 (1985), pp. 325–333 for a discussion of how candidate preference can affect ideological identification.

94. See Leonard Shyles, "Defining 'Images' of Presidential Candidates From Televised Political Spot Advertisements," *Political Behavior* 6 (1984), pp. 171–181.

95. See Joe McGinnis, *The Selling of the President 1968* (New York: Pocket Books, 1975); and Shawn Rosenberg, Lisa Bohan, Patrick McCafferty, and Kevin Harris, "The Image and the Vote: The Effect of Candidate Presentation on Voter Preference," *American Journal of Political Science* 30 (February 1986), pp. 108–127. For the argument that ability to manipulate images is limited, see Robert G. Meadow and Lee Sigelman, "Some Effects and Noneffects of Campaign Commercials: An Experimental Study," *Political Behavior* 4 (1982), pp. 163–175.

96. Joslyn, *Mass Media,* p. 256.

97. Doris A. Graber, *The Mass Media and American Politics,* 3rd ed. (Washington, DC: Congressional Quarterly Press, 1989), pp. 202, 203.

98. Flanigan and Zingale, *Political Behavior,* pp. 128, 129.

99. Wagner, "Media Do Make," p. 427.

100. Iyengar and Shanto, *News That Matters,* p. 63.

103. Laurily K. Epstein and Gerald Strom, "Election Night Projections and West Coast Turnout," *American Politics Quarterly* (October 1981), pp. 479–491.

104. Associated Press, "New View: Few Western Voters Stayed Home Because of TV Reports, Study Says," *Pittsburgh Post-Gazette,* November 9, 1984, pp. 1, 12.

101. Thomas E. Patterson, *The Mass Media Election* (New York: Praeger, 1980), pp. 123, 125.

102. Iyengar and Shanto, *News That Matters,* pp. 121, 95.

105. John E. Jackson, "Election-Night Reporting and Voter Turnout," *American Journal of Political Science* 27 (November 1983) pp. 615–635.

106. Joslyn, *Mass Media,* p. 225.

107. Flanigan and Zingale, *Political Behavior,* pp. 157–159.

108. Ibid., p. 158.

109. Thomas E. Patterson and Robert D. McClure, "Television News and Televised Political Advertising: Their Impact on the Voter." Paper presented at the National Conference on Money and Politics, Washington, DC, 1974.

110. Gerald M. Pomper with Susan S. Lederman, *Elections in America,* 2nd ed. (New York: Longman, 1980), Chapter 2.

111. Ibid., p. 15.

112. Ibid., p. 23.

113. Ibid., p. 73.

114. Ibid., p. 204. See also Conway, *Political Participation,* p. 154.

115. Schattschneider, *The Semisovereign People,* p. 131.

116. Ibid., p. 136.

117. Ibid., p. 138.

118. Benjamin Ginsberg, *The Consequences of Consent: Elections, Citizen Control and Popular Acquiescence* (Reading, MA: Addison-Wesley, 1982).

119. Ibid., p. 25.

120. Verba and Nie, *Participation in America,* p. 284.

121. Ibid., p. 308.

122. Conway, *Political Participation,* pp. 150–152.

123. Ibid., p. 151.

124. "Registration Drives Boost Turnout," *Elections '88* (Washington, DC: Congressional Quarterly Press, 1988), p. 143.

105. John E. Jackson, "Election-Night Reporting and Voter Turnout," *American Journal of Political Science* 27 (November 1983) pp. 615–635.

106. Joslyn, *Mass Media,* p. 225.

107. Flanigan and Zingale, *Political Behavior,* pp. 157–159.

108. Ibid., p. 158.

109. Thomas E. Patterson and Robert D. McClure, "Television News and Televised Political Advertising: Their Impact on the Voter." Paper presented at the National Conference on Money and Politics, Washington, DC, 1974.

110. Gerald M. Pomper with Susan S. Lederman, *Elections in America,* 2nd ed. (New York: Longman, 1980), Chapter 2.

111. Ibid., p. 15.

112. Ibid., p. 23.

113. Ibid., p. 73.1

14. Ibid., p. 204. See also Conway, *Political Participation,* p. 154.

115. Schattschneider, *The Semisovereign People,* p. 131.116. Ibid., p. 136.

117. Ibid., p. 138.

118. Benjamin Ginsberg, *The Consequences of Consent: Elections, Citizen Control and Popular Acquiescence* (Reading, MA: Addison-Wesley, 1982).

119. Ibid., p. 25.

120. Verba and Nie, *Participation in America,* p. 284.

121. Ibid., p. 308.

122. Conway, *Political Participation,* pp. 150–152.

123. Ibid., p. 151.

124. "Registration Drives Boost Turnout," *Elections '88* (Washington, DC: Congressional Quarterly Press, 1988), p. 143.

4

Political Parties and Elections

INTRODUCTION

Political parties provide the link between the people and their governors, and as such they play a vital role in bringing democracies to life. Once polities get beyond the size of city-states, there is a grave danger that politicians will become removed from citizens and isolated from their concerns. In representative democracies, frequent elections are supposed to ensure governmental responsiveness to constituents. But the framework of those elections itself is critical in determining to what extent "the people rule." In the United States, political parties have largely defined that framework, even though they are not mentioned anywhere in the Constitution.

Our political system is well served by political parties. In a sense, they act as personnel agencies, recruiting candidates for office. Parties normally do not have to work hard to get people to run for offices at the top of the ticket (such as the offices of president or state governor), but they often have to beat the bushes to get candidates for lower-level offices, particularly when the opposition is firmly entrenched. Even if the recruited candidates lose to the incumbents, the party has gained something, for it now has an experienced candidate who may well do better next time. It is important to the political system, as well as to the party, that such training take place, since it ensures a pool of experienced politicians available for higher positions. The experience of Ronald

Reagan notwithstanding, most people do not begin their political careers by running for governor.

Parties act to institutionalize the struggle for power. The U.S. Constitution leaves the running of elections to state governments. Aside from its provisions for the Electoral College, and its mandate that eligibility for voting in federal elections be determined by eligibility for voting in the most numerous branch of the state legislature, the Constitution says very little about elections. The Founders were suspicious of parties, but, in the absence of any other mechanism for organizing support for candidates, parties developed anyway.[1] Political parties have had tremendous influence on state legislatures and the electoral laws they pass. It is hard to imagine how our electoral system would work without parties there to nominate candidates and to promote platforms. Parties have helped ensure the peaceful transfer of power from one group to another, a process that has worked well with but one exception, and then we were on the brink of a civil war.

People lead busy, complicated lives, and many do not wish to devote much time to politics. Rightly or wrongly, it is not a high priority for many people. Parties help by organizing political information for us, helping to shape our view of the political world. This is a process that, for obvious reasons, works best for those who strongly identify with a political party. We may not know all the details of a given proposal, but if we know where our party stands on the issue, that can help us make up our minds. This is a shortcut decision-making process that we can use in the absence of complete information. By providing information on issues, parties help to educate the public. Issues that our party stresses will be issues that we, too, emphasize. At election time, parties help to mobilize the electorate with advertisements, campaign activities, rides to polling places, and so forth. Competition between the parties serves democratic interests because "they serve as mechanisms for achieving political equality by trying to increase the number of voters, thereby promoting participation in the political process."[2]

When we have problems with the government, we can turn to our party for help, because parties serve as intermediaries between citizens and public officials. Local party officials will have contacts with other party officials and with politicians, and they can use these connections to solve citizen problems, or simply to cut through red tape.

Our nation is vast in territory and diverse in demographics. Our two-party system helps to unify the citizenry, even as the two parties seek to divide the people. Every four years the parties come together to create party platforms based on broad issue concerns behind which all party members can unite (theoretically, anyway). It is true that political cultures, and political parties, differ from state to state, but it also is true that those differences are usually slight.

Through their platforms, the parties help set goals for the nation. Political parties often have promoted public policies. For example, the Republican party under Ronald Reagan promoted supply-side economics. The Democrats have promoted national health insurance. By keeping ideas alive and promoting their development, the parties have been able to step in when the time is right and offer solutions to public problems. Such activity also enables citizens to hold the parties accountable, for both the good times as well as the bad, and that is an essential ingredient for democratic government.[3]

Political parties thus have earned a special place in our political system because of these functions they perform. E. E. Schattschneider went so far as to write, "parties created democracy and . . . modern democracy is unthinkable save in terms of the parties."[4]

This chapter reviews the role of parties in the electorate and in nominations and elections. We will examine how the parties have evolved in reaction to a decline in party identification, a reduced party role in presidential elections, the increasing role of television in campaigns, and the rise of political action committees. We will consider the impact of party platforms and minor parties. It will be shown that, while many things have changed, the parties are far from dead.

THE EVOLUTION OF THE PARTIES—IN THE ELECTORATE

The Decline in Partisanship

Recall the discussion of campaign style eras in Chapter 1. From 1860 to 1896, we experienced a "militaristic" campaign era, a time in which parties were strong and voters were loyal. In the late 1800s, parties were important agents of socialization for their members. William Goodman wrote,

> Political speeches, pamphlets, and the party press communicated most political information and attitudes. Although most people were exposed only to their own party's messages, the information level, and the level of interest, were far higher than they were after parties lost this primary function of being "educators."[5]

But now we live in an era of commercial entertainment, mass media, and professional journalism. Much has changed in the political landscape. In particular, the 1960s were a volatile time in our history; the decade left an impact on practically every institution in our society. Political parties were not untouched. People began to turn away from parties, their loyalties weakened. Recall from Chapter 1 that parents were not as successful as those in previous generations in handing down party identification to their children.[6] Review of Tables 3–1 and 3–2 confirms these statements. It is clear from Table 3–1 that the number of people identifying themselves as strong Democrats is shrinking, from 21 percent in 1956 to 17 percent in 1984. (The shrinking was temporarily stopped in 1980 and 1986 as indicated by a rise in Democratic party identification to 18 percent.) The number of strong Republicans fell from 15 percent in 1956 to 8 percent in 1980, rebounding to 13 percent in 1984 and declining to 10 percent in 1986. The socialization process has not vanished completely, however. While many young voters reject identification with either of the major parties, those who do identify as Republicans or as Democrats tend to stay with the party of their parents.[7]

There is disagreement among political scientists as to whether or not the decline in partisanship means that people have developed negative attitudes toward parties. Perhaps the decline means that parties have simply ceased to be salient for many.[8] Either way, the decrease in the number of strong enthusiasts for parties means that the parties must work harder to drum up campaign workers and supporters.

Also note what has happened to the numbers of independents. While only 23 percent of the electorate in 1956, independents were 33 percent in 1986 (after rising to 36 percent in 1976). Party ties clearly were weakening. As suggested, many of these independents come from the younger age categories, as Table 3–2 shows. For example, 42 percent of those twenty-two to twenty-five called themselves independents, as compared with 27 percent of that age group who called themselves Republican and 31 percent who called themselves Democrat. Several explanations for the increase in independents have been presented by Robert H. Blank. First, as noted, party organizations and party workers have been displaced by the mass media as major sources of campaign information. People do not rely on parties for voting cues anymore. (In primaries and caucuses, they cannot.) It is hard work to use the media effectively to educate yourself about candidates and issues. Second, campaigns have become more candidate centered. As the characters of individual candidates have become more important, parties have become less important. Third, issues have become more important in campaigns, and many of these issues are personalized, not directly related to traditional party stands (for example, the issues of abortion and busing). Many prefer to rely on the media rather than their party when developing positions on these issues.[9]

Even when we consider that many independents "lean" toward one party or another, 33 percent is a high proportion of the electorate to be rejecting party labels. In recent presidential elections, independents have held the key to victory. As a result, the electoral climate is volatile, for it is difficult to predict which way the independent vote will go. Parties have had to work hard to attract the independent vote, and they cannot count on independents, who may have supported them for one election, to come back to the party for the next election. Democrats, in particular, have lost supporters to the independent group (and, sometimes, to the Republicans).

Ticket-splitting is more common among voters today than it was forty years ago. This occurs when voters support one party's candidates for some posts and the other party's candidates for other posts. When parties were strong, voters opted for straight-ticket voting, casting their votes for all of one party's nominees.[10] Today, voters can be swayed by candidates' personalities or by their stands on particular issues. As John F. Bibby writes, "at the turn of the century, ticket-splitting between presidential and congressional candidates was unusual, but . . . by the 1960s it was commonplace for almost one-third of the nation's congressional districts to have split outcomes between the presidential and congressional outcomes."[11] Only strong partisans are not likely to split their tickets. When strong partisans are eliminated from consideration, ticket-splitting is common. It occurs despite differences among voters in the level of interest in the campaign, media usage, and media preferences for television or for newspapers. Ticket-splitting is more likely with voters who decide on their choice during the campaign (as opposed to those who base an early decision on party affiliation). Deviation from party identification in such voting is related to candidate images, as we would expect.[12]

In the 1980s, candidate character has emerged as a significant campaign topic, one that sometimes overrides issues. Examples of this subject influencing a campaign include Gary Hart's temporary withdrawal from the 1988 presidential primary campaign because of an alleged extra-marital fling, Senator Joseph Biden's withdrawal from the same campaign due to charges of plagiarism, and the scandal surrounding Pat Robertson's announcement that he and his wife were not married when their first child was conceived. Although these incidents may have some importance, the focus on them detracts from more significant issues of party concern. In a general election, it could also mean that some weak partisans would abandon the party nominee to vote for a candidate of "higher" character.

Change in the New Deal Coalition

All the recent developments discussed previously signal important changes in the New Deal coalition that has dominated national politics and the Democratic party since the 1930s. The New Deal coalition was made up of union members, Roman Catholics, Jews, blacks, the poor, urban dwellers, and southerners. The main issues that held the coalition together were a feeling that government had a responsibility for dealing with unemployment and that government could legitimately intervene in the economy.[13] In the 1980s, however, only blacks, the poor, and urban dwellers remain strongly dedicated to the Democratic party.[14] Unfortunately for the Democratic party, voter turnout from these groups is usually low. In addition, while Mexican-Americans tend to be Democrats, Cuban-Americans tend to be Republicans. Asian-Americans have tended to vote Republican also. Since the 1950s, Republicans have been able to attract southern voters at the presidential level, and they have won a plurality of the white southern vote in every presidential election since 1968.[15] Changes in the South are partly due to an immigration of Republicans from the North, and partly due to weakening Democratic support among young white southerners. The Democratic New Deal coalition is thus weaker and less stable today than it was from the 1930s to the mid-1960s. Table 4–1 illustrates some of these changes. Note the decline in support among those with a college education. (Chapter 9 continues this discussion.)

Everett Carll Ladd provides an explanation for this decline:

> Since about 1960 . . . the New Deal coalitions have been unraveling in the face of complex social change. The United States has entered upon a new sociopolitical setting most aptly described as "postindustrial"—involving such conditions as a dramatic increase in national wealth, advanced technological development, the central importance of knowledge, the elaboration of national electronic communications processes, new occupational structures, and with them new lifestyles and expectations, which is to say, new social classes and new centers of power. The social and political world with which the parties must deal has changed so markedly from what it was in the age of Franklin Roosevelt that the party system could not help but be altered. A different mix of policy issues has been thrust upon the political agenda. Lines of social conflict have shifted. New interest groups have appeared and old groups have found themselves with new interests.[16]

The news is not completely bleak for the Democrats. Class-based differences in voting have declined since 1952, which means that, while Republicans have gained some support from those with lower incomes, the Democrats often pick up votes from those in the middle class. Democrats do well with professionals in the communications industry and in nonprofit institutions.[17] (The situation is different in the South, where the middle class is becoming increasingly Republican.) Democrats also regained some support from Jews in 1984, as Jews who voted Republican in 1980 became disaffected with the Reagan administration.

Along with these changes, remember that election turnout has decreased significantly. Again, this has made the job of parties more difficult; they cannot count on their supporters coming to the polls. They must now expend tremendous effort on registration drives and get-out-the-vote campaigns.

The *Times Mirror* Study

The *Times Mirror* commissioned the Gallup Organization to undertake a massive national survey in 1987, and the results are fascinating. The results

TABLE 4–1 Change in Support for Democratic Party, 1964–1980

VOTING FOR DEMOCRATIC PRESIDENTIAL CANDIDATE	1964	1968	1972	1976	1980
Jews	89%	92%	69%	66%	50%
Catholics	79	60	40	56	41
Blacks	100	96	87	94	93
Grade-school educated	80	60	40	69	62
College educated	52	38	38	43	32
Union members	83	53	43	63	51

SOURCE: American National Election Study Series, 1952–1980, Survey Research Center/Center for Political Studies, University of Michigan, as presented on p. 141 in Gitelson, Alan R., M. Margaret Conway, and Frank B. Feigert. *AMERICAN POLITICAL PARTIES: STABILITY AND CHANGE.* Copyright 1984 by Houghton Mifflin Company. Used with permission.

suggest that it is too simplistic today to speak merely in terms of Republicans, Democrats, and independents. The survey revealed eleven groups in the electorate, ten that vote and one that does not. Their findings are worthy of close examination.

The survey found nine basic values that help define political attitudes and behavior: "Religious faith" reflects a belief in God. "Tolerance" refers to a belief in freedom for those who don't share one's values. "Social justice" refers to a belief in the government's obligation to ensure social justice and social welfare. "Militant anticommunism" refers to a belief in a strong defense to halt the spread of communism. "Alienation" refers to the belief that the American system does not work for oneself. "American exceptionalism" refers to the belief that there are no limits to what Americans can do. "Financial pressure" refers to a belief about one's financial status (one either feels secure financially, or feels under pressure). "Attitudes about the government" refers to a belief about the proper role and effectiveness of government. And finally, "attitudes toward business corporations" refers to a belief about the goals and effectiveness of business corporations.[18] Voters are united or divided by their beliefs concerning these basic values. The survey showed that voters are "distinguished less by age, gender, race, or economic status than by values dominating their thinking and lives."[19]

The *Times Mirror* created a typology of the U.S. electorate based in large part upon these values. A description of these types follows, beginning with groups who tend to vote Republican.

Enterprise Republicans ("Enterprisers").

This group is 60 percent male and 99 percent white. It is made up of married men of northern European ancestry, who live in suburbia. They make up 10 percent of the adult population and 16 percent of the likely electorate. Key issues for enterprisers include support for cutting the budget deficit (without raising taxes); opposition to increased spending for health care, aid to the homeless, and programs for the elderly; opposition to more restrictions on abortion; opposition to quarantine measures for AIDS patients; and support for the "Star Wars" defense plan and for aid to the contras in Nicaragua.

Moral Republicans ("Moralists").

This group is middle-aged, earning a middle income. It is largely southern and 94 percent white, including a large number of "born again" Christians. They make up 11 percent of the adult population and 14 percent of the likely electorate. Key attitudes for moralists include strong opposition to abortion; strong support for school prayer; support for the death penalty and for quarantine measures for AIDS patients; strong support for anticommunism policies and for a strong national defense; support for social spending except when it is targeted for minorities; and concern about the problems of the deficit and unemployment.

Upbeats. These are young people under forty, earning a middle income. They are 94 percent white, with little or no college education. They are optimistic, not critical of the government's role in society, and strong Reagan supporters. They are 9 percent of the adult population and 9 percent of the likely electorate. Key attitudes for upbeats include concern about the deficit and other economic problems; moderate support for "Star Wars"; and opposition to aid for the contras.

Disaffecteds. This group is alienated and skeptical of big government and big business. They are middle-aged, earning a middle income. Their numbers include slightly more males, and they feel personal financial pressures. They lean toward the Republican party, but many have ties to the Democratic party. They are 9 percent of the adult population and 7 percent of the likely electorate. Key attitudes for the disaffecteds include strong opposition to government and to business; support for the military; strong support for capital punishment; strong opposition to gun control; and concern about unemployment and the deficit. They are divided on abortion.

Bystanders. This group is young, poorly educated, and lacks interest in political affairs. They tend to be under thirty. They are 82 percent white, 13 percent black, and largely unmarried. They make up 11 percent of the adult population and 0 percent of the likely electorate. When asked which party they prefer, they leaned toward the Democrats. Key attitudes for the bystanders include concern about unemployment, poverty, and the threat of nuclear war. They did not care who won the presidency in 1988.

Followers. Followers are young, poorly educated, blue collar, and from the East and South. They possess little religious commitment. In this group, 18 percent are Hispanics and 25 percent are black. They have limited interest in politics and little faith in the United States, yet they are uncritical of government and business. They are very persuadable and unpredictable, although they lean toward the Democrats. They are 7 percent of the adult population and 4 percent of the likely electorate. Key attitudes of followers include opposition to "Star Wars," and support for increased spending to reduce unemployment.

Seculars. This group does not profess religious belief. They are well educated, white, middle-aged people, heavily concentrated on the East and West Coasts, professional, and 11 percent Jewish. They make up 8 percent of the adult population and 9 percent of the likely electorate. Key attitudes for seculars include support for cuts in military spending; opposition to "Star Wars"; opposition to school prayer, anti-abortion legislation, and the relaxing of environmental controls. They are concerned about the deficit. They oppose increased aid for minorities and for farmers.

'60s Democrats. They are well educated and attend church. They are 60 percent female, and married with children. They are 16 percent black, and they are upper-middle-class, mainstream Democrats. They are 8 percent of the adult population and 11 percent of the likely electorate. Key attitudes for the '60s Democrats include support for increased spending on programs for minorities and for most other forms of social spending. They have strong opposition to "Star Wars," and support the peace, civil rights, and environmental movements.

New Deal Democrats ("New Dealers"). They are older people; 66 percent are over fifty. They are 29 percent Catholic. They are less likely to live in the West. Most are blue-collar workers, union members, with moderate incomes and with few financial pressures. Most are religious. They are 11 percent of the adult population and 15 percent of the likely electorate. Key attitudes for New Deal Democrats include support for social spending except when it is specifically targeted for minorities. They support more restrictions on abortions, favor school prayer, support "Star Wars," and have less concern about the environment.

God and Country Democrats. They are less well educated. They are southern, 31 percent black, poor, older, and solidly Democratic. They make up 7 percent of the adult population and 6 percent of the likely electorate. Key attitudes for God and Country Democrats include support for all forms of increased social spending, support for tax increases (more than any other group), and support for "Star Wars." They oppose defense cuts, and they are moderately anti-abortion.

The Partisan Poor. This group is 37 percent black. They have low incomes, and they are southern, urban, and poorly educated. They are the most firmly Democratic group in the country. They are 9 percent of the adult population and 9 percent of the likely electorate. Key attitudes for the partisan poor include strong support for all social spending, opposition to tax increases, and support for the death penalty. They support a constitutional amendment mandating school prayer. They are divided on abortion. They are concerned about unemployment.

The *Times Mirror* study suggests that political parties have their work cut out for them. Contradictions exist among the groups supporting Democrats and the groups supporting Republicans; the coalitions are thus unstable. Enterprise Republicans emphasize issues that are different from those emphasized by the Moral Republicans, for example. New Deal Democrats support restrictions on abortion, whereas '60s Democrats do not. These categories illustrate that many of today's issues do not lend themselves to the more government or less government dichotomy that traditionally separates liberals from conservatives. Today, it would seem, there is almost as much dividing party members as there is uniting them.

THE EVOLUTION OF THE PARTIES—IN NOMINATIONS AND IN ELECTIONS

Nomination Methods

As the nation has progressed through 200 years of its history, the process of selecting presidents has become more and more popularized. In the nation's early years, presidential nominees were selected by their party caucuses in Congress. In the 1800s, parties developed national nominating conventions as a more democratic method for choosing candidates. Caucuses and state conventions were used for selecting delegates to the conventions. Political parties and their leaders were able to dominate these proceedings. The nominee was almost always someone the party organization could support. In making their choices, party leaders were concerned not only with winning the present election, but also with promoting the long-term interests of the party.

As the country industrialized and became more educated, the need was felt once again for reform. States began to experiment with presidential primaries in 1905.[20] *Primary elections* allow the voters to bypass the party organization by voting directly for convention delegates. In the 1960s, primaries became popular as a reflection of the people's will, rather than having the choices made by a handful of party leaders in a "smoke-filled room." It took the 1968 Democratic national convention in Chicago, however, to make primary elections the dominant method for choosing convention delegates. Before one can fully understand the changes that occurred, it is first necessary to explain some more terms.

A *caucus* is a party meeting. States that use caucuses for the selection of national convention delegates begin at the local level with precinct caucuses. Public notice is made that the party will meet at a certain time and place, and all party members are invited to attend. At the precinct caucus, votes are taken to ascertain which candidates have support and how much. On the basis of those votes, delegates are selected for the next tier of the selection process, which is usually the county caucus. The same procedure is used at the county caucus, where delegates are selected for congressional district caucuses. And at the congressional district caucuses, delegates are chosen for the national and state conventions.

Voting in caucuses is usually quite visible (by a show of hands, for instance), and it can take all evening, so voter turnout tends to be lower than it is for states with primary elections. (The average voter turnout in presidential primaries in 1980 was 35 percent of the electorate.[21]) Because of the visibility of the decision-making process, party leaders are sometimes able to dominate the action at caucuses. Leaders can try to persuade party members to support the candidates that the leaders support. But caucuses are also vulnerable to takeover by activists. Since turnout is usually low, dedicated supporters of a particular candidate may be able to round up enough new participants to come in on caucus night and take over the nomination procedures. Broadcaster Pat Robertson, an on-the-air evangelical preacher, was able to do this in the Republican party in 1988, as was the Reverend Jesse Jackson in the Democratic party in the same year.

As stated, a primary election is an election that selects delegates to attend a convention to vote to nominate a particular candidate. Primaries are not all the same; they vary according to who can vote, and according to how the delegates are apportioned to candidates. Most states with primaries have *closed primaries.* These states require some pledge of party membership before allowing citizens to vote in the party's primary. In many states, this pledge involves declaring oneself to be a Democrat or Republican when registering to vote. In states with *open primaries,* there is no such test. Voters are simply given the Democratic or Republican ballot on request. Washington and Alaska have *blanket* or *wide-open primaries.* In these states, voters can move from one party's primary to the other party's primary as they vote for each office on the ballot. One could vote in the Democratic primary for president, in the Republican primary for governor, in the Democratic primary for Senator, and so forth.

Some states apportion presidential delegates in a *winner-take-all* fashion. The candidate who receives more primary votes than any other receives all of the state's convention delegates for that party. Many states now have *proportional* primaries. In a proportional primary state, candidates receive delegates in proportion to the amount of the vote they win in the state; a candidate with 40 percent of the vote wins 40 percent of the delegates, and the candidate winning 60 percent of the vote wins 60 percent of the delegates. Such a division of votes could encourage frivolous candidacies, so proportional primary states usually provide for a threshold amount of 10 or 15 percent of the votes. Candidates must earn enough support to pass this threshold amount before they will receive their share of delegates. There have also been *winner-take-more* primaries where the winning candidate in each congressional district gets a bonus delegate before the rest are divided proportionally. And some primaries are *beauty contests,* which is to say they play no role at all in the delegate selection process; they are merely popularity polls.

As if all this were not complicated enough, some states use a combination of methods for choosing delegates. In addition, the Republican party may use a method different from the method used by the Democratic party within the same state. And states sometimes change their delegate selection methods.

Nomination Reform

Table 4–2 illustrates the dramatic change in delegate selection after 1968. Both parties went from choosing a minority of delegates to choosing a majority of delegates through primaries. Even though the unpopular incumbent president Lyndon Johnson decided not to run for reelection in 1968, the Democratic convention was dominated by his forces. His vice president, Hubert Humphrey, received the nomination without winning a single primary. Humphrey did well in the party-dominated caucus states. Little of the anti-Vietnam war sentiment

TABLE 4–2   Number of Presidential Primaries and Percentage of Convention Delegates from Primary States, By Party

YEAR	DEMOCRATS		REPUBLICANS	
	# OF PRIMARIES	% DELEGATES	# OF PRIMARIES	% DELEGATES
1952	15	38.7%	13	39.0%
1956	19	42.7	19	44.8
1960	16	38.3	15	38.6
1964	17	45.7	17	45.6
1968	15	40.2	15	38.1
1972	22	65.3	21	56.8
1976	30	76.0	30	71.0
1980	35	71.8	34	76.0
1984	25	62.1	30	71.0
1988	34	NA	35	NA

NA: not available

SOURCE: William Crotty, John S. Jackson III, *Presidential Primaries and Nominations* (Washington, DC: Congressional Quarterly Press, 1985), p. 16. Reprinted with permission. Data for 1988 are from *Elections '88* (Washington, DC: Congressional Quarterly Press, 1988), p. 31. Reprinted with permission.

that fueled the campaigns of Eugene McCarthy and the late Robert Kennedy was reflected inside the convention hall. On top of this, antiwar protesters descended on Chicago during the convention, and the Democratic administration of Mayor Richard Daley responded with tear gas and violence. It was a public relations nightmare for the Democratic party.

In response, after the election of 1968, the party created a commission to study its rules and to make recommendations to open up the delegate selection process in order to make it more representative of the party as a whole. The commission was initially headed by Senator George McGovern, later by Representative Donald Fraser, and is known as the *McGovern-Fraser Commission*. The commission proposed a set of guidelines that were later adopted by the Democratic National Committee (DNC). The guidelines of the commission required that state parties take affirmative steps to ensure representation of blacks, women, and young people. The guidelines required that state parties have written rules of delegate selection and give public notice of all meetings. They forbade mandatory assessments of delegates and eased the requirements that a state party could impose in order for people to run for delegate. The guidelines banned the unit rule, which allowed all of a state's votes to be cast as a unit in accordance with the preferences of a majority of the state delegation. The guidelines restricted the amount of delegates that a party committee could select to 10 percent of the total size of the state delegation.[22]

These rules reduced the discretion of state party leaders and brought greater consistency to the delegate selection process. The DNC made it clear that it intended to enforce the new rules through its credentials committee. The states responded; many of them overhauled their delegate selection process through statutory changes as well as through changes in party rules. The new rules contained a contradiction: An open delegate selection process could result in delegations that were not representative of women, minorities, and young people. Fearful that their delegations might be challenged by the credentials committee, many states chose primary elections as the easiest route to fulfilling party requirements. Hence, the proliferation of primaries after 1968. In states where the changes were imposed through law, the Republican party was just as affected as the Democratic party. Members of the McGovern-Fraser Commission did not intend to increase the number of primaries; it was an unanticipated consequence that has had a great impact on the manner in which we nominate presidential candidates.

From the 1972 election on, those seeking the presidential nomination have had to pay more attention to winning primary votes than to pleasing party officials. The Democrats were hardly finished with reform, however. George McGovern, who had helped to write the new rules, was the party's nominee in 1972. McGovern was able to win the nomination, but he suffered a crushing defeat at the hands of incumbent president Richard Nixon. State party chairs and union leaders were unhappy at their loss of power at the 1972 convention. A new committee, the *Mikulski Commission,* named after chair Barbara Mikulski, was created. (At the time, Mikulski was a member of the Baltimore City Council; by 1988 she was a U.S. Senator.) The new commission did not throw out the McGovern-Fraser rules, but did modify them. It announced that strict quotas for blacks, women, and the young were not necessary, stating that affirmative action plans approved by the DNC would suffice. Of more significance, the Mikulski Commission required that states adopt proportional representation in their delegations. The threshold to qualify for a proportional share of the state's delegation was set at 15 percent of the vote. Proportional representation also was required for caucus states. The commission also discouraged states from using open primaries. The reforms of these two commissions were written into a Democratic Charter, adopted by the party in 1974.[23]

After the 1976 convention, another committee was formed to review the rules. This was the *Winograd Commission,* named for its chair, Michigan Democratic party chair Morley Winograd. In response to criticism that the proliferation of primaries had drawn out the length of the campaign, this commission attempted to reduce the time involved in the delegate selection process. Critics also charged that the rules encouraged too many "amateur" delegates and that they discouraged officeholders. The Winograd Commission responded by allowing state parties to select more elected officials and party officers as delegates. It reiterated and strengthened the ban on open primaries. The threshold needed to win a proportional share of votes was raised from 15 percent to 25 percent, making it tougher for the less well known candidates to qualify for delegates.[24]

The Democrats were not finished with reform. After the 1980 election, the *Hunt Commission* was formed under the leadership of chair Governor James Hunt of North Carolina. This commission went further than the previous one in encouraging "professionals." It provided for party and elected officials to have unpledged delegate status at the convention. State party chairs, vice-chairs, and two-thirds of the party's senators and representatives were made delegates. These delegates were dubbed "superdelegates." (In 1984 it turned out that few of these delegates were really unpledged; most of them announced their support for Walter Mondale.) This commission also unbound the delegates to the 1984 convention, saying they were free to follow their consciences in casting their votes. (This amounted to a symbolic gesture, since delegates are there in the first place because they support a particular candidate; they are not likely to change their minds at that point.) The commission also reaffirmed the party stands on open primaries, affirmative action, and shortening the campaigning period.[25]

Walter Mondale, the eventual Democratic nominee in 1984, benefited tremendously from the rules laid down by the Hunt Commission, and rivals Gary Hart and Jesse Jackson were vocal in their opposition to some of the procedures. Not surprisingly, the party responded to their criticisms with the establishment of yet another commission. Known as the *Fairness Commission,* this group increased the number of party and elected officials to be selected as delegates for the 1988 convention. The commission agreed to lower the threshold in proportional states to 15 percent (a position favored by Hart and Jackson). But the commission reaffirmed the right of states to hold winner-take-all or winner-take-more primaries. On the whole, the changes recommended by the Fairness Commission were minor compared with recommendations from previous reform groups.

The Supreme Court has upheld these reforms. In 1972, Illinois Democrats decided to choose their delegates in a manner that violated party rules. The dispute between the state party and the national party ended up in court, where the question was, which organization possessed the higher authority? In *Cousins* v. *Wigoda* (419 U.S. 477, 1975), the Supreme Court supported the national party, arguing that political parties were private organizations with rights of association that are protected by the Constitution. States are not free to abridge these rights in the absence of strong constitutional arguments. States can make their own primary election laws, but the party can set the criteria for representation at the convention.[26]

After this decision, challenges to national party rules dropped off, but another controversy arose around the 1980 delegate selection process. Wisconsin decided it would continue to hold an open primary, in violation of party rules. In *Democratic Party of the U.S.* v. *Wisconsin* ex. rel. *La Follette* (450 U.S. 197, 1981), the Supreme Court held that "a state had no right to interfere with the party's delegate selection process unless it demonstrated a compelling reason to do so."[27] The court felt that Wisconsin had failed to meet this test, and ruled that the Democratic party could refuse to seat delegates selected in a manner that violates its rules.

Not all court decisions have favored the national Democratic party. Connecticut's law prohibiting open primaries was challenged in 1986 by the

Republican party. Republicans desired open primaries because they hoped to attract independent voters. Unable to get the Democratic-controlled state legislature to change the law, Republicans challenged it in court. In *Tashjian* v. *Republican Party of Connecticut* (107 S.Ct. 544, 1986), the Supreme Court threw out the law on the grounds that it violated the First Amendment rights of freedom of association.[28]

Rather than continually fight state parties in court, the national party sometimes grants exceptions to the national rules. In 1984 the national party forced Wisconsin Democrats to use caucuses. Wisconsin Democrats were angry, and voter turnout decreased. The national party granted the Wisconsin party an exemption for 1988 that allowed it to return to an open primary.[29]

The Republican party has also had reform commissions. The first was the *Delegates and Organizations Committee,* which was in operation from 1969 to 1972. This committee made a series of recommendations that were similar to those of the McGovern-Fraser commission. For example, it suggested that the process for the selection of convention delegates be open, and that each state try to have an equal number of men and women in its delegation. State parties were not required to abide by these suggestions. The second Republican reform group was the 1972 *Rule Twenty-nine Committee,* which more or less recommended an affirmative action program for the state parties. Republicans have not been able to appeal to minorities successfully since the 1930s, and it was felt that an affirmative action program could help broaden the base of the party. The Republican National Committee (RNC) did not accept this recommendation, opting instead to merely urge the state parties to take "positive action" in order to attract minorities.[30]

Republican efforts at reform have been more subtle than Democratic efforts. The RNC cannot issue rules changes as can the DNC. Republican rules changes must be adopted by the national convention, which meets every four years prior to the presidential election. Suggested changes are not normally a source of controversy. Republican rules give the states some discretion in delegate selection.[31] Republicans still have winner-take-all delegate allocation. Whereas the Democratic party often has been torn apart by nomination fights, the Republicans have managed to retain unity, even in the face of hot contests. (One such contest occurred in 1976, when the party's incumbent president, Gerald Ford, faced a challenge from Ronald Reagan.) Republicans believe that power should lie with state parties rather than with the national organization, and their reform efforts amount to suggestions rather than mandates.[32] However, as has been shown, Republicans now rely just as much on primaries as the Democrats. For both parties, the ball game changed considerably after 1968.

The Impact of Nomination Reform

Political parties in the United States have never been deeply rooted in ideology, as are most European parties. U.S. parties have a tradition of pragmatism, of attempting to appeal to the vast numbers of voters politically in the middle of the road. Traditionally, U.S. voters have known liberal Republicans and conservative Democrats even though the majority of the members of those parties were ideologically in the opposite camp. In legislatures, popular nomination methods mean that party leaders have to accept a certain amount of voting that is contradictory to party positions. Everyone recognizes that incumbents must satisfy the voters back home if they want to be reelected, and sometimes the constituents disagree with the party. Since control of legislatures is based on which party has the majority, it is important to have legislators bearing the party label even if they do not always vote to support the party. For these reasons, and for a host of others associated with the U.S. political culture (including our dedication to individualism), "party responsibility" has been difficult to come by. Even so, there are times in our history when parties have been relatively successful in getting members to abide by the platform.

The changes brought about in nomination procedures since 1968 make it harder for parties to discipline members. Nominations are more popularized than ever before (and not just presidential nominations); the media are now an important factor. Parties now have less control over fund-raising, and party ties seem less and less important as voting cues. This means that officeholders have less reason to feel bound to their party upon election. Presidents may feel more beholden to specific blocks of voters and interest groups (the ones who helped them get nominated and elected) than they do to their party. Years ago, these blocks of voters and interest groups would have constituted the people who made up the party. Today, they may or may not be party supporters. Many of these individuals and groups now switch party allegiance from election to election. Members of Congress may feel beholden to political action committees.

The election of a Republican president and the Republican takeover of the Senate in 1980 did increase that party's unity for a few years. But all of this new independence among party members makes it more difficult for voters to hold politicians and parties accountable for their actions. It is dangerous to generalize on the basis of party affiliation. Instead, one must do research, digging out voting records and policy statements in an effort to nail down just where individual politicians stand. Our wealth of media makes such searches possible, but a process such as this asks a great deal of voters who are expected to go through it for state and local as well as for national candidates.[33]

Obviously, election campaigns have also been affected by the reforms. The nomination process has indeed been opened up by the rules changes. More people are allowed to participate, and minority representation at conventions has grown considerably, although it remains true that the income and educational levels of the delegates are higher than average. The power of party leaders has declined considerably.

The democratization of the delegate selection process has allowed issue and candidate activists to win places at the convention. Many of these activists are "purists" who resist attempts at compromise and make party unity difficult, if not impossible. This has been a particular problem for Democrats, with their broad coalition. It is the main reason for the creation of the super-delegates, the party professionals. It was hoped that the superdelegates would be more attentive to the interests of the party as a whole, and that their influence would lead to the nomination of candidates the entire party could support in the general election. In the 1970s, the Democratic party was greatly influenced by cause-oriented movements. Party organizations in some areas were too weak to act as mediators between the cause-oriented groups and candidates or office-holders. In some places the cause-oriented groups were able to take over the party organization. Such developments allowed feminists, minorities, environ-mentalists, and other groups to wield power in the party to the point that the party appeared to be fragmenting. Many older, New Deal Democrats felt alienated from these cause-oriented groups.

Scholars, however, are not in agreement on whether or not post-reform delegates differ significantly from pre-reform delegates. It is acknowledged that primary voters differ demographically from the general electorate. James I. Lengle, studying primaries in 1968 and 1972, argued that voter turnout in primaries reflects an upper-middle-class bias.[34] But Herbert Kritzer and Richard L. Rubin have concluded that there are few ways in which primary voters differ on issues from party identifiers and general election voters.[35] It appears that strong partisans are more likely to vote in primaries than weak partisans, but there is mixed evidence on whether or not primary voters are ideologically unrepresentative of their party's mass supporters or the general electorate.[36]

After the Watergate scandal, conservatives were frustrated because, while surveys showed strong support for conservative causes, identification with the Republican party was declining. They responded by developing the New Right, made up of "right to life" (anti-abortion) organizations, religious groups un-happy over the banning of school prayer, groups opposed to busing, and others unhappy over what they perceived as "reverse discrimination."[37] The New Right helped sweep Ronald Reagan into office, and it will be interesting to see whether the New Right will continue to dominate the Republican party now that Reagan has left office. Moral conservatives are not necessarily economic conservatives, and their influx into the party has caused tension among the Republicans.

The opening up of the nomination process and the proliferation of pri-maries have increased the role of the mass media. People are less willing today to take direction from their party. In primary elections all the candidates are from the same party, and the party is usually not able to publicly endorse a particular candidate. Since the candidates share the party's basic beliefs, it is not always easy to distinguish their individual positions on the issues. (This is one reason for the public's fascination with a candidate's character.) So the public turns to the media to help them sort out the faces, the issues, and the candidates' positions on the issues.

In the 1980s, presidential candidates have not always been well known to the public. Candidates have begun campaigning early in order to get their names across. The press has an important job to do in presenting these candidates. Unfortunately, the process is not as smooth as we might like. Journalists run stories providing candidate backgrounds and stands on issues early in the nomination struggle. But voters are not always interested in these things a year before the election. By the time voters are interested, such stories are "old news" to the press. Reporters have moved on to stories about campaign events, the "horse race" aspects of the campaign. Journalists are reluctant to write that one candidate has better policy ideas than another. Such articles would violate journalistic rules of objectivity, and, besides, reporters are usually not experts on public policy. They are experts on campaigns. Stories about poll results often dominate the news as journalists attempt to decipher the extent of support for each candidate. Campaigns are candidate-centered, with little discussion of party interests.

Candidate behavior is affected accordingly. Instead of spending time courting party leaders, candidates work hard to get "free" coverage on evening news programs. This often involves what are called *pseudo-events,* events that serve no purpose other than to get the candidate on television (for example, candidates may participate in ax-throwing contests, dog sled races, and so forth). These events have little or no issue content in them, but they help to make the candidate's name a household word. Candidates now hire media consultants to help them gain the most from such activities. These "hired guns," as critics call them, work for the candidate, not the party. We end up with "candidates who represent the parties without being sufficiently accountable to them."[38]

Because of the variety and complexity involved in the nomination process, the media have tremendous power through their ability to interpret primary and caucus results. Prominent journalists, after talking with voters, examining fund-raising reports, and meeting with candidates, often set benchmarks in the campaign. A candidate must win in New Hampshire, these pundits write, or his candidacy will be washed up. Or they may say that a candidate must get at least 40 percent of the vote in Iowa to keep his candidacy alive.[39] These reporters and columnists are not necessarily wrong in the predictions they make, but such predictions put a lot of pressure on candidates. And, once again, candidates are responding to influences outside of their political party.

Occasionally the media have made winners out of losers. In the New Hampshire Democratic primary in 1968, Senator Eugene McCarthy came in second to Lyndon Johnson, who was not even on the ballot. (Johnson supporters were able to write his name in.) This was prior to Johnson's withdrawal from the race, and no one was surprised to see an incumbent president do well in New Hampshire. The big story, instead, was that McCarthy did much better than expected. (McCarthy had been expected to get 5 to 15 percent of the vote; he ended up with 42 percent to Johnson's 50 percent.[40]) Not only was McCarthy's campaign off and running, Johnson soon withdrew from the race. Again in New Hampshire in 1972, George McGovern surprised the experts by winning 37 percent of the Democratic vote as compared with front-runner Senator Edmund Muskie's 46 percent.[41] McGovern received positive coverage, while the press was hard on Muskie, criticizing his performance. (Muskie was said to have cried in frustration and anger over a newspaper editor's criticisms about his wife. Muskie says it was melting snow on his face, not tears.) A similar approach was taken by the press in covering the Iowa caucuses in 1984. Walter Mondale, the front-runner, received the most votes, as expected. The press concentrated on the fact that Gary Hart did better than Senator John Glenn, who had been expected to be a hit with Iowa farmers. Such attention can help make those who do better than expected into serious contenders for the nomination. In the rush to inform the public about the emerging campaign star, the actual winner in these contests may be overlooked.

The media have every right to publish stories about the progress of the campaign, and commentators have a right to expound on the quality of candidates. In the 1930s and 1940s, though, media coverage was balanced by the provision of information to voters directly by their party. Today, the media are, for most, the only providers of political information. They are playing a difficult role, and it is not a role they asked to play. Their increased importance in campaigns is, to a great extent, the result of changes made by citizens (the decline in voter attachment to the parties) and political parties (the popularization of the nomination process). Readers seem to be better off than viewers. Those who rely on print for information can have access to a wide variety of periodicals, and they can thereby receive a variety of perspectives on campaigns. Those who rely on network television for news (and that is most citizens) get a headline news service that oversimplifies the nomination process.

But manipulation in presidential campaigns is a two-way street. Candidates with media savvy can find numerous ways in which to turn the press and its routine procedures to their advantage. Candidates learn to cultivate friendships with people such as newspaper publishers and prominent columnists, to plan campaign activities with pretty backdrops that will be appreciated by television reporters, to lower expectations about how well they will do in primaries, caucuses, and debates.

The role of the national conventions has also changed. In the 1980s, when candidates came to the national convention, it was routine for one candidate to possess enough pledged delegates to be the nominee. There is little suspense over the most significant choice the convention will make. The controversy, such as it is, at the convention is likely to be over the platform instead. A "brokered" convention, where party leaders and candidates bargain over the nomination, is still possible. But the conventions have not had to go beyond a first ballot for the nomination since 1952. Television coverage allows a united party to present the image of a love fest to the public (as was the case with the Republicans in 1984), a valuable beginning to the general election campaign. Conversely, television also can display party conflicts to the public. A divided party can look weak and petty, as did the Democrats in 1972. Party efforts to present a pleasant picture to the television audience can extend to changes in convention rules. In 1976 the Democrats adopted a rule stating that minority reports on the platform, rules, and credentials had to have the support of 25 percent of the members of these committees in order to be considered by the entire convention. The previous requirement had been 10 percent. Clearly, the party was attempting to avoid televised controversy.[42]

Have the reforms produced better nominees? This question can be answered only subjectively. If "better" is defined as the candidate who most appeals to the general membership of the party, the answer would be no. The rule changes, coupled with low voter turnout in primaries and caucuses, make it possible for activists who may not speak for the party as a whole to dominate the nomination process. The primary system allows parties to tear themselves apart, even though that can mean disaster in the general election. Nominations are the most valued prizes parties possess, and parties no longer control them. On the other hand, if "better" is defined as the candidate who can appeal to the greatest number of participants in primaries and caucuses, then the answer

SOURCE: Ed Gamble, Florida Times-Union. Copyright 1984. Reprinted with permission.

would be yes. The nomination system of the 1980s left the choice to those party members wishing to participate, and, in that sense, it is quite democratic.

To summarize, the arguments in favor of a reliance on primaries for delegate selection include the following:

- primaries are open and democratic
- primaries involve public opinion and a discussion of issues
- primaries force candidates to present themselves to the voters
- primaries test the organizational abilities of the candidates
- the primary process weeds out unappealing or disorganized candidates
- primaries allow voters more choice; party "renegades" such as George McGovern are given a chance at the nomination

Arguments against a reliance on primaries include the following:

- primaries are exhausting for candidates, the media, and voters; and they are expensive
- primaries encourage the invention of issues (for example, Does Ronald Reagan dye his hair?)
- primaries do not select candidates so much as they destroy them
- primaries can force a nominee on the party that the party masses do not want (for example, George McGovern)
- the long process disenfranchises voters; instead of getting a full-time Senator, Governor, and so forth, voters get part-time officeholders who run around the country campaigning for the presidential nomination
- primary results are difficult to interpret, allowing the media great influence
- primaries are divisive to political parties

The Democrats did reduce their reliance on primaries in 1984. Six states moved from primaries to the caucus-convention method for choosing delegates, and the proportion of primary delegates at the Democratic convention fell from 72 percent in 1980 to 62 percent in 1984. (See Table 4–2.) Richard A. Watson and Norman C. Thomas feel that this move, coupled with the use of super-delegates, constitutes a "counterrevolution" in nomination politics. They argue that we now have a "mixed" nomination system:

> It incorporates the selection of delegates by both the primary and caucus-convention methods. The participants include professionals representing blue-collar constituents, such as organized labor, as well as amateurs, who speak largely for white-collar constituents.[43]

Not all political scientists would go so far in their estimation of the extent to which the system has been changed. Primaries are defined as democratic, and are thus very popular. Both parties increased the number of states with primaries in 1988. For better or worse, the public now expects to have a role in the nomination process.

Some further proposals have been made by those who feel the nomination system remains flawed. These proposals include a national primary, a national postconvention primary, regional primaries, and the adoption of more standardized rules.[44] The proposal for a *national primary* would create a single, nationwide primary for each party on the same day. Candidates would obtain a spot on the ballot by filing petitions from seventeen states, with signatures equal to at least 1 percent of the state's vote in the previous presidential election. A runoff election would be held if no candidate received at least 40 percent of the vote. A one-day primary would solve many of the problems incurred in our current sequential system; states like Iowa and New Hampshire would no longer receive disproportionate attention. But the advantages of the current system would be lost as well; candidates would have little time to present themselves to the voters. Media campaigns would become even more important than they are now, since television is the only practical way to mount a national campaign.

A national primary would do little to stop the erosion of the power of political parties, but a *national postconvention primary* would increase the role of party leaders in the nomination. This plan is meant to combine the best of both worlds, conventions and primaries. Each state would use the caucus-convention method for selecting delegates to the national convention. A bloc of 25 percent of each state delegation would be reserved for party and elected officials, who would remain uncommitted. At the national convention, delegates would be bound to vote for the choice of their state conventions on the first ballot. On the second ballot, all but the top three candidates would be dropped, and all delegates would be unbound. A candidate receiving 70 percent or more of the national convention vote would automatically receive the party's nomination. If no candidate receives 70 percent of the vote, the top two or three finishers would appear on a national primary ballot, with, obviously, the primary scheduled *after* the convention. Party voters would then determine the nominee by plurality vote. Party members who registered for the caucuses would be eligible to vote in the postconvention primary. The nominee would then select his or her running mate from a list provided by the national convention.

This proposal would revive the national conventions. Winnowing of presidential candidates would take place at these conventions once again. With relatively few candidates to choose from in the postconvention primary, interest in the election and voter turnout might increase. The media still would play an important role; they are bound to in any national election. Such a plan would require massive changes in state nomination procedures and in the national parties. Since the proposal would further nationalize the presidential nomination process, it is doubtful that the state parties would voluntarily adopt it.

Still another reform proposes that the various state primary contests be grouped into several *regional primaries*. Senator Bob Packwood (R-Oregon) has suggested a plan that divides the nation into five regions. Within a region, states would be required to hold their primaries or initial caucuses on the same day. The dates would be assigned by lottery. Serious candidates would be placed on the ballot by a federal commission, with a petitioning procedure available for including those left out. Candidates would have to file statements disavowing interest in a presidential candidacy in any region in which they did not wish to be on the ballot. Voters would vote directly for candidates, and delegates to the national convention would be appointed by candidates in proportion to each candidate's vote in each state.

Regional primaries would eliminate the significance of the early contests in Iowa and New Hampshire. By shifting the order of the primaries, no region could gain undue prominence since no region would always vote first. Candidates would probably mount national campaigns and rely on television. The nomination contests would not take as long as current ones, but they would take more time than a national primary.

A final reform proposal involves *standardizing nominating procedures.* The current system, with different rules in each state, presents candidates with a difficult and expensive nomination process. One standardization proposal limits the dates for preconvention contests to three dates or a single month. Another proposal argues that primary votes should always commit delegates; that is, beauty contest primaries should be abolished. Filing deadlines, ballot qualification requirements, delegate commitments (the length of time delegates are bound at the convention), and so forth, would be standardized from state to state. A new federal commission (or the existing Federal Election Commission) would be authorized to police the national rules.

Such standardization would equalize the contests somewhat, but it would also nationalize the process, reducing the discretion and power of state parties. In addition, it is not always possible to anticipate the results of rules changes. Some of the goals sought would no doubt be achieved; unanticipated consequences might result as well.

All of these proposals involve a greater national presence in the nomination process. A greater national presence threatens political parties, which thrive at the state and local level. Past reform efforts and their results suggest that caution should be exercised before changing the rules again.

Campaign Financing

Major reform of campaign finance was another big change of the 1970s, but this was not the first time that Congress has attempted to regulate such matters. The Federal Corrupt Practices Act of 1925 required disclosure of receipts and expenditures for congressional races, but not for presidential campaigns. This law was not well enforced and not very effective. The Hatch Act of 1940 prohibited political activities by federal employees and attempted to limit the amount an individual could donate to any single candidate for federal office. The law contained a loophole that allowed contributions to multiple fund-raising committees.

These laws were not effective, but it took considerable difficulties to set the stage for stronger legislation. Reform in the 1970s was spurred by increasing campaign costs, controversy over the existence of "fat cat" contributors, and the Watergate scandal revelations, which showed how the system could be corrupted. In addition, total spending in presidential elections (including independent expenditures—money spent by groups with no connection to candidates or parties) went from $300 million in 1968 to $1,750 million in 1984.[45] President Richard Nixon signed the first of these reform bills, but insisted that it include a moratorium of sixty days. The Campaign to Re-elect the President (CREEP) raised $19.9 million during the moratorium period. Common Cause, a citizens' lobby, brought suit and forced CREEP to name the donors. It turned out that many of the contributions, including those from Gulf Oil, Goodyear Tire and Rubber, American Airlines, and Carnation Company, were illegal.[46]

Congress focused on four areas in its reform effort: public disclosure of contributions and expenditures, contribution restrictions, expenditure limitations, and public financing of presidential elections.[47] In 1971 Congress passed the *Revenue Act,* which set up a tax check-off system, allowing citizens to set one dollar of their tax money aside to pay for the presidential election campaign fund. *The Federal Election Campaign Act* (FECA) was passed the same year. Its major provisions include the following:

- it requires the disclosure of campaign contributions, expenditures, and debts
- it allows taxpayers to deduct small campaign contributions from their taxes
- it limits how much presidential and congressional candidates, and their families, can contribute to the candidate's campaign

The last provision was challenged in court in *Buckley* v. *Valeo* (424 U.S. 1, 1976). The Supreme Court allowed the rest of the act to stand, but ruled that limitations on personal spending were an unconstitutional violation of freedom of speech. Congressional candidates may spend as much of their own money on their campaigns as they like. Presidential candidates and their families are limited to $50,000 if the candidate accepts public funding. As it happened, the FECA was just the beginning. Amendments were passed in 1974 that placed restrictions on contributions, expenditures, disclosures, and reporting; established partial public funding of presidential primaries, elections, and nominating conventions; and created the Federal Election Commission (FEC) to enforce the FECA. Presidential candidates who wish to become eligible for federal matching funds during the nomination phase of the campaign must abide by various rules. In order to qualify for public funding, candidates must raise at least $5,000 in each of twenty states through individual contributions of $250 or less (thus discouraging "fat cat" contributions).[48] The first $250 of larger contributions also will be matched. To remain eligible for the matching money, candidates must win a minimum of 10 percent of the vote in each of two consecutive primaries or caucuses.[49] No individual contributions of more than $1,000 may be accepted. A maximum expenditure limit is set for each nomination campaign. (The limit is adjusted for inflation each election year. In 1984 it was $20 million.[50]) Candidates who do not wish to abide by these rules can refuse public money. State expenditure limits also are applied.

The FEC was set up as an independent, bipartisan group, but in *Buckley* v. *Valeo* the Supreme Court disagreed with the way its members were appointed. Congress had provided that some of its members be appointed by Congress and some by the president. In *Buckley,* the Supreme Court ruled that all members had to be appointed by the president with the advice and consent of the Senate. Amendments to the FECA in 1976 reconstituted the FEC and limited the amounts individuals can give to PACs and to the national parties. Other changes were made in 1976 and subsequently, but these have been minor, "fine-tuning" changes, many of which have made it easier for candidates to comply with the laws. Amendments in 1979 allow state and local parties to expand their role in the general election.

Public campaign funding is not without controversy. In favor of public funding, it can be argued that the subsidy frees candidates from being beholden to "fat cats" for their election. It prevents large donors from being able to "buy" an election. The advantages of wealthy candidates and of incumbents are diminished. On the other side of the argument, public funding may prop up frivolous candidacies, or keep failing campaigns alive. Limitations on contributions may violate First Amendment protections ensuring self-expression. Public financing also discriminates against minor-party candidates.[51] Major-party candidates receive·funds throughout the nomination campaign, but minor-party candidates get nothing until the election is over and unless they have polled 5 percent of the vote. Fund-raising groups that are independent of party and candidate committees are free to spend as much money on a race as they please, as long as their activities are not coordinated with the party or candidate on whose behalf the money is being spent.

While public funding of presidential elections has reduced the role of parties in campaign finance, some of the reforms have improved their position. Individuals can give $20,000 to parties, as opposed to $1,000 to candidates. The national parties are allowed to spend on behalf of their presidential and congressional candidates. The national and state party committees can directly contribute to congressional candidates. Public funds are provided to help pay the cost of the national conventions. A 1979 FECA amendment encourages "party-building activities" by allowing state and local parties to spend unlimited amounts on campaign materials (such as buttons), voter registration, and get-out-the-vote campaigns in presidential elections.[52]

The Impact of Campaign Finance Reform

The expenditure limits have had a variety of impacts on elections. Public funding of presidential elections has led many contributors to give money to congressional candidates instead, and spending in congressional races has risen accordingly. Campaign organization expenditures may have declined, but candidates have found ways to get around the limits.[53] Grass-roots activities have tended to be deemphasized, with an increasing proportion of campaign money going to pay media expenses. (In 1984, Walter Mondale and Ronald Reagan both spent about two-thirds of their campaign budgets on media.[54]) The mass media are an efficient way to reach millions of voters, and, again, reliance on the media means bypassing the parties.

The role of "fat cats" has been reduced. Individuals are limited to $1,000 donations per candidate per election. Services may be donated to candidates, however, and there is no limit placed on such gifts. More individuals contribute to parties and campaigns now than previously.[55] Nonparty groups and state and local party groups are playing an increasing role, spending money on behalf of candidates. Independent expenditures rose from $13.6 million in 1980 to $16.7 million in 1984.[56]

The FECA and its amendments have encouraged the proliferation of *political action committees* (PACs). Corporations and labor unions are still prohibited from making direct contributions to campaigns,[57] but the FECA and decisions by the FEC have made it clear that they can set up separate organizations, or PACs, through voluntary contributions. PACs may give up to $5,000 to a candidate and can spend an unlimited amount on independent expenditures on the candidate's behalf. In presidential elections, direct PAC donations play a small role due to public funding. (In 1984 such contributions made up almost 3 percent of the total amount raised during the election year.[58]) Independent expenditures, PAC voter mobilization efforts, and PAC contributions to state and local parties play a more significant role than direct PAC donations. (See Chapter 7 for a discussion of the role of PACs in congressional elections.) This kind of spending is not under the control of the candidate; this means that ads may appear that offend the candidate's taste or are inconsistent with the candidate's strategy. It is now routine for presidential candidates to form their own PACs prior to their formal announcements of candidacy. Such PACs are used to pay for organization-building activities, travel expenses, and donations to the campaigns of other politicians (a good way "to win friends and influence people").

By providing money directly to candidates, the reforms have decreased the role of political parties in presidential campaign financing. This is another reason why candidates are more independent from parties than they used to be. Since only contributions of $250 or less are matched by the government, candidates are encouraged to begin early. It takes more time to raise funds when your goal is small contributions from many donors than when the goal is to get large contributions from few donors. Professional fund-raisers are in big demand now. Direct mail fund-raising is a good way to try to tap large numbers of people for contributions. Such efforts are not cheap. According to William Goodman, "A direct mailing of a million letters from a computerized list can cost over a quarter of a million dollars."[59]

Because of the expenditure limits, campaigns tend to be more centralized now, allowing the candidate to exert more control over spending. Candidates may feel that it is easier to deemphasize grass-roots activities than it is to control and report them.[60] Campaign strategies are affected by the existence of state spending limits. The overall national spending limit is less than the total of the state limits, so candidates have to plan very carefully where and how they will spend their money.

The equal spending limits in the general election tend to work in favor of the incumbent, who already is well known and has regularly appeared in the news for years. Challengers get less "free" media coverage, and therefore must spend money to become better known. It appeared at first that the equal spending limits would favor the Democrats by neutralizing the funding edge Republicans have traditionally possessed, but that Democratic advantage disappears when other factors are considered. In 1980 and 1984, Republicans benefited from independent expenditures and state and local party activities more than the Democrats.[61] (It should be noted that Republicans also benefit from superior organization and fund-raising skills, not just from the FECA rules.)

Problems and unresolved questions remain. Some argue that congressional campaigns should be publicly funded. Some argue over whether presidential elections are underfunded or overfunded. The role played by PACs is controversial. Despite the reforms, incumbents retain many advantages over challengers.

The FECA and its amendments have made a difference in terms of disclosure: It is easy now to discover who is getting money from whom. The rules have changed, and the route money takes is different now. But the role money plays is important still.

THE RESPONSE OF THE PARTIES

The changes that have been discussed here have meant difficult times for political parties. There is less and less certainty about how the electorate will behave, about what each party's coalition will look like. Many scholars have gone so far as to tag these developments as signaling the "decline" of parties in the United States.[62] But the parties are finding ways of making a comeback. The rules of the game may have changed, but the parties are making some of the rules, at least, work in their favor.

We have already examined some of the ways the parties have fought back. Both parties have mounted massive voter registration drives in an effort to attract more people to the polls. The Democrats have created superdelegates, ensuring that a big block of voting delegates at their conventions will be professional politicians and party leaders. The DNC has flexed its muscles and won in the court battles over rules. Both parties have developed schools and seminars for candidates in order to help them keep up with the latest in polling methods and public relations procedures. Today's candidates are better equipped than ever to manipulate the media rather than be manipulated by the media.

Perhaps the most significant response came from the Republican party and has to do with money. After the Watergate scandal, the congressional elections of 1974, and the presidential election of 1976, the Republican party took stock. Its candidates were decimated in the congressional elections, and the White House was lost to Jimmy Carter. Some were arguing that the United States had developed into a one and a half party system, with the Republican party counting as the half.[63] The party responded by gradually purging itself of liberals, by opening up to the religious right, and by appointing William Brock (a former senator from Tennessee) as chair of the RNC.

One of the first actions taken by Brock was to shore up the financial position of the party. The Republicans studied the direct mail fund-raising efforts that had been so successful for Democrat George McGovern in 1972, and they then raised the direct mail system to a fine art, using it to build a large core of small contributors. Conservative activist Richard Viguerie, a direct mail expert, played a significant role in this development. The effort was quite successful. In the 1977–1978 election cycle, expenditures of $7,973,000 brought in $25,128,000. The list of contributors had grown to more than 2 million by 1980.[64]

The money collected through the direct mail operation was used in a variety of ways. Federal law allows national and state party committees to make direct contributions to congressional candidates, and much of the money went to this. (Party committees are limited to direct contributions of $5,000 per candidate per election in House races; the limit for Senate races is determined by a formula taking population into account.[65]) The party also funded *Commonsense,* a public policy quarterly, and *First Monday,* which provided a forum for attacks on the Carter administration. It produced television commercials that promoted the party and ridiculed President Carter and House Speaker Thomas P. "Tip" O'Neill. Advisory councils were created on foreign policy, energy and environmental policies, economic policy, "human concerns," and government in general. More than 400 politicians and policy experts served on these councils, and their work became the basis for the 1980 Republican platform. A division of the RNC was created to recruit candidates for state legislatures and resuscitate state and local party organizations. In some cases, the RNC went so far as to support particular candidates in primary contests.[66]

The RNC supplied the funds for recruiting and training campaign staff as well. During the 1983–1984 election cycle, the RNC was able to provide direction to party groups in 650 strategic counties, which held 57 percent of the national electorate.[67] Regional political and finance directors were appointed to help state parties and to coordinate state efforts with the RNC.[68]

Both parties have congressional campaign committees in addition to the national committees. The National Republican Senatorial Committee and the Congressional (House) Committees for both parties improved their fund-raising efforts and began providing more services to candidates. In the 1981–1982 election cycle, the Democratic committees raised $12 million, while the Republican committees raised $107 million—about twice what they had raised in the 1979–1980 cycle. The Republican committees have made data banks on issues available to candidates, and they have supplied advice on advertising, polling, fund-raising, and demography. And, of course, they have supplied money.[69]

As the gap between the Democrats and the Republicans in party identification began to close, and as the Republican organization began to thrive, the Democratic party realized that it would have to catch up. Charles Manatt, a California lawyer, became chair of the DNC in 1981. Manatt faced a difficult situation: Not only had the Democrats lost the White House, but also they had lost the Senate for the first time in twenty-eight years. Fund-raising is a perennial problem for the Democrats, since so many of the groups in the Democratic coalition (such as the poor, minorities, and blue-collar workers) have little money to donate to political parties. On top of its usual problems, the DNC had been shouldering a $9 million campaign debt from the 1968 campaigns of Hubert Humphrey and Robert Kennedy. So Manatt focused on raising money, just as Brock had done for the Republicans. The DNC attempted to copy the tactics that were working so well for the Republicans, but the Democrats had less money to work with and lagged behind the RNC. Democrats still are unable to provide the same range of services as do the Republicans. Recognizing that many of the people who do not vote have been in groups that tend to lean toward the Democrats, the DNC made a major push for voter registration for 1984. The RNC responded with a drive of its own, which, by most accounts, was the more successful of the two. The Democratic drive was aimed at registering any and all potential voters; the Republican effort was targeted at those likely to vote Republican.[70]

The Democrats did make some progress in terms of the Democratic Senatorial and Congressional campaign committees. Democratic Congressional Committee chair Representative Tony Coelho of California was able to substantially increase contributions for the 1983–1984 election cycle. Coelho even was successful in persuading some senior Democrats with safe seats to share some of their excess funds with colleagues facing tough opponents. The Democratic Congressional Committee also opened a television studio on Capitol Hill in 1984, which it shares with Democratic senatorial candidates. While the Democratic committees lag behind the Republican ones in the amount of money raised, their new efforts have helped to keep some races winnable for the Democrats. This has forced the Republican committees to attend to races that otherwise would not need their help.[71] The gap in fund-raising is still large. In 1984, the Republican committees raised about $300 million, while the Democratic committees raised $96.7 million.[72] PACs have tended to give more money to incumbents than to challengers, and that has helped the Democrats, since so many of their candidates are incumbents. In particular, Democratic candidates are often aided by organized labor.

In addition to aid from party organizations, the RNC also has worked to coordinate PACs that wish to contribute to Republican candidates. Through the Republican senatorial and congressional campaign committees, compatible PACs are steered toward races identified by the party as winnable but in need of help.[73] Again, the Democrats have tried to emulate this behavior. According to Bibby, in 1984, "The Democratic Congressional Campaign Committee . . . was unusually effective in channeling PAC contributions to candidates involved in close races."[74]

Funds and services are not provided without strings. The parties are reluctant to provide support for those who are not fully in the fold ideologically, and they expect those receiving aid to be supportive of the party whenever they can. Indeed, party unity in Congress has been increasing. Republican unity from 1980 to 1984 was particularly high by historical standards. This unity was spurred by a Republican president, as well as by the money and services made available by party groups. But Democratic unity rose as well. The parties are thus experiencing a change that takes us closer to the ideal of party responsibility.[75]

M. Margaret Conway succinctly summarizes the consequences of these party changes. First, national committee activity is not without drawbacks for state and local party organizations. The local organizations are often bypassed by citizens who prefer working directly with candidate organizations. Second, the more national committees control fund-raising, the more they control who gets to compete successfully for offices. Third, candidates who receive aid are indebted to the national party, not to the local organization. Fourth, Republican success has shown that party rivals—interest groups and the media—can be used to help achieve party goals. Fifth, the FECA, despite its limitations on contributions and expenditures, provides an opportunity for a larger party role in fund-raising.[76]

Thus we have a system in which the national parties do not control presidential nominations, but are involved in rule enforcement, fund-raising, and the provision of goods and services. Compared with where the parties stood in the mid-1970s, they have grown in strength as institutions.[77]

CONVENTIONS AND PARTY PLATFORMS

Despite the changes in the nomination process, the political parties continue to use nominating conventions. Conventions have several traditional functions. These include deciding party rules and regulations, choosing the presidential and vice-presidential nominees, deciding on the platform, and providing a forum for uniting the party and launching the campaign. Before the national convention, most of the important decisions have already been made in the primaries, in the caucuses, and in the subcommittees of the party national committees. Convention delegates largely ratify decisions that have been made elsewhere. Television covers conventions closely, and it is difficult for delegates to bargain in a fishbowl.

The national committees determine the convention sites, the apportionment of the delegates, and the major speakers. The convention cities must have adequate hotel space, and convention sites must accommodate the needs of the mass media in order to be considered. Political factors also play a role; parties like to meet in cities with mayors who are members of that party. Or the personal feelings of an incumbent nominee may be influential. The party may choose to make a political statement in its choice, meeting in the South, for example, to show support for that region, or in Detroit to show concern for the country's industrial base. In apportioning delegates to states, the parties consider the size of a state's congressional delegation (based on the state's population), and its record in supporting the party's candidates in the past.

The first day of the national convention includes the keynote address, aimed at unifying the delegates. The second day includes committee reports on credentials, rules, and the platform. The reports are debated, amended, and adopted.

The *credentials committee* reviews each delegate's credentials to determine if he or she was legally selected. Normally there is no controversy about credentials, but there are exceptions. At the 1972 Democratic convention, two groups from Chicago claimed legitimacy: Mayor Richard Daley's "regular" delegation and one headed by Alderman William Singer and the Reverend Jesse Jackson. The Singer-Jackson group claimed that Daley's delegation was not selected in accordance with the McGovern-Fraser guidelines requiring proportional representation of minorities and women. The convention agreed to seat the Singer-Jackson delegation.[78]

The *rules committee* determines the procedures that will be followed at the convention. The creation of superdelegates is an example of a rules change at a convention. Some rules have to do with whether or not delegates are bound to support the candidate they pledged to support in the primary or caucus. In 1980, the Democrats bound the delegates to vote for their declared choice on the first ballot; after that the delegates were free to vote their consciences. In 1984, the Democratic delegates were free to vote as they chose from the first ballot on. Allowing the delegates such discretion can be useful if late-breaking events tarnish the appeal of the candidate to whom they were pledged. In 1976 Ronald Reagan asked the Republican convention to amend its rules and require candidates to name their running mates prior to the balloting on presidential candidates. (Reagan had already announced Senator Richard Schweiker from Pennsylvania as his choice as his running mate.) Gerald Ford's supporters defeated Reagan's request.

The *platform committee* drafts the statement on which party members will run for the next four years. Platform committees (or subcommittees) begin their meetings well before the convention meets, holding hearings in different areas of the country so that a variety of voices can be involved in preparing the platform. (They are also trying to work out intraparty differences in a setting relatively removed from media attention.) The statement itself normally includes some pats on the back about party accomplishments; it also includes goals for the future, priorities, and it assigns blame for national problems to the other party. Delegates take the platform seriously. Some southern delegates walked out of the 1948 Democratic convention because it adopted a civil rights plank they deemed too liberal. Some went so far as to form a third party, the States' Rights party, which nominated Strom Thurmond, then governor of South Carolina. Thurmond carried four southern states in the election.[79] Nominees sometimes decide not to argue with their rivals over the platform in an effort to promote the appearance of party unity. The Jimmy Carter forces allowed Edward Kennedy supporters to win several platform fights in 1980.

Remember that the decisions made by these committees and subcommittees are subject to ratification by the convention body as a whole. The delegates are capable of overriding committee decisions if they can muster enough votes.

The third day of the national convention is when the presidential candidate is chosen, and on the fourth day the vice-presidential candidate is selected and the nomination acceptance speeches are given. Delegates tend to support the vice-presidential choice of the presidential nominee. With today's nomination process, the presidential nominee is often known before the convention meets. This gives the candidate some time to think over his or her choice and to interview prospective "veeps." This in contrast to the pre-reform era, when there was often little time to deliberate the vice-presidential choice. (The classic example of confusion on this matter is the 1960 convention choice of Lyndon Johnson for vice president by John Kennedy. One version of the story has it that Kennedy offered the spot to Johnson as a courtesy, assuming he would prefer to remain Senate Majority Leader. The Kennedy people were shocked and disappointed when he accepted.) Most presidential nominees attempt to "balance the ticket" in choosing their running mate. Often this involves seeking a regional balance; it can also involve gender and ideology. The idea is to get a vice-presidential nominee who can appeal to those segments of the electorate who are not natural supporters of the presidential nominee. In 1984, Democrat Walter Mondale chose Geraldine Ferraro, partly in an attempt to appeal to female voters. Ferraro was similar to Mondale in ideology, but came from New York instead of Mondale's Minnesota. Another concern, of course, is choosing a running mate qualified to take over if anything should happen to the president.

Nominees confer with party leaders as well as with their own advisers in making their choice. In 1976, with the Democratic nomination in hand well before the convention, Jimmy Carter took the unusual step of inviting prospective running mates to his home in Plains, Georgia, for interviews and consideration as potential vice-presidential nominees. (Some candidates were interviewed in New York.) Given Carter's position as an outsider to Washington, and given the difficulties in making a last-minute choice, the procedure seemed like a good idea, and appeared to work well for Carter. The interviews gave him an opportunity to determine his level of compatibility with the vice-presidential hopefuls. But when Walter Mondale tried the same approach in 1984, it backfired. Mondale interviewed many black, Hispanic, and female politicians, and critics claimed he was pandering to special interests, a serious charge in that Mondale had made gathering group endorsements a centerpiece of his campaign to win the nomination. The 1988 nominees tried to avoid such controversy by attempting to keep their vice-presidential deliberations out of the limelight. This is difficult to do, however, and the politicians under consideration are usually proud that they are being considered for the ticket and want the world to know. And when the presidential nominations are secured before the convention, the vice-presidential deliberation then provides the only suspense. Naturally, the mass media will focus on this choice. For the Republicans in 1988, media attention was largely negative as nominee George Bush surprised everyone by choosing the relatively inexperienced junior senator from Indiana, Dan Quayle, as his running mate.

The acceptance speeches can be important in providing themes for the general election campaign, and in rousing the party faithful. It is extremely important to achieve party unity, if at all possible. The party that is most divided at the end of the conventions has lost every election since 1964, whether the party has an incumbent president or not.[80] Challenges to incumbents who are seeking renomination can seriously damage the party's chances. For these reasons, the front-runner may decide not to argue over platform issues, believing that winning the nomination and achieving the appearance of unity is more important than winning fights on planks of the platform.

Planning has become very important so that the party's shining moments—the acceptance speech by the presidential nominee and speeches showcasing up and coming "stars" of the party—will coincide with prime time television viewing. George McGovern's 1972 acceptance speech was delivered at 2:48 A.M., due to protracted arguments about the platform. Many commentators felt it was the best speech he ever gave, but few viewers saw it. The parties now make strenuous efforts to avoid a reoccurrence of this mistake.

Today the media do not just cover the convention; they are part of the story. Correspondents often convey information from one delegate to another, or from candidates to delegates or vice versa. In 1980, CBS anchor Walter Cronkite was instrumental in the debate about whether or not Gerald Ford would become Ronald Reagan's running mate. (See Chapter 6.) Television concentrates on events that are dramatic visually. The networks often ignore what is happening at the podium and instead feature interviews, stories about disunity, or correspondents' speculations. Delegates, particularly Democratic delegates, form into caucuses organized around race, gender, state delegations, regions of the country, and so forth. The media attempt to follow the interaction between these caucuses and the candidates. As stated, many of the important decisions have been made by the time the delegates convene. Television sometimes imparts a drama to conventions that does not exist.

Given the preceding discussion, it would be natural for one to suspect that party platforms are empty exercises, gobbledygook put forward for public relations purposes and then ignored by all. In fact, just the opposite is true. The vast majority of public officials want to support their party's platform, and the majority of the time they are able to do so without any contradictory pressure from their constituents. For all the independence that exists in the electorate, it still is true that one of the main reasons a candidate gets elected is because constituents support that candidate's party. Party may not be as strong an influence as it was in the 1940s, but it is often a stronger influence than anything else.

The platforms adopted by the national parties every four years at their national conventions reveal distinct differences between Republicans and Democrats on a host of issues including the Equal Rights Amendment, taxes, balancing the federal budget, employment, and foreign policy.

If voters are to make informed choices, platforms must be meaningful pledges. But do politicians take the party positions seriously? According to Gerald M. Pomper and Susan L. Lederman, they do. Pomper and Lederman set out to test how well public officials follow, or attempt to follow, their party's platforms. They began by arguing that platforms, in order to serve democratic purposes, must be "specific, policy-oriented, and relevant to the voters' concerns."[81] Pomper and Lederman showed that the platforms of the major parties fulfill these requirements. They found that about one-third of the statements in platforms are evaluations of the parties' records. Thus platforms provide information for those voters wishing to make retrospective judgments about the party's performance. Platform statements contain information aimed at attracting voters, statements that reveal party campaign strategy. Platforms also include pledges for the future. Pomper and Lederman found such statements to be clustered in the areas of foreign policy, economic policy, and social welfare policy. Such pledges are useful for voters wishing to make prospective judgments.[82]

Pomper and Lederman found that the party that is considered to be behind in an election tends to emphasize future pledges and to be more specific in the pledges made. The party that is considered ahead may be afraid that detailed promises will disrupt its coalition.[83]

After studying platforms from 1944 to 1978, Pomper and Lederman found that once party members hold office, platform pledges are usually fulfilled. These authors found that, when actions similar to those promised as well as actions actually promised were included, nearly three-fourths of all platform promises were kept. As we would expect, controlling the White House helps. The in-party was found to achieve about four-fifths of its platform goals.[84]

Platforms therefore play a vital role in helping parties perform their role as a link between the governed and their governors. They are another reason why parties are meaningful in a democracy.

MINOR PARTIES

The stability of a two-party system in the United States is a curious phenomenon. When most of the world is dominated by multiparty systems, why are two sufficient for the United States? Part of the answer is that we have separation of powers, a single executive, and a presidential system instead of a parliamentary one. (Only one party can win the White House.) The Electoral College is another factor. Electoral votes are distributed on a winner-take-all basis, an advantage for the major parties. That most legislative elections in the United States are in single-member districts that must be won by a majority of votes also may contribute to our two-party system. Major party gerrymandering helps protect their incumbents. (*Gerrymandering* refers to the drawing of district boundaries to the benefit of one party or group over another). Another possible reason for our two-party system is that the initial political conflict in this country—to revise the Articles of Confederation or adopt a new Constitution—was two-sided, with the anti-Federalists fighting the Federalists. Also, major parties in the United States are not strictly ideological; they are flexible enough to change with the times. Whatever the reason, Americans have shown an affinity for two-party politics.

Minor or third parties have, however, played a significant role in our history, one of them—the Republicans—eventually becoming a major party. In every presidential election since 1872 there have been more than two candidates.[85] Various types of minor parties have developed. Some are organized around a single issue (for instance, the Prohibition party); some around a charismatic politician (Theodore Roosevelt and the Bull Moose party, or George Wallace and the American Independent party); some around ideologies of the left (the Socialist party); some have been confined to a particular region (New York state's Liberal and Conservative parties, or Minnesota's Democratic Farmer-Labor party); some are splinters from the major parties (the Breckinridge Democrats of 1860, the Dixiecrats of 1948); and some are true minor parties with a broad base of electoral support (the Populists of 1892 and 1896, and the Libertarian party in the elections of the 1970s and 1980s). The single-issue parties have disappeared when the issues they promoted were resolved. The parties organized around politicians have usually died with the candidacy. The ideologically extreme parties have failed to garner enough support to be taken seriously. In fact, minor-party presidential candidates usually poll only two to three percent of the vote.[86]

Third parties have not been without impact. Often the major parties have co-opted some of the minor-party proposals, making them their own. For example, the antislavery proposals of the Free Soilers were adopted by the Republicans. Populist and Progressive ideas on the graduated income tax, minimum wages, and Social Security were adopted by the major parties. It is not clear how much credit should be given to minor parties for these developments. The major parties might have adopted such positions anyway, given time.[87]

While minor parties may not have enough support to win presidential elections, they can disrupt them. If no presidential candidate wins a majority of electoral votes, the election goes into the House of Representatives, where each state has one vote. Also, a minor party might drain support away from just one of the major parties. If the election is close, it is conceivable that such a minor party could throw the election to the other major party's candidate. While scholars cannot say that such a scenario has ever occurred, according to Blank it is mathematically possible that the results of the elections of 1848, 1892, 1956, 1960, and 1968 could have been reversed without the third-party voting that took place in those years.[88]

Third parties face a variety of obstacles today. It has been shown that media attention is crucial for effective candidacies, and third parties and their candidates receive little coverage from the major media. Journalists look at the small number of party members and the relatively small amounts of money raised for the campaign, and they declare that such candidates do not have a chance and are therefore not newsworthy. Lack of media attention can help ensure that such predictions come true. Presidential candidates from the Socialist and Communist parties are given so little attention that most voters do not even know their names.

One of the biggest obstacles to minor party presidential candidates is found in the system of public funding. As stated earlier, major-party candidates receive matching funds as the nomination fight progresses; new minor-party candidates receive nothing until after the election is over and only if they have polled 5 percent of the vote. By that time, the money is good only for paying off campaign debts; it cannot be used for strategic campaign purposes. Consequently, third-party candidates rely on loans, which can be difficult to get. Third parties that qualify for public funding in one election will automatically qualify for it in the next, but it is difficult for such parties to survive that long.

Third-party candidates also encounter problems getting on the ballot in many states. It often is difficult for such parties to acquire the number of signatures on petitions needed to get on the ballot. (George Wallace in 1968 and John Anderson in 1980 were able to meet ballot requirements in all fifty states; such success is rare for minor-party candidates.[89])

Perhaps the unkindest cut of all is that many of the voters who voiced support for a minor-party candidate during the campaign will abandon that candidate on election day. When push comes to shove, many feel that a vote for a minor-party candidate is a "wasted" vote, given the odds. Rather than waste their vote, they force themselves to choose a major-party candidate they can live with.

With all of these obstacles, one might wonder why third parties continue to exist. Obviously, their members are committed to a set of ideas not represented in the major parties. Through their activities, third parties hope to educate the public. Perhaps one day some of their ideas, at least, will be acceptable. The major parties concentrate their focus on middle-class Americans. To some extent, minor parties provide representation for the rest.[90] Third parties help fulfill the needs of democracy by providing a voice for those whose ideas are not represented in the major parties.

SUMMARY

This chapter illustrates how much the political landscape has changed since 1960. Party affiliation, while still important, is not as significant to voters as it once was. Evidence for this is shown in ticket-splitting, in voting for the person and not the party, or in not voting at all. Presidential campaigns are now candidate-centered, prolonged affairs with a reduced role for political parties. The mass media have an increased role to play, as they sort out the primaries and caucuses for confused voters. Political parties have responded by providing services and coordinating fund-raising to the point where parties are more nationalized today than ever before. Democrats have concentrated on reforming nomination rules, while Republicans have built up the Republican National Committee to provide services to candidates.

The end result of these changes is that election outcomes are less predictable than before and the electorate more volatile. Specific evidence for this will be provided in the next two chapters as we examine presidential elections since 1960.

SUGGESTED READINGS

BLANK, ROBERT H., *Political Parties: an Introduction*. Englewood Cliffs, NJ: Prentice-Hall, 1980.

COTTER, CORNELIUS P., and JOHN F. BIBBY, "Institutional Development of Parties and the Thesis of Party Decline," *Political Science Quarterly* 95 (Spring 1980), pp. 1–28.

CROTTY, WILLIAM, and JOHN S. JACKSON III, *Presidential Primaries and Nominations*. Washington, DC: Congressional Quarterly Press, 1985.

FIORINA, MORRIS P., "The Decline of Collective Responsibility in American Politics," *Daedalus* 109 (Summer 1980), pp. 25–45.

FREEMAN, JO, "The Political Culture of Democrats and Republicans," *Political Science Quarterly* 101 (1986), pp. 327–356.

GOODMAN, WILLIAM, *The Party System in America*. Englewood Cliffs, NJ: Prentice-Hall, 1980.

IPPOLITO, DENNIS, and THOMAS WALKER, *Political Parties, Interest Groups, and PACs*. Englewood Cliffs, NJ: Prentice-Hall, 1980.

MAISEL, L. SANDY, *Parties and Elections in America: The Electoral Process*. New York: Random House, 1987.

NICE, DAVID C., "Polarization in the American Party System," *Presidential Studies Quarterly* 14 (Winter 1984), pp. 109–116.

POMPER, GERALD M., "The Decline of the Party in American Elections," *Political Science Quarterly* 92 (Spring 1977), pp. 21–41.

PRICE, DAVID E., *Bringing Back the Parties*. Washington, DC: Congressional Quarterly Press, 1984.

SANDMAN, JOSHUA H., "The Re-emerging Role of the Political Party: Campaign '84 and Beyond," *Presidential Studies Quarterly* 14 (Fall 1984), pp. 512–518.

SULLIVAN, DENNIS G., JEFFREY L. PRESSMAN, BENJAMIN I. PAGE, and JOHN J. LYONS, *The Politics of Representation: The Democratic Convention 1972*. New York: St. Martin's Press, 1974.

SUNDQUIST, JAMES L., "Whither the American Party System?—Revisited," *Political Science Quarterly* 98 (Winter 1983–84), pp. 573–593.

DISCUSSION QUESTIONS

1. What are the contributions made to our political system by parties?

2. What is *your* attitude toward political parties? Do you favor party loyalty, or do you prefer to weigh each candidate's qualifications regardless of their party? What are the advantages and disadvantages of party loyalty?

3. How important are questions about a candidate's character as compared with questions more related to party platforms and job qualifications?

4. Why are primary elections a popular method for selecting delegates to conventions? How do you feel about the role primaries play in the nomination process?

5. How has increased reliance on primaries changed the role of the mass media in covering nomination campaigns?

6. How have campaign finance reforms altered the role of parties in campaigns?

7. How much attention should voters pay to party platforms? How important should platforms be compared with a candidate's personality, a candidate's political skills, campaign events, and so forth?

8. Should minor parties and their candidates receive treatment equal to that of the major parties in the election laws and in media attention?

NOTES

1. Alan R. Gitelson, M. Margaret Conway, and Frank B. Feigert, *American Political Parties: Stability and Change* (Boston: Houghton Mifflin, 1984), p. 12.

2. Ibid., p. 14.

3. See Morris P. Fiorina, "The Decline of Collective Responsibility in American Politics," *Daedalus* 109 (Summer 1980), pp. 25–45.

4. E. E. Schattschneider, *Party Government* (Holt, Rinehart & Winston, 1942), p. 1.

5. William Goodman, *The Party System in America* (Englewood Cliffs, NJ: Prentice-Hall, 1980), pp. 71, 72.

6. Paul R. Abramson, "Developing Party Identification: A Further Examination of Life-Cycle, Generational, and Period Effects," *American Journal of Political Science* 23 (February 1979), pp. 78–96. See also the rejoinder by Philip E. Converse in the same issue.

7. Robert H. Blank, *Political Parties, An Introduction* (Englewood Cliffs, NJ: Prentice-Hall, 1980), p. 254.

8. See Martin P. Wattenberg, "The Decline of Political Partisanship in the United States: Negativity or Neutrality?" *American Political Science Review* 75 (December 1981), pp. 941–950, and Stephen C. Craig, "Neutrality, Negativity, or Both? A Reply to Wattenberg," *Political Behavior* 9 (1987), pp. 126–138.

9. Blank, *Political Parties*, pp. 291, 292.

10. Frank B. Feigert disputes the idea that ticket-splitting is widespread or increasing. See "Illusions of Ticket-Splitting," *American Politics Quarterly* 7 (October 1979), pp. 470–488.

11. John F. Bibby, *Politics, Parties, and Elections in America* (Chicago: Nelson-Hall, 1987), p. 260.

12. William S. Maddox and Dan Nimmo, "In Search of the Ticket Splitter," *Political Science Quarterly* 62 (September 1981), pp. 401–408.

13. L. Sandy Maisel, *Parties and Elections in America: The Electoral Process* (New York: Random House, 1987), p. 44.

14. Gitelson, et al., *American Political Parties,* p. 138.

15. John F. Bibby, *Politics, Parties and Elections,* p. 270.

16. Everett Carll Ladd, "The Shifting Party Coalitions—From the 1930s to the 1970s," in Seymour Martin Lipset, ed., *Party Coalitions in the 1980s* (San Francisco: Institute for Contemporary Studies, 1981), pp. 127–149. The quotation is from p. 128.

17. Bibby, *Politics, Parties, and Elections,* p. 268.

18. *The People, Press, and Politics* (Los Angeles: Times Mirror, 1987), p. 1. Originally, one of the classifications used was "The Passive Poor." In April 1988 Times Mirror announced they were changing the name of this category to "God and Country Democrats." Times Mirror discovered in polls that people in this category *could* be roused to political action under some circumstances.

19. David S. Broder, "The American Voters' New Stripes," *The Washington Post National Weekly Edition* 4 (October 19, 1987), p. 6.

20. William Crotty and John S. Jackson III, *Presidential Primaries and Nominations* (Washington, DC: Congressional Quarterly Press, 1985), p. 14.

21. Gitelson, et al., *American Political Parties,* p. 181.

22. Bibby, *Politics, Parties, and Elections,* pp. 171, 172.

23. Ibid., p. 173.

24. Maisel, *Parties and Elections,* p. 176.

25. Ibid., p. 177.

26. Stephen J. Wayne, *The Road to the White House,* 3rd ed. (New York: St. Martin's Press, 1988), p. 98.

27. Ibid., p. 98.

28. Ibid.

29. Ibid., p. 99.

30. Crotty and Jacobson, *Presidential Primaries,* pp. 46, 47.

31. Bibby, *Politics, Parties, and Elections,* p. 179.

32. Maisel, *Parties and Elections,* p. 180.

33. A. James Reichley disagrees. In "The Rise of National Parties" in John E. Chubb and Paul E. Peterson, eds., *The New Direction in American Politics* (Washington, DC: The Brookings Institution, 1985), he argues that the responsible party system recommended by the American Political Science Association in 1950 is arriving due to increasing ideological consistency in the two parties.

34. James I. Lengle, *Representation and Presidential Primaries: The Democratic Party in the Post Reform Era* (Westport, CT: Greenwood Press, 1981).

35. Herbert Kritzer and Richard L. Rubin, "Representativeness of the 1972 Presidential Primaries," in William Crotty, ed., *The Party Symbol: Readings on Political Parties,* (San Francisco: W.H. Freeman, 1980); and Richard L. Rubin, "Presidential Primaries: Continuities, Dimensions of Change, and Political Implications," in William Crotty, ed., *The Party Symbol* (San Francisco: W.H. Freeman, 1980).

36. Crotty and Jacobson, *Presidential Primaries,* p. 89.

37. James L. Sundquist, "Whither the American Party System?—Revisited," *Political Science Quarterly* 98 (Winter 1983–1984), pp. 573–593.

38. Crotty and Jacobson, *Presidential Primaries,* p. 64.

39. Timothy Crouse, *The Boys on the Bus* (New York: Ballantine Books, 1973), pp. 47–49.

40. Gary R. Orren and Nelson W. Polsby, eds., *Media and Momentum, The New Hampshire Primary and Nomination Politics* (Chatham, NJ: Chatham House, 1987), pp. 12, 191.

41. Ibid.

42. Herbert B. Asher, "The Media and the Presidential Selection Process," in Louis Maisel and Joseph Cooper, eds., *The Impact of the Electoral Process* (Beverly Hills, CA: Sage, 1977), p. 223.

43. Richard A. Watson and Norman C. Thomas, *The Politics of the Presidency,* 2nd ed. (Washington, DC: Congressional Quarterly Press, 1988), p. 61.

44. William Crotty and John S. Jackson III, *Presidential Primaries and Nominations* (Washington, DC: Congressional Quarterly Press, 1985), pp. 220–230.

45. Maisel, *Parties and Elections,* p. 235. Figures were compiled by Herbert Alexander and the Citizen's Research Foundation.

46. Gitelson, et al., *American Political Parties,* p. 209.

47. Ibid., p. 207.

48. William Goodman, *The Party System in America* (Englewood Cliffs, NJ: Prentice-Hall, 1980), p. 106.

49. Crotty and Jacobson, *Presidential Primaries,* p. 161.

50. Gitelson, et al., *American Political Parties,* p. 202.

51. Ibid., p. 208.

52. William J. Keefe, Parties, Politics, and Public Policy in America, 4th ed. (New York: Holt, Rinehart, and Winston, 1984), p. 140.

53. Elizabeth Drew, *Politics and Money, The New Road to Corruption* (New York: Macmillan, 1983.)

54. Wayne, *The Road to the White House,* p. 41.

55. Keefe, *Parties, Politics,* p. 139.

56. Wayne, *The Road to the White House,* p. 41.

57. Reasons for prohibiting direct contributions from corporations and labor unions include the fear of electing presidents who would be beholden to such groups if the groups were allowed to contribute, and the fear that corporations and unions would dominate contributions, reducing the influence of individual contributors.

58. Wayne, *The Road to the White House,* p. 44.

59. Goodman, *The Party System In America,* p. 107.

60. Bibby, *Politics, Parties, and Elections,* p. 182.

61. Wayne, *Road to the White House,* pp. 49, 50.

62. William Crotty, *American Parties in Decline,* 2nd ed. (Boston: Little, Brown, 1984); Walter Dean Burnham, *The Current Crisis in American Politics* (New York: Oxford University Press, 1982) and "The Eclipse of the Democratic Party," *Society* 21 (July/August 1984), pp. 5–11 and reaction articles.

63. Everett Carll Ladd, *Where Have All the Voters Gone?* (New York: W.W. Norton, 1982).

64. Reichley, "The Rise of National Parties," p. 188.

65. Bibby, *Politics, Parties, and Elections,* pp. 205, 206.

66. Reichley, "The Rise of National Parties," p. 198.

67. Ibid., p. 175.

68. Maisel, *Parties and Elections,* p. 278.

69. Reichley, "The Rise of National Parties," p. 189.

70. Ibid., pp. 192–194.

71. Ibid., pp. 194, 195.

72. Keefe, *Parties, Politics,* p. 141.

73. Reichley, "The Rise of National Parties," pp. 189, 190.

74. Bibby, *Politics, Parties, and Elections,* p. 206.

75. Reichley, "The Rise of National Parties," p. 197.

76. M. Margaret Conway, "Republican Political Party Nationalization, Campaign Activities, and Their Implications for the Party System," *Publius* 13 (Winter 1983), pp. 1–17.

77. See Cornelius P. Cotter and John F. Bibby, "Institutional Development of Parties and the Thesis of Party Decline," *Political Science Quarterly* 95 (Spring 1980), pp. 1–28.

78. Crotty and Jackson, *Presidential Primaries,* p. 191.

79. Richard A. Watson, *The Presidential Contest,* 2nd ed. (New York: John Wiley, 1984), p. 45.

80. Crotty and Jackson, *Presidential Primaries,* p. 205.

81. Gerald M. Pomper with Susan S. Lederman, *Elections in America,* 2nd ed. (New York: Longman, 1980), p. 129.

82. Ibid., pp. 128–145.

83. Ibid., pp. 145, 146.

84. Ibid., pp. 161–165.

85. Goodman, *The Party System,* p. 16.

86. Ibid., p. 16.

87. Blank, *Political Parties,* p. 47.

88. Ibid., p. 44.

89. Gitelson, et al., *American Political Parties,* p. 61.

90. Ibid., pp. 65, 66.

Presidential Elections, 1960-1976

INTRODUCTION

The Electoral College

The system used in the United States for selecting its chief executive is the most democratic in the world. Nominations are not controlled by party officers; the franchise is extended to virtually all citizens eighteen years or older; and both the mass media and public opinion play a role in the process that is unsurpassed in the Western world.

This is not to argue that the United States has the best system for electing presidents, or that it necessarily picks the best person to hold that office. As reported in other chapters, our electoral system results in many problems, including low voter turnout rates. But the option for citizen involvement exists to an extent not found in other countries, providing real opportunities for the people to participate, if they wish to.

In a strict sense, though, these elections are not so democratic. Their results do not actually select the president; the Electoral College does. Before we review the presidential elections since 1960, it is necessary to describe the purpose and method of the Electoral College.

The Founders were frightened of concentrated power, wherever it might be found—in the executive, the legislature, the judiciary, or in the people. The framers of the Constitution knew that people can be subject to emotions, to fads that can sweep them away against their better judgment. However, an electoral system that eliminated popular participation would not be legitimate. A compromise was found: Citizens would be allowed to vote, but not directly for presidential candidates. The popular vote would not select presidents, but it would select electors. They would then meet in December of election years, in their state capitals, and cast their votes. The votes from the states would be gathered in Washington, D.C. in January and counted. This would be the action that formally elects presidents. Electors originally were meant to be respected, experienced persons who would make wise decisions. With the rise of political parties, however, electors became party functionaries, putting aside their discretion to support their parties' nominees.

The number of electors for each state is determined by taking both statehood and population into account: The number of U.S. senators from a state (two) is added to the number of members of the U.S. House of Representatives for that state. The total is the number of electors that the state will have. States gain or lose electoral votes as they gain or lose population, as determined by the U.S. Census taken every ten years. This system of allocation gives great power to populous states, which control large blocks of electoral votes, but it over-represents small states, which are guaranteed three electoral votes no matter how tiny their populations. The individuals chosen to be electors are determined by party rules and state laws.

State laws also control the manner in which popular votes are translated into electoral votes. All states but one (Maine) allocate electors in a winner-take-all fashion. A candidate can thus win a state by just one vote and still win *all* the state's electors. This means candidates can be successful by winning the most populous eleven states, even while losing the rest. It also means a candidate can win many small states by large margins, lose some key big states by small margins, lose in the Electoral College, but win the popular vote. This occurred in 1876, when Rutherford B. Hayes was elected, and in 1888, when Benjamin Harrison was elected.

The Constitution requires that if no candidate receives a majority (270 votes) in the Electoral College, then the election must go into the U.S. House of Representatives, where each state has one vote. This occurred in 1824, when the House chose John Quincy Adams. There is some evidence that the Founders did not expect most elections to be decided by the Electoral College. Rather, they expected the Electoral College to perform a winnowing function, thereby allowing the House to determine the winner.[1] The development of political parties and party loyalty among electors changed this scenario.

The House also decided the election of 1800. The Constitution made no provision for identifying electoral votes for presidential candidates as distinct from votes for vice-presidential candidates. In 1800, the Democratic-Republicans nominated Thomas Jefferson for president and Aaron Burr for vice president. The electors who won by being on this ticket cast an equal number of ballots for both Jefferson and Burr, tying the election. The House, after much political maneuvering, chose Jefferson. Later the Twelfth Amendment was added to the Constitution, providing a separate vote for the offices of president and vice president.

The Electoral College has many opponents because it can give an election to a president who has the popular support of only a minority. Another problem with the college has to do with *faithless electors.* Electors are selected because they are expected to support the party's candidate, but they are not bound to do so. (Some states have laws requiring electors to vote for their state's popular winner, but if an elector chooses to defy the law, there is no way to change the vote. The elector could be fined or jailed, but the state cannot change his vote.) They can vote for whomever they wish. On occasion, some electors have done just that: A Nixon elector voted for Democratic Senator Harry F. Byrd in 1960, a Nixon elector voted for George C. Wallace in 1968, a Ford elector voted for Ronald Reagan in 1976,[2] and an elector voted for Lloyd Bentsen in 1988. In our history, fewer than twenty-five electors have been faithless, and none of these instances has changed the outcome of an election. The possibility is there, though, and many find it disconcerting.

The winner-take-all feature discourages independent and minor-party candidates. Few such candidates are popular enough to win entire states. Their support might be substantial, 35 to 45 percent of the vote, but unless they have enough votes to come in first in a state, it does not ensure them electoral votes.

Because of these undemocratic features, proposals have been made to alter or abolish the Electoral College. The *proportional plan* would do away with the winner-take-all system and allocate the electoral votes according to the popular vote. Under this system, a candidate winning 45 percent of the popular vote in a state would receive 45 percent of that state's electoral votes. This reform addresses the minority winner problem. Another reform is aimed at faithless electors. The *automatic plan* would do away with the position of elector; the electoral votes would automatically be counted toward the proper candidate.

The *national bonus plan* proposes that the Electoral College be retained but altered to prevent the minority vote-getter in the popular vote from winning the electoral vote. Under this plan, a pool of 102 votes would go to the candidate who receives the most popular votes, added to the candidate's regular electoral vote. The majority required for winning would then be 321. If no one receives a majority, an unlikely development, then a runoff election would be held between the top two candidates.[3]

The most popular reform idea is the *direct election* proposal. This does away with the Electoral College completely. The states would have no role in presidential elections under this plan; presidential elections would be truly national contests, and every vote would count. (With the winner-take-all-Electoral College system, a person's vote for a candidate who wins 35 percent of the state's vote is wasted; it does not count toward the commitment of electoral votes.) The direct election proposal is popular with the public, but political

TABLE 5–1 *(Continued)*

	1984 VOTE COUNT	CHANGE AFTER 1980 CENSUS
Virginia	12	– –
Washington	10	+1
West Virginia	6	– –
Wisconsin	11	– –
Wyoming	3	– –

SOURCE: Census changes are from William J. Keefe, et al., *American Democracy, Institutions, Politics, and Policies,* 2nd ed. (Chicago: The Dorsey Press, 1986), p. 182. Reprinted with permission of Brooks/Cole Publishing Company, a division of Wadsworth, Inc.

Recent Presidential Elections

We turn now to the post-World War II presidential elections. While that war officially ended in 1945, it had lingering effects through the presidencies of Harry S Truman (who made the decision to drop the atomic bomb that ended the war) and Dwight D. Eisenhower (a war hero turned politician). The election of John F. Kennedy in 1960 marked a new era in U.S. politics. This election saw an early start to campaigning, the use of primary elections to sway party leaders, a reliance on personal campaign staffs, the coming to power of the post-World War II generation, and an important role for the mass media. It also may have been the last presidential election in which the New Deal coalition behaved in more or less its traditional manner.

So we begin with this election, and we trace important events and trends that followed in the elections through 1976. (The elections of 1980 through 1988 are discussed in Chapter 6.) First, we briefly examine the nomination campaigns for each election. Next, the issues important in the campaign and the role they played are discussed. Third, how the public evaluated the candidates is covered, as are the election results. Information on campaign finances and the mass media is included where pertinent. In these two chapters, we will trace the increasing importance of primary elections for winning nominations, and the increasing independence of candidates from their parties. Chapter 6 concludes with an examination of the role of political consultants and voting rationales.

Two chapters cannot possibly discuss each of these elections exhaustively, but focusing on these areas should equip the reader to better understand the history of recent presidential elections and put the latest one into perspective.

THE 1960 ELECTION

The Nominations

The Democrats lost the presidency to Republican Dwight Eisenhower in 1952 and 1956, but not because the country had problems with the Democratic leadership per se. Eisenhower was an extremely popular war hero, a former general who had commanded the Allied troops in Europe, whose political background was so blank that both major parties had attempted to recruit him to run for president. Any candidate who ran against Ike was likely to be defeated, as was former Illinois governor Adlai Stevenson, the Democrats' choice in both 1952 and 1956. By 1960 the Democrats were ready to reclaim the White House, but there was no obvious standard bearer for the party. In addition to John Kennedy, a young senator from Massachusetts who had been in contention for the vice-presidential nomination in 1956, the field included Senate Majority Leader Lyndon B. Johnson of Texas, Senator Hubert H. Humphrey of Minnesota, and Senator Stuart Symington of Missouri. Stevenson and Tennessee Senator Estes Kefauver were available to be drafted if the convention became deadlocked. (This turned out to be a good year for candidates who were members of Congress, as opposed to candidates who were governors.)

From the start, Kennedy's Catholicism was a problem. The last time a major party nominated a Catholic was in 1928 when the Democrats nominated Alfred Smith. Smith lost to Herbert Hoover after a campaign marked by anti-Catholic sentiments. There was no evidence that public attitudes had changed. And Kennedy was relatively young and inexperienced to boot. His strategy was to impress party leaders with wins in carefully selected primaries. He addressed the Catholic issue in the West Virginia primary campaign and in an important speech delivered to the Greater Houston Ministerial Association. Kennedy won West Virginia, a state that was overwhelmingly Protestant, and sought in Houston to reassure those who feared that he would take his direction from Rome:

> I believe in an America where the separation of church and state is absolute—where no Catholic prelate would tell the President (should he be a Catholic) how to act and no Protestant minister would tell his parishioners for whom to vote—where no church or church school is granted any public funds or political preference—and where no man is denied public office merely because his religion differs from the President who might appoint him or the people who might elect him.[4]

The West Virginia primary victory and the Houston speech impressed the political elites, but the "Catholic problem" still did not go away.

Kennedy also scored an important victory against Humphrey in Wisconsin, a state close to Humphrey's home in Minnesota. Kennedy had two factors working strongly in his favor: his father's money, which enabled him to purchase time on television, and his brother Robert, who managed his campaign. Although Robert was even younger than John, he was an excellent strategist and delegate counter. He understood the tasks that were necessary in a campaign, and saw to it those tasks were accomplished. In addition to these advantages, Kennedy was a war hero, having served on PT boats in the Pacific during World War II.

resisted efforts by his staff to brief him on the staging of the debate. A poised Kennedy held the stage with the vice president of the United States. In terms of televised images, Kennedy looked stronger than he had before; Nixon looked less formidable. Nixon was a skilled debater, however, and polls showed that listeners believed that Nixon had won the debate. Polls of television viewers found just the opposite. An estimated 70 to 75 million people saw the first debate; audiences for the other three debates were around 50 million.[7]

Kennedy, true to his campaign, promoted a more activist national government, whereas Nixon emphasized the similarities between the candidates. Ideological differences were not stressed, allowing the candidates' personal characteristics and images to play an important role in the perceptions of viewers.[8]

Much has been made of these debates. It is true that Kennedy made a good impression, that the value of Nixon's status as vice president was reduced. But few voters said they changed their minds because of the debates. Because the 1960 election was so close, it is tempting to credit Kennedy's victory to his performance. It is possible that the debates swayed enough voters, or reached enough of those uncommitted, to bring Kennedy success. We will never know for certain. After 1960, though, candidates not only paid much more attention to their looks but also to how they came across on television. Did they appear relaxed, competent, confident, and sincere? Did they appear to want the presidency too much? Most of all, they wanted to avoid making the kind of impression that Nixon made in the first debate, prompting critics to ask, "Would you buy a used car from this man?"

Another groundbreaking event in 1960 was the publication of Theodore H. White's *The Making of the President 1960.*[9] White traveled with the candidates, watched them closely, and wrote in detail about their campaigns and decisions. His approach set a standard for the years that followed. According to Timothy Crouse,

> The book struck most readers as a total revelation—it was as if they had never before read anything, anywhere, that told them what a political campaign was about. They had some idea that a campaign consisted of a series of arcane deals and dull speeches, and suddenly White came along with a book that laid out the campaign as a wide-screen thriller with full-blooded heroes and white-knuckle suspense on every page. The book hit the number-one spot on the best-seller lists six weeks after publication and stayed there for exactly one year.[10]

According to Crouse, the book inspired editors of major newspapers to strengthen their own coverage of presidential campaigns. Crouse wrote that the Associated Press told its reporters in 1972, "When Teddy White's book comes out, there shouldn't be one single story in that book that we haven't reported ourselves."[11] For better or worse, campaign reporting would never be the same. White was a lonely figure on the campaign trail in 1960; today, the reporters sometimes outnumber the audiences that the candidates address.

The Results

The Democrats took back the White House in 1960 in one of the closest presidential elections in U.S. history, an election where voter turnout reached a remarkably high level (62.8 percent). Kennedy won 34.2 million popular votes; Nixon 34.1 million. Kennedy's winning margin was about one-tenth of 1 percent. The Electoral College vote was 303 for Kennedy; 219 for Nixon. (Democratic Senator Harry F. Byrd of Virginia received fifteen electoral votes.) Kennedy was successful in the Northeast, in most of the South, in cities, and with blacks and union workers. Nixon did well in upper New England, the Midwest, and the West.[12] (See Table 5-3 for election results from 1960-1988.)

While Catholics strongly supported Kennedy, his religion hurt him in the overall popular vote. One estimate is that Kennedy's religion cost him 1.5 million votes. But these votes were not spread throughout the country; they were concentrated in particular areas, such as in the South. This geographical concentration of the anti-Catholic sentiment means that the issue cost Kennedy popular votes but did not hurt him in the Electoral College. While there were

TABLE 5-3   Popular and Electoral Votes, 1960-1988

YEAR	CANDIDATES	ELECTORAL VOTE	POPULAR VOTE
1960[a]	Kennedy (D)	303	34,221,344
	Nixon (R)	219	34,106,671
1964	Johnson (D)	486	43,126,584
	Goldwater (R)	52	27,177,838
1968[b]	Humphrey (D)	191	31,274,503
	Nixon (R)	301	31,785,148
1972	McGovern (D)	17	29,171,791
	Nixon (R)	520	47,170,179
1976	Carter (D)	297	40,830,763
	Ford (R)	240	39,147,793
1980	Carter (D)	49	35,483,883
	Reagan (R)	489	43,904,153
1984	Mondale (D)	13	37,577,137
	Reagan (R)	525	54,455,074
1988[c]	Dukakis (D)	111	41,809,030
	Bush (R)	426	48,901,046

[a]Harry F. Byrd received 15 electoral votes.
[b]George C. Wallace received 46 electoral votes.
[c]Lloyd Bentsen received 1 electoral vote.
SOURCE: Data for 1960-1984 are from Harold W. Stanley and Richard G. Niemi, eds., Vital Statistics on American Politics (Washington, DC: Congressional Quarterly Press, 1988), pp. 82, 83. Figures are from Congressional Quarterly's Guide to U.S. Elections. Reprinted with permission. Data for 1988 are from B. Drummond Ayres, Jr., "Electoral College's Stately Landslide Sends Bush and Quayle Into History," The New York Times, December 20, 1988, p. 13; and Richard L. Berke, "50.16% Voter Turnout Is 64-Year Low," The New York Times, December 18, 1988, Section 1, p. 18. Copyright 1988 by The New York Times Company. Reprinted by permission.

High percentages of voters believed that racial antagonism or the international situation were the most serious problems facing the United States. They favored the Democrats on these issues.[20] The 1964 race differed from those in 1952, 1956, and 1960 in that the candidates were more clearly differentiated in their positions on national issues.[21]

Voter Evaluations of Candidates

Johnson was preferred over Goldwater by most voters in 1964. The Republicans were helped by the race issue in the South, but virtually all other

'There's Only One Economic Indicator I Go By'

SOURCE: Tom Engelhardt, St. Louis Post-Dispatch. Copyright 1980. Reprinted with permission.

issues favored the Democrats. Johnson had the image of a progressive who was a "warm and friendly person with good judgment." Very few voters felt the same was true of Senator Goldwater.[22] Many voters thought that Goldwater was a radical; few felt that way about Johnson.

The Mass Media

As noted, no debates took place between the nominees in 1964. Johnson, a popular incumbent, had nothing to gain and something to lose by appearing on the same stage with Goldwater. Television did make a lasting impression, though, in terms of spot commercials. This was the year that the campaign industry produced the "daisy spot," a commercial for the Johnson campaign that aired only once but was extremely controversial. It played off fears about Goldwater's stand on the use of nuclear weapons. In this spot, a little girl was shown pulling petals off a daisy as a voice began a countdown. Then a mushroom shaped cloud appeared in the sky. As the words "Vote for President Johnson on November 3" appeared on the screen, a voice said, "The stakes are too high for you to stay at home."[23] There is no evidence that this spot affected voters, but it was a precursor of things to come. Before too long, negative advertising would become popular with all kinds of candidates.

While the national conventions had felt the effects of television in previous years, the electronic media had an explicit impact in 1964. There were preconvention shows and postconvention shows. The length of the demonstrations for candidates at the conventions and the number and length of speeches at the conventions were affected by television. The Republicans, in an effort to conserve prime time, combined the roles of temporary chair and keynote speaker. In the midst of controversy, the Republicans stalled for time by having the entire proposed platform read to the delegates (and the viewing audience). This meant that the fights over the planks were delayed until after most viewers in the East and Midwest had gone to bed.[24] (The Republicans met in San Francisco.)

The Goldwater delegates were antagonistic toward the delegates pledged to other candidates. Television showed viewers the Goldwater supporters' "impatience, ill-breeding, [and] unwillingness to accord the courtesy of a fair hearing to opponents."[25] The Goldwater group was equally harsh with the press, denouncing journalists in speeches from the podium. At one point, security was asked to clear the aisles, which were crowded with delegates and reporters. John Chancellor of NBC was in the middle of an interview and did not hurry to leave the floor. He was escorted out, saying, "This is John Chancellor, somewhere in custody."[26]

This election marked two important developments in how the media cover election night. The networks and some of the print media arrived at a joint arrangement providing for a fast and common count of the vote as it was reported. Such cooperation previously had been a rarity. The other develop-

Soviet Union than he had been in 1960. In the meantime, Agnew's campaign sounded a lot like that of third-party candidate George Wallace, with attacks on bureaucrats, civil rights, and protesters.

As for Wallace himself, this was the year in which he ran for president as the nominee of the American Independent party. His campaign was fairly successful for a third-party effort. His was an antiestablishment campaign, which addressed law and order, taxes, and desegregation, as well as the issues that Agnew was pursuing for the Republicans. His running mate was General Curtis LeMay, former Air Force chief of staff.

Voter Evaluations of Candidates

Five issues accounted for most of the problems mentioned by the electorate as being the most important: the Vietnam War, law and order, civil rights, poverty, and the urban riots. The Democrats were preferred on the issues of civil rights and poverty, the Republicans on the other issues.[33] Nixon enjoyed good standing in the polls from the start.

Wallace supporters were very concerned about issues, particularly the Vietnam War, law and order, and civil rights. Support for Nixon and Humphrey was much less tied to issues. This difference is probably because Wallace was less ambiguous about his stance on these issues than were the major-party candidates.[34]

The Mass Media

Michigan Governor George Romney had been a major contender for the Republican nomination at one time. A televised interview proved to be his undoing. Romney agreed to an interview on Detroit television shortly after his return from a trip to South Vietnam. He was tired and unaccompanied by advisors. He was asked if his position on the Vietnam War was not inconsistent with earlier beliefs. Romney answered, "I have been brainwashed by generals and diplomats in Vietnam." This comment received tremendous attention from editorialists, and the reaction was negative. Governors are not supposed to be susceptible to brainwashing. It was the end of the race for Romney, and provided an instructive lesson to the other candidates: Do not give interviews when you are tired, and have an aide present at interviews, someone who can tell the candidate when a statement has been made that can be misconstrued.[35]

Media coverage of the Democratic convention was controversial. Some believed that the demonstrations would have developed quite differently had not "the whole world" been watching. It is possible that the presence of cameras encouraged protesters to be more aggressive; some threw rocks and bottles at the police. (A government commission, however, called the melee a "police riot.") Such questions are beyond the scope of this text. What is important here is that the images projected from Chicago were detrimental to the Democrats' chances of winning the November election. Their chances may not have been high anyway, but the violence and disarray at the convention produced negative images of the party. The party was clearly split in its attitudes toward the demonstrators. Connecticut Governor Abraham Ribicoff, in his nomination speech for Senator George McGovern, referred to Chicago police as using "Gestapo tactics." Some cheered his words; some booed, including Chicago Mayor Richard Daley, clearly seen on television shouting at Ribicoff. (Lip readers have said he was yelling ethnic slurs.) The pervasiveness of the mass media meant that the party could not hide its quarrels behind closed doors.

Nixon's campaign used slick marketing and advertising techniques to sell a "new" Nixon. The details of this marketing strategy were revealed in a book by Joe McGinniss entitled *The Selling of the President 1968*.[36] This book served as a reminder that, with the decline in party loyalty, advertising was becoming more and more important in efforts to reach voters.

The Results

The 1968 election was very close; Humphrey's campaign picked up steam in the last weeks of the campaign. Some speculate that if the campaign had lasted two more weeks Humphrey might have won. As it was, Nixon received 31.8 million votes to Humphrey's 31.2 million. The Electoral College vote count was 301 to 191.[37] Nixon won thirty-two states; Humphrey thirteen. Nixon won six southern states, all of the West except Texas, Washington, and Hawaii, and all the midwestern states except Michigan and Minnesota. Humphrey was strong in the East. Wallace received 9.9 million votes, winning five southern states. He won forty-six electoral votes.[38]

About 97 percent of black voters chose Humphrey; the remaining 3 percent voted for Nixon. Democrats won 35 percent of the white vote, Republicans 52 percent, and Wallace 14 percent. Wallace ran better among younger people than older; younger citizens have weaker attachments to political parties, and are more likely to support a third-party candidate.[39]

The Wallace candidacy, had it been successful enough to deny one of the major-party candidates a majority, would have threatened to disrupt Electoral College voting. It appears that Wallace took votes away from Nixon, even though most of his supporters were registered Democrats.[40]

Both 1968 candidates began their campaigns early; McCarthy made a special effort to develop grass-roots support. The tumultuous convention and campaign provided the impetus for nomination reform in the Democratic party. The primaries were not important in 1968, but after this year a majority of convention delegates would be chosen through them. No longer would party leaders dictate the nominee. (See Chapter 4.) This also was an election where the cracks in the New Deal coalition became apparent. Not only did many registered Democrats vote for Nixon, quite a few turned to the third-party candidate.

polled would describe McGovern as someone who "sticks to principles," while 40 percent described Nixon this way. While evaluations of Nixon on various qualities were rarely high, they were higher than evaluations of McGovern.[48]

Campaign Finances

In keeping with the trend toward candidate-centered campaigns, the Nixon campaign in 1972 decided to separate itself from the Republican National Committee. The Committee for the Reelection of the President (CREEP) was created to finance and run the campaign. Nixon did not engage in much traditional campaigning, though, and CREEP was free to get involved in other matters, such as raising money and burglarizing the Democratic National Committee headquarters at the Watergate hotel in Washington, D.C. The highest level of contributions by individual donors was reached in 1972. A total of $51.3 million was donated by just 1,254 individuals. The largest single contribution was made by W. Clement Stone, who gave $2,141,655.94.[49]

Some corporations disguised illegal contributions (ones that came from their company treasuries) by "laundering money." There were a variety of ways to launder money.

> American Airlines, for example, sent money from one U.S. bank to an agent in Lebanon for supposed purchase of an aircraft; it came back to a second U.S. bank and then on to the Finance Committee for the Reelection of the President. Other firms drew on secret slush funds, sold bogus airline tickets, or created fictitious bonus schemes for employees. The employees then contributed the bonus to a campaign.[50]

Investigations revealed that in the early 1970s illegal corporate contributions existed on a huge scale. Many of those convicted of illegal contributions said they committed the crime because the fund raisers included high officials such as Maurice Stans, the former secretary of commerce, and Herbert Kalmbach, Nixon's personal attorney.[51]

Another campaign finance issue that came out in the Watergate scandal revelations was the awarding of ambassadorships to contributors of large sums to the campaign. While Nixon was not the first president to so reward supporters, his choices, though confirmed by the Senate, were controversial. For example, Ruth Farkas, a sociologist and director of a New York department store, was appointed ambassador to Luxembourg. Farkas had given $300,000 to the Nixon campaign. Exchanging a federal job for campaign support is a federal crime. Herbert Kalmbach later went to jail for fund-raising activities that were partly related to "ambassadorial auctions."[52]

The McGovern campaign took Goldwater's direct mail fund-raising tactics to heart. The Democratic party was still laden with debts from Robert Kennedy's and Hubert Humphrey's 1968 presidential campaign bids; the usual donors had already been hit hard by the party. The McGovern campaign faced this problem by developing lists of potential contributors—antiwar activists and others—and by soliciting small contributions through the mail. They started early, in January of 1971. Ironically, the Republicans would renew their use of direct mail fund-raising after the Watergate scandal and make successful use of the technique in later elections.

The Mass Media

It is difficult to determine just how influential coverage of Muskie's "crying" incident was. It is quite possible that something else might have proved equally troublesome for Muskie. Whatever the scene did or did not reveal about Muskie, it illustrates how powerful the press can be in their coverage of primary elections. Reporters cover candidates day in and day out, and are bound to catch the candidates at their worst as well as at their best. While one can argue that it is good to see candidates when they are tired and distraught (that it is good to see their weaknesses), one can also argue that, with this kind of scrutiny, no candidate's image will survive. *The Washington Post* reporter and columnist David S. Broder was one of the reporters who wrote stories saying that Muskie had wept. Looking back on this incident in 1987, Broder wrote:

> What Muskie did not know and what I certainly did not know at the time I wrote the Manchester story was that there was another set of facts which would have put the incident into a very different context. Those facts related to a series of actions, ordered and coordinated by the Nixon White House and designed to harass, to vex, and to embarrass the front-running Democrat, who was judged as a serious threat to Nixon's reelection. . . . Had those facts been known, I might have described Muskie in different terms: not as a victim of his own overambitious campaign strategy and his own too-human temperament but as the victim of a fraud, managed by operatives of a frightened and unscrupulous President. That story surely would have had a different impact.[53]

In the early stages of this campaign, many reporters clearly had a high opinion of McGovern. Their early stories about his campaign were perhaps too positive, since no one thought he had a chance at getting the nomination. He was not put under the same scrutiny as Muskie. Once McGovern won the nomination, the scrutiny was there, a media spotlight illuminating all the campaign's gaffes and weaknesses. Perhaps if the media attention had come sooner, the McGovern campaign would have been more savvy by the time the nomination was clinched. Or, McGovern's weaknesses, revealed sooner, might have kept him from winning the nomination.

Reporters complained about a lack of access to Nixon; the McGovern campaign may have given the press too much access. An imbalance was created; Nixon could make mistakes in private, while McGovern's were made virtually in front of the press. Crouse, writing about press coverage of this campaign in *The Boys on the Bus,* wrote:

victories, even though they were early in the campaign, and began giving Carter serious coverage. In fact, journalists were quick to call Carter "the man to beat" after Iowa.

The liberals in the group often did well at the polls, but with so many in the contest the liberal vote was split among them. Governor Brown, in particular, did well in later primaries, but by then it was too late to parley those wins into the nomination. In spite of all the candidates in contention, the Democrats enjoyed a united convention for a change. Carter, an outsider to the federal government, chose a Washington insider, Senator Walter F. Mondale of Minnesota, as his running mate. Since Carter's presidential nomination was not in doubt, he had time before the convention to contemplate his vice-presidential choice. As noted previously, he invited a variety of Democratic elected officials down to Plains, Georgia, so he could meet them and size them up. It was a far more ordered process than the old-fashioned, wait-until-the-last-minute approach.

The Issues

The campaign was dominated by gaffes on both sides. Carter gave an interview to *Playboy* magazine, which seemed an odd choice for a self-described "born again" Christian. (Carter admitted that he had experienced lust in his heart in this interview.) He made a statement about ethnic purity in neighborhoods that was misunderstood. Ford's comment about Eastern Europe and Soviet domination was also misunderstood. He was making the point that Eastern Europeans did not consider themselves to be controlled by the Soviet Union, that they had a sense of national identity, but the remark was said to imply that Ford was naive about the Soviet Union's influence in Eastern Europe.[59]

Voter Evaluations of Candidates

Both Ford and Carter were perceived positively by the electorate, but for different reasons. Carter made a favorable impression because of his personal leadership and his connection with Democratic ideology. Carter campaigned against the Washington establishment, a logical approach after the debacle of the Nixon years. Ford was seen as reliable, decisive, and competent in terms of his previous public service.[60] He conducted a "Rose Garden" strategy, staying close to the White House and acting presidential rather than campaigning out on the hustings.

Unemployment and inflation headed the list of problems considered most important by the electorate, and the Democrats carried an advantage on these issues. They were also preferred on the three other issues receiving mention: national economic health, the energy crisis, and crime.[61]

Ford's pardon of Nixon was not a frequent topic of debate in the campaign, but there is some evidence that it did sway some voters. One study showed that approval versus disapproval of the pardon was connected with vote choice. This remained true when party identification was ruled out as an influence.[62] In other words, those who disapproved of the pardon were likely to vote against Ford, regardless of whether they were Republicans or Democrats.

The social issues that were so important and controversial in 1972—abortion, drugs, an amnesty for draft dodgers—were still of concern, but they did not play a significant role in 1976. Economic problems had become more salient. Both candidates, however, tried to make personality the major theme of the campaign.[63]

Campaign Finances

The Federal Election Campaign Act (FECA), described in Chapter 4, was passed in 1971 and amended in 1974. The 1976 election was the first to come under the new finance rules. Recall that the FECA created limits on campaign expenditures and mandated disclosure of receipts and expenditures. The Revenue Act of 1971 provided for the income tax check-off that created a pool of money for public funding of presidential campaigns.

The *Buckley* v. *Valeo* Supreme Court decision mandated that the Federal Election Commission (FEC) be reconstituted so that all its members were appointed by the president. The necessity of doing this caused delays in paying out government funds to presidential candidates in 1976. Also, instead of simply reconstituting the FEC, Congress embarked on significant revisions in the law, dealing with the compliance and enforcement procedures and the advisory opinions. The FEC was not remade until May 1976. Obviously, campaigns that were not well financed suffered from the delay.[64] Independent expenditures played only a small role in 1976; in the 1975–1976 election cycle, less than $800,000 was spent independently.[65]

The Mass Media

The mass media were particularly important for Jimmy Carter, since he began the campaign as a relative unknown outside his home state. A Federal Communications Commission (FCC) ruling allowed televised debates in 1976, as long as an outside sponsor presented the events. The League of Women Voters was happy to do so, and the candidates agreed to debate, much to Carter's benefit. Carter handled himself well, appearing to be in command of an array of facts and figures. The presidential candidates had three debates; the vice-presidential contenders had one. Viewership of the debates was high, but it apparently changed few candidate choice decisions.[66] For most, the debates simply reinforced the voters' previous choices.

As noted elsewhere, voters were not quick to pick up on Ford's Eastern Europe gaffe. One study found that, while Ford did not suffer from the remark in polls taken immediately after the debate, later polls showed that respondents were much more likely to say that Carter was the winner of that debate. It is likely that people were influenced by the commentary that followed the debate, commentary that was critical of Ford.[67]

2. Assess the history of nomination reform in the Democratic party. Are amateurs given too much or too little power? What about professionals? What is the reasoning for your position?
3. What are the pros and cons of beginning the nomination contest as early as one year before the election?
4. Compare the status of the New Deal coalition in 1960 with the coalition in 1976.

NOTES

1. A. James Reichley, "The Electoral System," in A. James Reichley, ed., *Elections American Style* (Washington, DC: The Brookings Institution, 1987), p. 6.

2. "The Electoral College," *Elections '88* (Washington, DC: Congressional Quarterly Press, 1988), p. 75.

3. Stephen J. Wayne, *The Road to the White House,* 3rd ed. (New York: St. Martin's Press, 1988), p. 297.

4. Theodore H. White, *The Making of the President, 1960* (New York: Atheneum, 1961), p. 391.

5. Herbert B. Asher, *Presidential Elections and American Politics,* 4th ed. (Chicago: The Dorsey Press, 1988), p. 142.

6. Ibid., p. 139.

7. Ibid., p. 254.

8. "Modern Presidential Elections," *Elections '88,* p. 4.

9. White, *The Making of the President, 1960.*

10. Timothy Crouse, *The Boys on the Bus* (New York: Ballantine Books, 1973), pp. 33, 34.

11. Ibid., p. 36.

12. "Modern Presidential Elections," *Elections '88,* p. 5.

13. Asher, *Presidential Elections,* pp. 139, 140.

14. "Modern Presidential Elections," *Elections '88,* p. 5.

15. J. Leonard Reinsch, *Getting Elected: From Roosevelt and Radio to Television and Reagan* (New York: Hippocrene Books, 1988), p. 192.

16. "Modern Presidential Elections," *Elections '88,* p. 5.

17. Milton C. Cummings, Jr., ed., *The National Election of 1964* (Washington, DC: The Brookings Institution, 1966), p. 110.

18. Frank J. Sorauf, *Money in American Elections* (Glenview, IL: Scott, Foresman, 1988), p. 26.

19. Stanley Karnow, *Vietnam: A History* (New York: Viking, 1983), p. 395.

20. Cummings, *The National Election,* p. 45.

21. Ibid., p. 269.

22. Ibid., p. 45.

23. Ibid., p. 61.

24. Ibid., pp. 36, 37.

25. Ibid., p. 120.

26. Reinsch, *Getting Elected,* p. 191.

27. Cummings, *The National Election,* p. 143.

28. "Modern Presidential Elections," *Elections '88,* p. 6.

29. Cummings, *The National Election,* p. 150.

30. "Modern Presidential Elections," *Elections '88,* p. 7.

31. Ibid., p. 8.

32. Joe McGinniss, *The Selling of the President, 1968* (New York: Trident Press, 1969.)

33. Asher, *Presidential Elections,* p. 158.

34. Ibid., p. 157.

35. Reinsch, *Getting Elected,* p. 210.

36. McGinniss, *The Selling of the President, 1968.*

37. Harold W. Stanley and Richard G. Niemi, eds., *Vital Statistics on American Politics* (Washington, DC: Congressional Quarterly Press, 1988), p. 83.

38. "Modern Presidential Elections," *Elections '88,* p. 8.

39. Asher, *Presidential Elections,* p. 160.

40. Ibid., p. 157.

41. The burglary was at the Democratic National Committee headquarters in the Watergate Hotel building in Washington, DC.

42. Asher, *Presidential Elections,* p. 166.

43. "Modern Presidential Elections," *Elections '88,* p. 8.

44. Ibid., p. 8.

45. Ibid., p. 9.

46. See Crouse, *The Boys on the Bus,* pp. 344–353.

47. Asher, *Presidential Elections,* pp. 164, 165.

48. Ibid., p. 167.

49. Herbert E. Alexander, *Financing Politics,* 3rd ed. (Washington, DC: Congressional Quarterly Press, 1984), pp. 60, 61.

50. Ibid., p. 86.

51. Ibid., p. 87.

52. Ibid., p. 65.

53. David S. Broder, *Behind the Front Page: A Candid Look at How the News is Made* (New York: Simon & Schuster, 1987), p. 37.

54. Crouse, *The Boys on the Bus,* pp. 361, 362.

55. Stanley and Niemi, *Vital Statistics on American Politics,* p. 83.

56. Asher, *Presidential Elections,* p. 162.

57. Kenneth J. Meier and James E. Campbell, "Issue Voting: An Empirical Examination of Individually Necessary and Jointly Sufficient Conditions," *American Politics Quarterly* 7 (January 1979), pp. 21–50.

58. "Modern Presidential Elections," *Elections '88,* p. 10.

59. Ibid., p. 10.

60. Asher, *Presidential Elections,* p. 174.

61. Ibid., p. 174.

62. Arthur H. Miller and Warren E. Miller, "Partisanship and Performance: 'Rational' Choice in the 1976 Presidential Election." Paper presented at the annual meeting of the American Political Science Association, Washington, DC, September 1–4, 1977, as noted in Asher, *Presidential Elections,* p. 176.

63. Asher, *Presidential Elections,* pp. 174, 177.

64. Alexander, *Financing Politics,* pp. 42, 43.

65. Ibid., pp. 63, 64.

66. Asher, *Presidential Elections,* p. 178.

67. Ibid., p. 178.

68. "Modern Presidential Elections," *Elections '88,* p. 11.

69. Ibid., p. 11.

points among men, but by less than 8 percent among women.[6] Note tl.at more women supported Reagan than Carter, but their support for Reagan was weaker than the men's support. Much of the support for Reagan was negative; many of his supporters favored Reagan because they were against Carter. Much of Carter's support was negative as well. Many voters went into the 1980 election unhappy with both candidates.

Campaign Finances

In 1980, independent expenditures increased dramatically, totaling about $2.7 million (up from $800,000 in 1975-1976). Independent spending was used to enhance candidate spending in the crucial early primary states and in later primaries when the candidates were approaching the national spending limit.[7] Independent spending also was high in congressional races. New Right groups, such as the National Conservative Political Action Committee (NCPAC), targeted a number of prominent liberal Democratic senators, and six were defeated at the polls. It is impossible to say how influential the independent spending was in these campaigns; other factors were involved as well.

Independent spending is not regulated by the Federal Election Campaign Act. Other ways of spending money and avoiding the regulations of the FECA include draft committees and presidential PACs. Groundwork can be laid for a candidate by groups that work without the candidate's authorization to draft the candidate. There were many such committees in 1980 working to draft Senator Kennedy. Each committee could accept individual donations of up to $5,000 and spend unlimited amounts of money. Four eventual presidential candidates—Reagan, Bush, Connally, and Senator Robert Dole of Kansas—formed political action committees to aid fellow party members and party committees. While the purpose of these PACs was to aid others, they also brought their founders good will from federal, state, and local candidates and from local party organizations. They gave their founders excuses to travel throughout the country, gaining the attention of the media. And the costs did not count against future spending limits that were to apply once candidacies were announced. Both Mondale and Kennedy set up PACs in 1981.[8]

In addition to using direct mail to raise money, candidates experimented with other fund-raising innovations. Concerts by rock and country musicians were used to generate funds. In 1980 the proportion of the population giving money to candidates and causes increased significantly. Studies show that between 1952 and 1976 from 4 to 12 percent of the population donated to politics at some level in presidential election years. A 1980 survey found that 13 percent of the population contributed to candidates and causes in that year.[9] The main goal of campaign finance reform, replacing a handful of "fat cats" with large numbers of contributors, seemed to be realized.[10]

Republican candidate John Connally decided to forgo public funding, believing that he could do better unbound by the rules which accompany the receipt of public money. A wealthy man, Connally raised and spent $12.72 million, but he was not a popular candidate. He received only one vote at the Republican convention.[11] It is likely that his experience discouraged later candidates from doing without public funding.

As an independent candidate, John Anderson faced certain disadvantages in the campaign finance laws. Minor-party candidates from new parties do not receive matching funds from the government until after the election, and then only if they poll at least 5 percent of the vote. But Anderson was running as an independent, and the law was silent on such candidates. An FEC ruling in September of 1980 made Anderson eligible for retroactive public funds if he received the same 5 percent or more of the popular vote in the general election. In the meantime, Anderson attempted to rely on bank loans and loans from individual contributors. Anderson raised only about half the amount that the major-party candidates had at their disposal, and some of this money was not received until after the election. Anderson was at a decided disadvantage, as are all minor-party and independent candidates.[12]

The Mass Media

The campaigns of George McGovern and Jimmy Carter had been given boosts by the Iowa caucuses. By 1980, the media were paying close attention to these contests, just in case they were to have any predictive power. It is a commitment they have continued to the present day.

One 1980 news practice, unconnected to the campaign in the beginning, added to Carter's troubles. When the U.S. embassy personnel were taken hostage in Iran, the network news shows included in each broadcast a message announcing how long the hostages had been held ("This is the fiftieth day of captivity. . . .") No doubt the broadcasters had noble intentions; American citizens had been held in prisoner of war camps or held hostage before, and some had criticized the news media for announcing such events but then forgetting them. No one wanted that to happen with the Iran hostages, and no one knew that their torment would last 444 days. In the end, the network news was a constant reminder that the Carter administration had not been able to free U.S. citizens. Out of necessity, the negotiation efforts of the Carter team were taking place without much publicity, but the failure of the administration to free the hostages received publicity every day. The one-year anniversary of the hostage taking was election day, 1980, and the hostages were returned on inauguration day, 1981.

The medium of television played a particularly strange role at the 1980 Republican convention. Polls showed that Gerald Ford would add more to the ticket as a vice-presidential candidate than any other Republican. Even though he had turned Reagan down on the nomination once, the Republican convention was full of talk of Ford on the ticket. This talk was spurred by an interview Ford gave to Walter Cronkite of CBS News. Television became a vital means of communication among Ford, Reagan, and the delegates as negotiations were carried out.[13] Reagan balked when the term "co-presidency" surfaced, and he chose George Bush instead of Ford.

The well-funded Republican party spent a great deal of money on institutional advertising in 1980, in part because of FEC decisions allowing expenditures for party-building purposes. The most widely seen of these commercials presented a House Speaker Thomas P. ("Tip") O'Neill look-alike espousing big-spending values. The tag line was "Vote Republican—for a Change." These ads were funded by the Republican National Committee.[14]

Despite a campaign filled with gaffes and misstatements, Reagan remained popular. There was controversy about whether or not the press was taking it easy on him, but such charges were unfair. The press ran plenty of stories about Reagan's mistakes; the majority of the public simply did not care. Even when the stories on television were critical of Reagan, the pictures presented an image of a warm, kind, trustworthy man—a man who was not Jimmy Carter.

The FCC again allowed televised debates, as long as they were sponsored by an outside organization. The Reagan forces were anxious to have a debate with Carter, knowing that challengers normally have much to gain from such encounters. The Carter forces knew that incumbents normally have much to lose, but Carter's popularity ratings were so low, and their confidence that Reagan would make mistakes so high, they agreed. But Reagan made a good impression; he appeared to be a much more reasonable and knowledgeable person than Carter had portrayed him to be. And he scored big with this closing:

> Next Tuesday all of you will go to the polls, will stand there in the polling place and make a decision. I think when you make that decision, it might be well if you would ask yourself, are you better off than you were four years ago? Is it easier for you to go and buy things in the stores than it was four years ago? Is there more or less unemployment in the country than there was four years ago? Is America as respected throughout the world as it was? Do you feel that our security is as safe, that we're as strong as we were four years ago? And if you answer all of those questions yes, why then, I think your choice is very obvious as to whom you will vote for. If you don't agree, if you don't think that this course that we've been on for the last four years is what you would like to see us follow for the next four, then I could suggest another choice that you have.[15]

A short-lived controversy arose after the election when it was revealed that the Reagan campaign had access to Carter's briefing books before the debate. These books were used to help Reagan prepare.

On election night, Reagan's victory was announced on television at 8:15 P.M. (EST), raising a controversy over the effect this announcement would have in the West, where the polls were still open. To make matters worse, Carter made an early concession speech an hour before polls closed on the West Coast.

This was not the first time a presidential victory had been announced early; Johnson's 1964 win was announced as early as 6:48 P.M. (EST).[16] Studies have not been able to show conclusively that early election calls affect turnout or voting decisions, but many believe an impact exists. Some have called for legislation that would create uniform closing times for polls across the nation; others have argued that news organizations should exercise restraint.

The Results

Polls had predicted that the 1980 election would be close; they were wrong. Many voters were undecided up until the last minute, but those voters went for Reagan in large numbers. Reagan won 44 million popular votes to Carter's 35 million; Reagan won 489 electoral votes to Carter's 49. John Anderson received 7 percent of the popular vote.[17] It is believed that Anderson took votes away from Carter rather than from Reagan.

Reagan beat Carter by more than a two-to-one margin in nine states. He had support from virtually all groups except blacks. The Republicans also gained a majority in the Senate for the first time since 1958, outnumbering Democrats fifty-three to forty-seven.[18] It is common to view this election as a mandate for Republicans and conservatism. Studies have shown, however, that the vote in 1980 was retrospective, being an anti-Carter vote, not a pro-Reagan vote.[19] Majorities still disapproved of the conservative position on social issues. The Reagan "landslide" was also tempered by a low voter turnout (52.6 percent); nonetheless, the Republican victory paved the way for changes in budget policies.

THE 1984 ELECTION

The Nominations

Despite controversies over his policies, President Reagan has remained personally very popular among the voters. The economy, which skidded into a major recession shortly after Reagan took office, picked up as the 1984 election approached, helping the Republicans. Reagan had no trouble gaining renomination, and the Republican convention was a love-fest that resembled a coronation.

Former Vice President Walter Mondale was an early and obvious favorite for the Democratic nomination, but he faced opposition from senators Gary Hart of Colorado, John Glenn of Ohio, Alan Cranston of California, and Ernest Hollings of South Carolina, and from the civil rights activist the Reverend Jesse Jackson. Former governor Reubin Askew of Florida and former presidential nominee George McGovern also entered the race.

This broad field of candidates was quickly narrowed to Mondale, Hart, and Jackson. Hart was taken seriously after finishing second in Iowa and first in New Hampshire, but his campaign was not well organized or well financed and so it did not take full advantage of these victories. Jackson's prospects for winning the nomination were never good, but he remained in the race in order to push his liberal agenda.

After winning the nomination, Mondale repeated Jimmy Carter's procedure in searching for a vice-presidential candidate, inviting Democrats of various backgrounds (both in terms of offices they had held and in terms of electoral demographics) for interviews. While such a careful process makes a lot of sense compared with last-minute headhunting, it backfired on Mondale. The Republicans had accused the Democrats of pandering to special interests— organized labor, teachers, and welfare recipients—all through the campaign, and now they argued that Mondale was going to "cave in" to special-interest pressure in making his running mate choice. In the end, Mondale made history by choosing a woman, Representative Geraldine Ferraro of New York, and the Republicans, indeed, made their charge about interest group pressure. (The Republicans already were suffering from the gender gap, and Ferraro's nomination was likely to take at least a few more women's votes away from the GOP.)

Reaction on the convention floor to Ferraro's nomination was euphoric, but the euphoria soon turned sour. Ferraro was a Catholic with a pro-choice stand on abortion, and that position and her husband's financial dealings soon became matters of controversy. It took weeks for these matters to settle down.[20]

Religion was introduced into the presidential election in a significant manner with the candidacy of an ordained minister, Jesse Jackson, and with the actions of black churches on his behalf. While religious activists had been present in the Republican party for some time, helping to shape its platforms, it would not be until 1988 that a conservative minister, Pat Robertson, made a run for the nomination.

Jackson's goal was to build a "Rainbow Coalition," a group of supporters with varied ethnic, racial, and religious backgrounds. In the end his supporters were, for the most part, black. He alienated Jews with comments that included references to them as "Hymies," and to New York City as "Hymietown." He raised further concerns by his association with the anti-Semitic black Muslim leader Louis Farrakhan and by his overtures to the Palestine Liberation Organization, which at that time advocated the destruction of Israel. Still, Jackson won almost 20 percent of the votes cast in Democratic primaries, winning two primaries in the District of Columbia and in Louisiana. He received more than 25 percent of the vote in New York, Tennessee, Maryland, and North Carolina. He won almost 500 delegates to the convention, and was one of the featured speakers at that gathering.[21]

Concern about the role of amateurs versus professionals had been growing in the Democratic party, and the party rules for 1984 addressed the issue by providing for *superdelegates,* elected officials (party professionals) who would be guaranteed voting seats at the convention. The purpose of the superdelegates was to provide a counterbalance to the amateurs. It was a mechanism for introducing the experienced opinion of politicians who knew what it took to win votes in a general election. While the amateurs might let their hearts carry them away, the superdelegates were supposed to be ruled by their heads. Technically, the superdelegates were uncommited, but in 1984 the majority of them let it be known they were for Mondale well before the convention. The timing of this reform was not an accident; the Mondale-Carter forces controlled the Democratic National Committee, and the rules were written to favor the former vice president.

The Issues

The economy was still the major concern in 1984. In his acceptance speech, Mondale asserted that, due to the deficit, whoever won the election would find it necessary to raise taxes. He said that Reagan would never admit to such a necessity, but he, Mondale, was honest enough to do so. It was a risky move; the public was concerned about the deficit, but still opposed tax increases. It is interesting to note that those most concerned about the deficit also felt that the Republican party could handle the problem better than the Democrats, even though the deficit had increased tremendously during a Republican administration.[22]

The issues cited as most important in 1984 were lessening the deficit, decreasing unemployment, preventing nuclear war, preventing conventional war, and stemming inflation. The Democrats were favored in dealing with unemployment and nuclear war; the Republicans were favored on the other issues.[23]

As noted, the issues of race and religion also played roles in the 1984 election. Jesse Jackson was unable to win the Democratic nomination, but his presence in the contest reminded voters of the issues of social welfare and race. Henry A. Plotkin described how the two issues intertwined when he wrote:

> In a fundamental way, the attack by the Republicans on the welfare state can be seen as an attack on black aspirations as well. For many Americans, the welfare state and blacks are seen as coterminous, so that talk of dramatically cutting social programs is merely a subtle form of racism. This is not to say that the President is a racist; rather it is to argue that criticism of the welfare state and the reluctance to expand it have a disproportionate effect on black America.[24]

The selection of the pro-choice Ferraro as Mondale's running mate sparked activity on the part of pro-life activists, who often demonstrated at Ferraro's rallies. The Roman Catholic archbishop of New York, John J. O'Connor, called abortion the critical issue in the campaign, and questioned whether Catholics could in good conscience vote for pro-choice candidates.[25]

Voter Evaluations of Candidates

Reagan was a popular incumbent, rated highly in terms of integrity, leadership, and competence. According to Herbert B. Asher, "Reagan's major advantage rested not in specific issues, but in the feeling of pride and confidence he fostered in his fellow citizens."[26]

Mondale was perceived as a traditional liberal, and one who wanted to raise taxes. He could not counteract Reagan's personal popularity; many citizens continued to support Reagan even when they disagreed with him on issues.[27] Mondale campaigned as a traditional Democrat, seeking and receiving endorsements from a variety of labor unions and interest groups. Reagan used these endorsements to characterize the Democrats as a party of "special interests."

Campaign Finances

Independent spending was high in 1984, hitting $17.5 million. While NCPAC was not as effective as it had been in 1980, total independent spending was very much weighted in favor of the Republicans; $16.3 million of the money spent in independent campaigns (93 percent) was spent promoting Republican candidates. Relatively few PACs accounted for most of this money; four accounted for 84 percent of all the money spent independently on the 1984 presidential campaign. They were NCPAC, the Fund for a Conservative Majority, Ruff PAC, and Senator Jesse Helms's National Congressional Club. All spent either for Reagan or against Mondale. These figures exaggerate the political spending done by these groups; much of this money went toward fund-raising costs, not to the campaign efforts themselves.[28]

The support given Mondale by organized labor helped the Democrats to offset somewhat the spending on behalf of the Republican party. It is estimated that

> labor/corporations/associations spent $3.5 million for Reagan, but $20.1 million for Mondale, much of the difference coming from organized labor. Republican state and local parties had more to spend, though: $15.6 million to the Democrats' $6.0 million.[29]

The Republican National Committee (RNC) was able to help Republican candidates by providing coordination for money raised at the state and local level ("soft" money). Some state laws allow such money to be used in states other than the ones in which it was raised. The RNC took advantage of the Republican party's ability to raise this money, and then targeted places where the money could best be used. The presidential ticket was used to help raise these funds, even though its own campaign was publicly funded.

Asher writes that campaign practices have seriously weakened campaign finance reforms.[30] He argues that there are now three campaigns for the presidency: the candidate-centered campaign, the political-party campaign, and the independent campaign. According to Asher, these campaigns are *not* independent of each other. Asher argues that only the candidate-centered general election campaign is run as the law intends. This is, of course, the campaign that is funded by public money. Some state and local party expenditures violate the spirit of the campaign finance laws by providing coordination where none was intended. Independent spending, according to Asher, is easily coordinated with the other two campaigns, given the information that is available to the public. (It is not difficult to figure out where expenditures will help a candidate, even without officially talking to the candidate's campaign staff.)

> If one accepts the argument that the three campaigns for president are coordinated to varying degrees and are not independent, where does the major responsibility for coordination lie? The answer is clear—in the candidate-centered campaign. It is the candidate's team of pollsters, media experts, and the like that plays the major role in directing expenditures in strategically effective ways.[31]

The Mass Media

During the nomination campaign, the media made a controversial decision in their coverage of the Iowa caucuses. In the Democratic contest, Mondale finished with 45 percent of the vote, not unexpected. Instead of concentrating on Mondale's win, the media focused on Gary Hart, who came in second (actually third, behind uncommitted voters) with 15 percent of the vote. Hart surprisingly trounced Glenn, who received a paltry 5 percent. Glenn, a popular former astronaut and Korean War hero, had been expected to do much better. It was surprising that Hart outpolled him, but many questioned whether or not Hart deserved the avalanche of publicity that followed. About 85,000 people had attended the Democratic caucuses on February 20, less than one-sixth of the people who usually vote Democratic in presidential elections in Iowa. George McGovern won 13 percent of the vote, even more of a surprise, but the media barely gave this any attention at all! Reporters had already made up their minds to not take McGovern seriously this time. These media choices had obvious effects, helping Hart and hurting Glenn and McGovern.[32]

John Glenn received a great deal of publicity—much of it favorable—when the movie *The Right Stuff* was released in the fall of 1983. The movie was about the early days of the space program, and Glenn was portrayed as a forceful person and a loving husband. But the movie, and the publicity, did not do Glenn much good. Maybe it was timing, since the movie came out before most people were interested in the campaign. Maybe it was that few people saw the movie. Maybe it was because voters in primaries and caucuses were paying more attention to Glenn the campaigner, and were not impressed with what they saw. Whatever the reason, Glenn failed to benefit from this publicity. This example illustrates that trying to gain politically from media attention is a tricky business.

There were quite a few televised debates during the nomination season, particularly among the Democrats. By April 23, there had been eight debates presented on local stations. PBS (the Public Broadcasting Service) and CBS also aired debates, but viewership was low.[33] The three commercial networks did not provide gavel-to-gavel coverage of the national conventions, deciding instead to begin coverage each evening at 9:00 P.M. Low viewer ratings and conventions at which the presidential nominees were already determined well in advance led to the cutbacks in TV coverage. Network officials believed there was less news being made at conventions. Ratings were low in 1984. Conventions now compete with movies on cable channels, MTV (a music-video channel), and rented videotapes. C-SPAN (the Cable-Satellite Public Affairs Network) and Ted Turner's CNN (Cable News Network) took up the slack, providing gavel-to-gavel coverage. Political scientists and other political news junkies rejoiced, but in 1984 only 43 percent of homes with television had access to cable.[34] Thus some would find it easier to watch the conventions than others.

Reagan and Mondale appeared in two debates, their running mates in one. Mondale's strategy in the first debate was to avoid attacking a popular incumbent; instead, he took the approach of "retiring an oldtimer," giving Reagan credit for contributing to a resurgence of patriotism and to the debate on education.[35] Reagan gave a poor performance in the first debate, appearing tired and confused. His age was briefly resurrected as a campaign issue, but he bounced back in the second debate, reassuring his supporters. He jokingly remarked that he would not exploit Mondale's youth and inexperience.

Among the television spot advertisements, noteworthy was an ad for Reagan which proclaimed that it was "morning again in America." It was an ad with no issue content, an ad that summoned feelings of patriotism and dedication to family. The implied message, without addressing specifics, was that things were going pretty well in the country, and voters should choose to continue the present leadership. Mondale's spots on the deficit paled in comparison.

Again the media made early projections of the winner, CBS announcing Reagan's victory at 8:00 P.M. (EST). ABC made the announcement at 8:13, and NBC showed the most restraint, waiting until 8:31 to call Reagan the winner.[36]

The Results

Reagan was consistently more popular than Mondale in preelection polls. Once again Reagan achieved a resounding victory, winning 54.5 million popular votes to Mondale's 37.6 million, and 525 electoral votes to Mondale's 13. Mondale won only the District of Columbia and Minnesota.[37] The gender gap was in evidence; one poll showed that men preferred Reagan to Mondale by a 61 to 37 percent margin, while women supported Reagan by a 57 to 42 percent margin.[38] Jews were not as supportive of Reagan as they had been four years earlier; they favored Mondale by a two-to-one margin. Catholics voted for Reagan by about a three-to-two margin. White "born again" Protestants supported Reagan by a four-to-one margin; other white Protestants voted for Reagan by more than two to one.[39] Once again, voters were retrospective in their approach to the election; while they did not agree always with Reagan's policies, they found enough with which to be satisfied in the previous four years to grant him another term.

The Republican party, however, suffered a net loss of two seats in the

Senate, and went on to lose control of the chamber to the Democrats in 1986. The party gained fourteen seats in the House of Representatives. The Republican victories at the presidential level since 1968 have led many to argue that the United States is in the process of a partisan realignment that will result in a Republican majority. This topic is addressed in Chapter 9.

Did Mondale's choice of a female running mate help or hurt the ticket? Most voters are not greatly concerned about vice-presidential candidates when deciding for which ticket they will vote. An NBC poll found most voters saying Ferraro's candidacy made no difference to them, but among the remaining voters Ferraro slightly hurt the ticket. This reaction may well have been due to the controversy over her family finances, or her relative inexperience as a politician, rather than to her gender per se.[40]

Mondale attributed his defeat, in part, to his lackluster performance on television, saying that "modern politics requires the mastery of television."[41] He expressed concern that presidential politics is lacking in substance, relying on imagery and deemphasizing the tough questions facing the nation. The Reagan team made sure that one story emerged from their campaign each day, and they chose the theme and provided the "sound bites" (short, sometimes humorous quotes) that the television news programs could not resist. There is no question that Reagan came across on television better than Mondale; how-

SOURCE: Clyde Wells, The Augusta Chronicle. Copyright 1987. Reprinted with permisison.

ever, even a media-savvy Mondale would have had difficulty unseating a popular president when the economy was perceived to be in such good shape.

Jackson's candidacy paved the way for a second run in 1988. It also served notice to Democrats who, in the face of Republican success at the presidential level, argued that the party should become more conservative. Jackson's presence in the race meant that minorities and the poor had not been forgotten by the Democratic party.

THE 1988 ELECTION

The Nominations

As the 1988 campaign approached, the Republican party faced some tough issues. The federal deficit had doubled during the Reagan years, and there had been a stock market crash on October 19, 1987. President Reagan had made two unsuccessful nominations to the Supreme Court (Robert Bork and Douglas Ginsburg). And, in November of 1987, it was revealed that the administration had secretly entered into an illegal arms-for-hostages deal with Iran. (The hostages this time were not U.S. diplomats, but businessmen and reporters who had traveled to or stayed in Lebanon despite State Department warnings.) This scandal became known as the Iran-contra scandal after it was discovered that funds from the sale of arms to Iran had been transferred to the contras in Central America. President Reagan continued to enjoy unprecedented popularity for a second-term president, but his popularity ratings as measured by polls did slide, and public opinion appeared to be swinging away from the Republican party. But two important factors favored the GOP: The nation was at peace, and most people felt the economy was doing well. The deficit was high, but inflation and unemployment were low.

Vice President George Bush was the favored candidate on the Republican side in a field that included Senator Robert Dole, former Delaware Governor Pierre S. "Pete" DuPont, evangelical broadcaster Pat Robertson, and retired General Alexander Haig. The Iran-contra scandal was one threat to Bush. If he knew about the details of the overtures to Iran, he could be criticized for not stopping the arms-for-hostages trade. If he did not know, he could hardly argue that he had been a knowledgeable and involved vice president. But the public seemed to lose interest in the scandal, and Bush settled the issue when he appeared on the CBS Evening News for an interview with anchor Dan Rather. Rather repeatedly attempted to draw out Bush on the role he played in the scandal, but Bush turned the tables by making Rather the issue. He objected to repeated questioning on the trade, arguing that he had answered the questions already. Bush suggested that people should be judged by their entire records, not by one incident in their careers. Bush mentioned that one evening Rather caused CBS to "go black." (Rather had walked away from his desk when CBS had decided to stay with a sporting event and begin the news late.) Bush said that Rather should not be judged by that single incident, but by his entire career. The exchange between the two was heated, and it served not only to suppress further questions about the Iran-contra scandal, but also to eradicate Bush's image as a "wimp."[42]

Bush's campaign was by far the best financed, and he collected the necessary number of delegates early in the primary season. He surprised everyone when he chose the relatively unknown forty-one-year-old Indiana Senator Dan Quayle for his running mate.

On the Democratic side, quite a few politicians touted as contenders chose not to run. New York Governor Mario Cuomo, New Jersey Senator Bill Bradley, and Georgia Senator Sam Nunn, among others, let it be known they were not interested in the nomination. Still, there was no shortage of candidates. Jesse Jackson once again threw his hat into the ring, as did Senator Joseph Biden of Delaware, Governor Michael Dukakis of Massachusetts, Senator Albert Gore of Tennessee, Senator Paul Simon of Illinois, former Senator Gary Hart of Colorado, and Representative Richard Gephardt of Missouri. This was, with the exception of Jackson, a group of experienced and talented politicians, but none was particularly well known at the beginning of the campaign. They were dubbed the "seven dwarfs." Televised debates were very popular this campaign season, and eventually voters who were interested began to develop impressions of the individuals in the group.

The 1988 campaign illustrates better than any other the vulnerability of caucuses to takeover maneuvers by amateurs. On the Democratic side, loyal supporters of Jackson gave him victories in seven caucus states (including Michigan and Texas), while on the Republican side, equally loyal supporters of Pat Robertson gave their man victories in three caucus states (including Iowa).[43] Since voter turnout in caucuses tends to be low, a relatively small group of dedicated supporters can have an impact. The same group, however, can be a drop in the bucket as compared with all the voters participating in a primary. Robertson failed to win any primaries, while Jackson again won seven.

Jackson was aided by a change in the threshold requirement for qualifying for delegates in proportional states. This threshold was 20 percent in 1984; in 1988 it was lowered to 15 percent. (See the discussion in Chapter 4 on the Fairness Commission.)

The attention given to the Iowa caucuses was in jeopardy after 1988. The candidates finishing first, Gephardt for the Democrats and Dole for the Republicans, did not do well in the nomination contest, dropping out well before the conventions.

What amounted to a regional primary was held, for the first time, in the South early in the primary season. The conservative wing of the Democratic party believed that one reason the party had had trouble winning the White House in recent years was because its nominees had been too liberal, especially for the South. Most of the southern states agreed to hold their primaries or caucuses on March 8, 1988 (dubbed "Super Tuesday"), believing that a conservative candidate would win big and gain the momentum necessary to do well in future contests. This strategy failed for several reasons. First, none of the popular conservative southern politicians (such as Senator Nunn of Georgia) decided to run. Tennessee's Gore was considered too young by some voters, and not conservative enough by others. Second, a large proportion of the Democratic southern electorate is black, and black voters are not terribly supportive of conservative candidates. Third, a black candidate, Jesse Jackson, was in the race, and did quite well, gaining an average of 10 percent of the white vote and 95 percent of the black vote.[44] In the end, Dukakis won in Florida and Texas, the populous, important states; Jackson and Gore won in the others, but no candidate emerged as a regionwide winner. Gore's campaign was given a brief boost by six Super Tuesday victories, but his failure to win any primaries outside the South ended his campaign.

As discussed previously, Senator Hart temporarily dropped out of the race after a scandal involving a woman fashion model and suggestions of infidelity. Later a lack of votes weeded him out, as well as most of the other candidates.

Michael Dukakis emerged as the nominee, with Jackson dogging him all the way to the convention. Jackson's campaign made history, garnering more votes than any previous black candidate. Jackson won 29 percent of the primary vote and 37 percent of the first-round caucus votes.[45] Dukakis, ignoring pleas from Jackson supporters that Jackson had "earned" the vice-presidential nomination, went for old-fashioned ticket-balancing and chose Texas Senator Lloyd Bentsen as his running mate. As in 1960, the Democrats ran a "Boston-Austin" ticket. In spite of the disappointment felt by the Jackson supporters, the convention ended with apparent party unity.

Jackson may have lost the vice-presidential nomination, but he won some points with the Rules Committee charged with drawing up the rules for the 1992 Democratic nomination contest. Jackson won a change that ties more closely the selection of delegates to a candidate's share of the primary or caucus vote.[46]

The Issues

The most important issues facing the country, as measured by a Gallup poll taken for *The New York Times* in May 1988, were illicit drug use, unemployment and recession, the budget deficit, and the economy in general.[47] Abortion and the state of the environment also concerned the electorate. These topics did not receive much discussion during the campaign. This was a banner year for negative campaigning. Bush attacked Dukakis for Dukakis's opposition to a Massachusetts bill requiring teachers to lead their classes in the Pledge of Allegiance and his opposition to the death penalty. Bush also made attacks on Dukakis for a Massachusetts prison furlough program for convicts, which made Dukakis appear soft on crime. Dukakis accused Bush of not being involved in major Reagan administration decisions, and of being packaged by his campaign "handlers." Bush appeared to be more comfortable with the negative approach than Dukakis, and he succeeded in putting Dukakis on the defensive for most of the campaign.

Dukakis said in his nomination acceptance speech that this election was not about ideology, but about competence. The electorate agreed with him. According to a CBS/*New York Times* poll, when voters were asked whether issues or competence were more important in how they voted, 19 percent chose issues, while 67 percent chose competence.[48] Unfortunately for Dukakis, the candidate that the electorate felt most competent was George Bush.

Voter Evaluations of Candidates

Once again, voters were not thrilled with either major party's nominee. Dukakis rode high in the polls after the Democratic convention, but soon plummetted in the face of Bush's negative ads. Dukakis promoted his competence as a public official, but many came to see his campaign as inept, responding too late and with too little to Bush's attacks. Dukakis was not well known when the campaign began, and Bush was able to define Dukakis to the voters. What Bush presented was a Dukakis who was liberal (the dreaded "L" word as it came to be known) and soft on crime and defense. Bush did not merely define Dukakis; he virtually set the agenda for the entire campaign through his speeches and advertisements. Bush defined himself in favorable terms even as he defined Dukakis in negative terms.

Bush himself was not viewed well by the electorate. One major poll, with a margin of error of plus or minus 3 percent, found that only 7 percent expected him to be a very good president, while 31 percent expected him to be a good president.[49] However, another major poll with the same margin of error found that respondents believed Bush to be more competent than Dukakis, 51 percent to 32 percent. Dukakis's running mate, Lloyd Bentsen, however, was preferred to Bush's vice-presidential candidate, Dan Quayle, 43 percent to 33 percent. Only one-third of those polled found Quayle qualified to be president.[50]

An ABC/*Washington Post* poll taken in October, with a margin of error of plus or minus 3 percent, found that 56 percent of those polled agreed that both Bush and Dukakis would "get things done." The same poll favored Dukakis on caring about the concerns of "people like me"; 63 percent thought Dukakis exhibited empathy, while only 52 percent said the same about Bush. Of those asked, 65 percent described Bush as possessing a vision for the country's future, and 64 percent said the same about Dukakis.[51]

Campaign Finances

Independent spending was high in 1988. For example, the National Security Political Action Committee said it raised almost $8 million to help the Bush campaign. Citizens for Dukakis said it raised over $200,000 for spending on behalf of the Democratic candidate. Party and campaign spokespersons complained that such efforts interfered with the messages the candidates were trying to communicate.[52]

Some of the negative advertisements that were run in this campaign were paid for by independent groups. The National Security Political Action Committee sponsored a television ad that showcased a photograph of Willie Horton, a black man who had stabbed a white man and raped his fiancee while he was out of prison on the Massachusetts furlough program. The Bush campaign complained to federal agencies about the committee, charging that it had misled people into thinking it was an arm of the Bush campaign. Such complaints aside, the ad ran throughout the campaign. Most of the independent spending done on behalf of presidential candidates was in support of Bush.[53]

The election of 1988 also was a high point in the spending of "soft money," the money that can be spent for party-building purposes. Activities such as mailings and field operations were being paid for with soft money through the parties instead of by the campaigns. Both Bush and Dukakis put their finance staffs on national party payrolls "to play key roles in raising and spending money for indirect applications."[54] Critics of the use of soft money argue that it provides an outlet for "fat cat" money, the kind of money that federal campaign finance reform was aimed at reducing. Corporations and labor unions, which are prohibited from making direct contributions to federal candidates, are allowed to make contributions for party-building activities. Clearly some party-building activities also benefit federal candidates. And when the costs of field organizations are paid for out of soft money, it frees up regulated contributions to pay for television advertising. Defenders of soft money argue that its use increases public interest and participation in elections, and that it revitalizes local party organizations.[55] Both the Democratic and Republican campaigns had expected to raise $50 million in soft money by election day.[56]

The Mass Media

The 1988 election was dominated by the character issue during the pre-convention nomination campaign. The Hart scandal was not the only incident to raise the issue of character. Early in the campaign it was revealed that Joe Biden had lied about his university record, and had committed plagiarism in a campaign speech. The hullabaloo that resulted forced him out of the campaign. It also was revealed that Pat Robertson's first child was conceived prior to his marriage.

These episodes raised important questions. How much does the public have a right to know? How heavily should such revelations be weighed by the electorate, and how related are these facts to performance in office? What about information on spouses? Children? How far should reporters go to get this kind of information? Biden's fate was sealed by a videotape provided to the press by Dukakis's campaign manager, who was then fired, only to be rehired during the general election campaign. Even some journalists questioned the *Miami Herald's* use of a stakeout to watch Hart. When candidate personalities and their personal campaigns mean so much more in an election than political parties and party loyalty, questions such as these are encouraged.

This campaign saw candidates take advantage of new ways to reach voters and activists. Most candidates prepared videotapes and distributed them at meetings and fund-raisers where they could not be present. The tapes were supposed to give viewers a feel for the candidate as a person. For the candidate this was the next best thing to being there. Another popular technique was to have televised call-in shows connected to other locations by satellite. Not only could local voters and reporters ask the candidate questions, but also voters and reporters from a continent away, allowing the candidate to get more mileage out of a single appearance.

During the nomination contest, there developed an embarrassment of riches as far as debates went. Instead of too few, there were perhaps too many debates, particularly among the Democratic candidates. Although aimed at voters in the current primary or caucus state, some of these debates were broadcast across the nation as well. The debates were no doubt useful to voters in the states, but the schedule was a heavy one for the candidates, and, toward the end, candidates began bowing out.

Jesse Jackson's candidacy presented a different set of questions. Some felt that the press, which was engaged by Jackson's rhetorical abilities and convinced that he had no chance to win the nomination, was too easy on Jackson. Some said the press did not examine Jackson's proposals critically. Others argued that the press was too hard on Jackson, that the press constantly reminded readers and viewers that Jackson had little chance of winning. They blamed the press for saying that Jackson's presence as a vice-presidential candidate would doom the Democratic ticket. Jackson received a good deal of press coverage when compared with most of the other Democratic candidates. Certainly not all of this coverage was favorable. As the campaign neared the convention, and as Jackson refused to concede defeat to Dukakis, headlines asked "What Does Jesse Want?" Critics of the press answered that Jackson wanted the same thing as any white candidate—he wanted to win. The press was in a difficult position.[57] Jackson had accomplished tremendous achievements as a candidate, going far beyond his protest candidacy of 1984. But that fact, in fairness, had to be put into perspective. Other facts existed, including poll results showing that Jackson would hurt the Democratic ticket if he was the vice-presidential candidate.

Again the three major networks refused to air gavel-to-gavel coverage of the conventions. Again network ratings were low. Again C-SPAN and CNN picked up the slack.

The general election campaign was an extremely negative race, especially in terms of television ads. Republicans claimed the Democrats started it with chants of "Where was George?" at their convention, accusing Bush of not being part of the decision-making structure at the White House. Bush quickly retaliated. Vulnerable on environmental issues, he filmed an ad in Boston's harbor that blamed Dukakis for the pollution there. (Of course, these ads avoided reference to the Reagan administration's cuts in antipollution programs.) In a debate, Bush, using what he said were Dukakis's own words, called the Massachusetts governor a "card-carrying member of the ACLU [American Civil Liberties Union]." Democrats accused the Bush campaign of calling up the language of McCarthyism (personal attacks based on indiscriminate allegations).

As noted, Dukakis had vetoed a Massachusetts bill that would have required teachers to lead students in the Pledge of Allegiance. Acting on the advice of the state's attorney general, Dukakis vetoed the bill on the grounds that, in light of U.S. Supreme Court decisions, it was unconstitutional. Bush repeatedly attacked Dukakis's decision, but denied he was impugning Dukakis's patriotism. This issue became a centerpiece of a campaign that avoided discussions of the budget deficit and foreign trade, two critical election issues.

The most controversial of Bush's television ads was one featuring the Massachusetts furlough program. The ad showed a line of convicts moving through a revolving turnstile. It suggested that 268 murderers had escaped while on furloughs or overstayed their furloughs, when that number actually represented *all* escaped or overdue furlough prisoners. Another ad featured relatives of Willie Horton's victims decrying the furlough program. The ads did not mention that Dukakis did not personally determine the prisoners who were released on furloughs, that the program was started by a Republican governor, or that many other states use furlough programs. Campaign advertising expert Kathleen Hall Jamieson said, "Never before in a presidential campaign have televised ads sponsored by a major-party candidate lied so blatantly."[58] Because of these ads and the one funded by the independent committee about the black prisoner, Willie Horton, Dukakis supporters accused Bush of bringing racism into the campaign.

Dukakis's own ads were generally agreed to be less effective than Bush's. One ad showed campaign "handlers" working on what was supposed to be Bush strategy. The message was that Dukakis was not a "managed" candidate, and that Bush was. But many viewers were confused, thinking this was a pro-Bush ad.

While slugging it out on the airwaves, both candidates restricted their availability to the press. The campaigns kept journalists busy with "themes of the week" and "messages of the day," but allowed few interviews or casual exchanges between the candidates and the press. Dukakis initially ran a relatively open campaign, but soon discovered the press was more interested in getting his response to Bush attacks than in the message he was attempting to put forth. For their part, the media were quick to include stories about press manipulation in their campaign coverage. They did little to withdraw from the manipulative environment, however. Still, it is difficult for the press to adequately cover serious issues when the candidates so assiduously avoid the issues.

All campaign coverage was not superficial. Magazines and newspapers still provided in-depth coverage for those who were interested. On television, PBS shone with a series of campaign-related broadcasts that were heavy with issue content. As usual, its "MacNeil/Lehrer NewsHour" provided coverage that went far beyond "sound bites." And, as usual, most people were not reading the in-depth stories or watching the issue-oriented broadcasts.

Behind in the polls, Dukakis was all over television in the last weeks of the campaign, doing interviews on network news shows, ABC's "Nightline," and the Larry King show on CNN. It was not enough to save his campaign. Bush began the campaign as a relatively unpopular candidate with a "wimpy" image. He and his strategists devised an effective program for blasting that negative image and for making their opponent the issue. Given the peace and prosperity that reigned, and which benefited the Republican party, Bush might have taken a less-aggressive approach to the campaign. He also might have lost the election. Dukakis, advised by a relatively inexperienced campaign team, made errors that he could ill afford to make.

There were two debates between Bush and Dukakis and one between their running mates. The League of Women Voters had competition in 1988 in obtaining debate sponsorship. A bipartisan commission was formed by the Democratic and Republican national committees for the purpose of sponsoring debates. Originally, the bipartisan commission was to sponsor the first presidential debate, the League of Women Voters the second. The League withdrew from the second, however, complaining that the campaigns were given too much power to dictate the terms under which the debate would take place. The bipartisan commission sponsored the second debate as well.

Dukakis faced high expectations in the second debate. Critics had charged him with lacking the passion and zeal necessary to be a leader. He and his campaign were also criticized for not responding effectively to Bush's attacks. It was said that he needed to exhibit both passion and toughness in this debate. The first question Dukakis faced was how he would react on learning that his wife had been raped and murdered. Would he still oppose the death penalty? Dukakis was stiff in his answer, reiterating his position that the death penalty was not an effective policy. He quickly moved to another topic, and many viewers were dismayed by the coldness of his response. The three major television networks decided not to declare any winner in the first presidential debate and in the vice-presidential debate, but NBC News and ABC News did declare Bush to be the winner of the second presidential debate.

In the end, it was a campaign that almost everyone agreed was shallow and offensive. Candidates found their messages reduced to "sound bites." Journalists were frustrated at the inaccessibility of the candidates, and at the ease with which they themselves were manipulated. The public was turned off by the negative tone of the campaign. Who is to blame for this state of affairs? All of the above. If negative campaigning works, and it does, candidates will continue to use it. The press complains about manipulation but continues to cooperate with candidates, following them out to cover pseudo-events and reporting charges and countercharges, when they could be doing more interesting and enlightening stories. The public has yet to insist that they not be condescended to by shallow campaigns and shallow coverage. Until the public stops voting for candidates who rely on shallow campaigns, candidates will run shallow campaigns. Until the public stops buying the magazines and newspapers that feature shallow coverage, and stops viewing the news programs that feature "sound bite" coverage—until the public hits the media where it counts, in the pocketbook—media coverage is unlikely to change.

But the biggest problem is the lack of importance of political parties to U.S. voters. Parties represent a statement of beliefs about political values, about the state of the country, about what politics can and cannot accomplish. When this is taken away from the electoral environment, campaigns have to turn on other matters, matters such as a candidate's personality and campaign imagery and issues. In the meantime, media advisers play a crucial role in campaigns. Campaign communication specialist Jamieson said of 1988, "If Roger Ailes [Bush's top media advisor] was working for Dukakis, he [Dukakis] would be the front-runner."[59] Such a statement has chilling implications for democratic theory.

CBS was the first network to project a winner, calling the election at 9:17 P.M. (EST). Once again, West Coast voters complained since their polls were still open.

The Results

George Bush won the 1988 election with an Electoral College vote of 426 to Dukakis's 111. (Lloyd Bentsen received one vote.) The popular vote went 49 million for Bush, with 42 million for Dukakis.[60] Bush's victory came in an election where voter turnout dropped to its lowest level in forty years; just 50 percent of those eligible cast ballots.[61] Many believed that the negative tone of the campaign kept some potential voters from going to the polls. A CBS/*New York Times* poll found that, if the nonvoters had participated, George Bush would still have won the election, and by a greater margin. The actual vote had Bush beating Dukakis by 54 percent to 46 percent, a difference of 8 percentage points. If the nonvoters had voted, according to the poll results, Bush would have won by 11 percentage points.[62] The poll's margin of error was plus or minus 3 percentage points.

Preliminary estimates suggested that black voter turnout significantly declined from 1984, a blow to the Dukakis campaign. Blacks who did vote supported Dukakis by a nine-to-one margin.[63] Low black voter turnout may have reflected the distance that Dukakis put between himself and Jesse Jackson.

The party winning the White House in 1988 lost seats in the House of Representatives. (Nearly 99 percent of the House incumbents who sought reelection won.) Democrats gained a net of three seats in the House, and a net of one in the Senate.[64]

TWENTY-EIGHT YEARS OF CAMPAIGNS

Presidential campaigns have become more democratized since 1960, for better or worse. Popular participation is to be valued, of course, but our country's Founders would be amazed at the demands our current political system makes on voters. Does the average citizen really want or need to be involved in the nomination process? In this section, we examine some of the consequences of this democratization, including the increasing use of political consultants and the rationales used by voters.

The Use of Political Consultants

As presidential candidates have grown more independent of political parties, and as televised images have become more important in campaigns, contenders have come to rely more and more on consultants. These consultants work for the candidates, not for the parties, and they provide advice on an array of subjects—fund-raising, computer use, media coverage, polling, even the issues. Whereas congressional candidates (especially Republican ones) can get some help on these subjects from the party, presidential candidates tend to go outside the party.

Some definitions are in order. According to Larry J. Sabato, a *political consultant* is "a campaign professional who is engaged primarily in the provision of advice and services . . . to candidates, their campaigns, and other political committees."[65] A generalist advises candidates on all aspects of the campaign, while a specialist develops expertise and offers advice in one or two areas of campaigning. The trend today is toward specialists and away from generalists, and specializations are getting narrower. Yesterday's specialist in fund-raising is today's specialist in fund-raising from those making small contributions, for example.

The political consulting profession is closely related to public relations. Many consultants began their careers in advertising. In 1960 there were few political consultants; today there are thousands, if local consultants are included.[66] The development of consulting as a profession is signaled by organizations such as the American Association of Political Consultants, the Graduate School of Political Management in New York City, and the Campaign Management Institute at Kent State University in Ohio. Political consulting was made possible and flourished because of technological developments, many of which were first used in advertising products. Companies refined the art of polling, the use of direct mail, demographic targeting, and the use of the media in efforts to sell more products. The development of computers made these tasks easier. It was relatively easy to transfer these skills to political campaigns; easy, that is, if the candidate can afford it. Political consultants do not work cheaply. Consulting expenses went from $1.8 billion in 1983-1984 to an estimated $2.5 billion to $3 billion in 1987-1988.[67]

Consultants want to work for winners; their reputations suffer if they are routinely associated with losing campaigns. Because of this concern, most clients of consultants are incumbents. Some consultants consider ideology and political party in deciding whether or not to take on a client, working almost exclusively for liberals or conservatives and Democrats or Republicans. But according to Sabato, consultants rarely let ideological concerns interfere with their business sense. They do what they do to make money, and that naturally influences most of the decisions they make. Most consultants are not strongly committed to a political party.[68] They are more concerned about how well they get along with prospective clients on a personal basis. Sabato quotes consultant David Garth on his decision not to work with Bill Bradley, running for the U.S. Senate in 1978, but to work with Bradley's opponent, Richard Leone, instead:

> I didn't like Bradley. I interviewed him. It was awful. I asked him five or six questions. I asked him questions about energy, housing, the kind of things I think as a candidate for the U.S. Senate from the state of New Jersey he ought to know. He didn't know anything. I didn't ask him any questions like "Do you want to win?" or "Will you change your clothes?" I don't like that. Dick Leone was a personal friend of ours. We had worked with him in several campaigns. He probably would have been the best qualified guy in that race. He was also an Italian and I felt there was a shortage, quite frankly, of Italians in office, that we needed more because it's a group that really feels unrepresented, the same as the blacks do.[69]

Sabato points out that these comments raise some interesting issues. Top political consultants are in great demand. Their decision to work for some candidates and not for others may have a substantial impact on a campaign. There is a danger that consultants will become "kingmakers," encouraging some kinds of candidates, discouraging others, in general performing a role that used to be performed by political parties. Parties are responsible to their members; to whom are consultants responsible?

Washington Post reporter and columnist David S. Broder voices a concern about the closeness between reporters and consultants. Consultants are in big demand by the press as sources and as interviewees to interpret campaign events. Broder fears that consultants are becoming "sacred cows," that reporters who rely heavily on them for information will be reluctant to write anything critical about consultants.[70]

Another complaint is that consultants, particularly media consultants, trivialize political debate by emphasizing image and style over substance. In the 1988 campaign it was said that Illinois Senator Paul Simon's advisors attempted to convince him to stop wearing bow ties because they were old-fashioned and projected the wrong kind of image. Simon refused this advice. Consultants are also blamed (perhaps unfairly) for the increasing use of negative advertising.

Political consultants do perform important services for candidates. As long as the parties remain weak, presidential candidates will look elsewhere for advice. And as long as nominations are determined by primaries and caucuses that pit party members against each other, contenders will want the best advice money can buy. This desire does not end with victory. Some consultants, such as pollster Pat Caddell in the Carter administration, follow their candidates into the White House.

Voting Rationales

We know that many factors affect voting decisions, among them party identification, a long-term influence. Short-term factors also play a role, and economic concerns have been especially important in presidential elections since 1980. But in what sense is the economy important—in terms of voters' personal finances, or in terms of the national economy? A voter might feel that things are going well for himself or herself, but that the national economy is in bad shape. Or vice versa. It turns out that both kinds of evaluation are important. In a study using survey data from 1956 to 1984, Gregory Markus found that, at an individual level, personal finances moderately influenced individual votes, but that macroeconomic conditions are more important in determining election outcomes.[71] Markus found that the proportion of people feeling personally "worse off" did not change much in the years studied; if there is little change, then feelings about personal finances cannot explain election outcomes, which varied in these years, with Democrats winning some elections and Republicans winning others.

We have seen that some critics of our electoral system argue that voters are too easily swayed by a candidate's image and personality rather than by the candidate's positions on issues. It is not just the poorly educated who make voting decisions in this manner. David P. Glass found, in fact, that it was the better educated who have the most concern for a candidate's personal attributes. Their interest in personality does not come at the expense of interest in issues, but in addition to it. Glass speculates that those who are well educated are aware that policy promises made in campaigns are not always met after the election is over. With this in mind, it is rational to consider personality characteristics as well. Glass also points out that the personal attributes people are interested in are important ones—competence, leadership capacity, and integrity.[72]

If voters are overly concerned with image and personality, it is not completely the fault of the public. Candidates themselves often stress image over substance. Eugene Declercq and his associates wrote:

> Perhaps we should come to accept the fact that the quality of public voting is a successful adaptation by the public to a relatively enduring political environment. *Voting candidate image rather than issues may thus reflect the paucity of issues and the abundance of image in the campaign or in media coverage, and voting one's party identification may be entirely rational given a very slow change in the positions advocated by the major parties.*[73]

Vagueness on the issues can be a rational strategy for candidates. James E. Campbell found, in a study of presidential candidates from 1968 to 1980, that winning candidates were less likely to espouse clear positions when issues were salient to the public, and were more likely to have ambiguous positions when public opinion was divided. Candidates were most likely to be ambiguous when their position was different from that held by the public.[74] Campbell notes that ambiguity does not always benefit a candidate; its value depends on the issue, the salience of the issue to the public, and the popularity of the candidate's position with the public.

While presidential elections may be full of imagery and symbolism, research has shown that ideology is playing an increasing role in the nomination process.[75] And Arthur H. Miller and Martin P. Wattenberg found that in general elections incumbents are judged on retrospective evaluations of their performance in office. Challengers are judged on their prospective policies, as are candidates in open races. They discovered that, from 1952 to 1980, policy and performance factors were increasingly related to voting decisions.[76] Despite political consultants, despite televised images, issues and policies still matter.

SUMMARY

During the past twenty-eight years, presidential elections have become more expensive and the campaigns longer, and they have become more vulnerable to intrusion by the mass media. Voters have come to expect the kinds of debates that were so significant in 1960, and they want debates between vice-presidential nominees as well as between the candidates at the top of the tickets. Campaigns are candidate-centered and rely on stops at airport Tarmacs and "sound bites" on network news shows. Millionaires not currently employed seem to have an edge in winning the nomination. Legions of reporters cover the contests, beginning well before the first primary or caucus, and while press coverage often exaggerates the trivial, it also presents the attentive public with an incredible amount of information. The major networks have cut back on coverage of the conventions, but PBS, CNN, C-SPAN, and a variety of publications give voters the conventions and much more.

Gary R. Orren writes that elections need to fulfill three functions in order to serve democracy: They must create a government with enough legitimacy and authority to govern; they must ensure that government represents the interests of the people; and they must serve as a mechanism for educating citizens about government and politics, for binding the people into a community. He concludes that our system fails in all three.[77] In 1980 and 1984, almost two eligible citizens refrained from voting for every one who voted for Ronald Reagan.[78] Since 1960 there has been an erosion in concern about presidential election outcomes.[79] The decline of political parties, the selling of candidates like products, the turmoil of the 1960s, and the Watergate scandal have produced a dissatisfied electorate that is often unimpressed with the candidates and the policy alternatives offered to them. People lack confidence in the parties, do not trust politicians, and do not seem to know in which direction they want the country to go.

It is no wonder, under such circumstances, that we have a divided government, one party controlling the White House and another the Congress. In the next chapter, we turn our focus on those congressional elections.

SUGGESTED READINGS

The 1980 Election

ABRAMSON, PAUL R., JOHN H. ALDRICH, and DAVID W. ROHDE, *Change and Continuity in the 1980 Elections.* Washington, DC: Congressional Quarterly Press, 1982.

FERGUSON, THOMAS, and JOEL ROGERS, eds., *The Hidden Election: Politics and Economics in the 1980 Presidential Campaign.* New York: Pantheon Books, 1981.

GERMOND, JACK W., and JULES WITCOVER, *Blue Smoke and Mirrors: How Reagan Won and Why Carter Lost the Election of 1980.* New York: Viking Press, 1981.

POMPER, GERALD, ed., *The Election of 1980: Reports and Interpretations.* Chatham, NJ: Chatham House, 1981.

ROBINSON, MICHAEL J., and MARGARET A. SHEENAN, *Over the Wire and On TV: CBS and UPI in Campaign '80.* New York: Russell Sage, 1983.

SANDOZ, ELLIS, and CECIL V. CRABB, JR., eds., *A Tide of Discontent: The 1980 Elections and Their Meaning.* Washington, DC: Congressional Quarterly Press, 1981.

The 1984 Election

ABRAMSON, PAUL R., JOHN H. ALDRICH, and DAVID W. ROHDE, *Change and Continuity in the 1984 Elections* (revised ed.). Washington, DC: Congressional Quarterly Press, 1987.

GERMOND, JACK W., and JULES WITCOVER, *Wake Us When It's Over: Presidential Politics of 1984.* New York: Macmillan, 1985.

NELSON, MICHAEL, ed., *The Elections of 1984.* Washington, DC: Congressional Quarterly Press, 1985.

ROBINSON, MICHAEL J., and AUSTIN RANNEY, eds., *The Mass Media in Campaign '84.* Washington, DC: American Enterprise Institute, 1985.

POMPER, GERALD, ed., *The Election of 1984: Reports and Interpretations.* Chatham, NJ: Chatham House, 1985.

SANDOZ, ELLIS, and CECIL V. CRABB, JR., eds., *Election '84.* New York: New American Library, 1985.

The 1988 Election

BRODER, DAVID S., "Bush Gets the Prize, But It's a Split Decision," *The Washington Post National Weekly Edition,* 6 (November 14–20, 1988), p. 10.

——— and PAUL TAYLOR, "The Democrats' Problem: It's the Message, Not the Medium," *The Washington Post National Weekly Edition,* 6 (November 14–20, 1988), pp. 11, 12.

Congressional Quarterly Weekly Report 46 (November 12, 1988).

COOK, RHODES, "Despite Gains in Some Groups, Democrats Still Have Far to Go," *Congressional Quarterly Weekly Report* 46 (December 3, 1988), pp. 3442–3448.

NELSON, MICHAEL, ed., *The Elections of 1988.* Washington, DC: Congressional Quarterly Press, 1989.

ORESKES, MICHAEL, "G.O.P. to Offer a Theme a Day for TV Viewers," *The New York Times,* August 15, 1988, p. 1.
SABATO, LARRY J., *Election '88.* Glenview, IL: Scott, Foresman/Little, Brown, 1989.

DISCUSSION QUESTIONS

1. What is the *proper* role for television in presidential campaigns? How should the media handle the "character" question? Was it right for the *Miami Herald* to stake out Gary Hart's townhouse?
2. Are you for or against public funding of presidential elections? Why?
3. Why do you think voters have been so unhappy with their choices in recent presidential elections?
4. How would you solve or address the problem of early network projections of winners on election nights? (Keep in mind the First Amendment.)
5. Assess the role of political consultants in campaigns. Is it better or worse for political parties to perform these functions? Why?

NOTES

1. "Modern Presidential Elections," *Elections '88* (Washington, DC: Congressional Quarterly Press, 1988), p. 11.

2. Kennedy drove his car off a bridge, and the young woman in the car with him drowned.

3. Herbert B. Asher, *Presidential Elections and American Politics,* 4th ed. (Chicago: The Dorsey Press, 1988), p. 184.

4. Ibid.

5. Jack W. Germond and Jules Witcover, *Blue Smoke and Mirrors: How Reagan Won and Why Carter Lost the Election of 1980* (New York: The Viking Press, 1981), p. 256.

6. Asher, *Presidential Elections,* p. 188.

7. Herbert E. Alexander, *Financing Politics,* 3rd ed. (Washington, DC: Congressional Quarterly Press, 1984), p. 64.

8. Ibid, pp. 117, 118.

9. Ibid., pp. 72, 73.

10. See Frank J. Sorauf, *Money in American Elections* (Glenview, IL: Scott, Foresman, 1988), pp. 46, 47.

11. Ibid, p. 190.

12. Alexander, *Financing Politics,* p. 130.

13. Germond and Witcover, *Blue Smoke,* Chapter 8.

14. Sorauf, *Money in American,* pp. 131, 132.

15. "Text of Debate Between Carter and port 38 (November 1, 1980), p. 3289. Reagan," *Con-*

gressional Quarterly Weekly Report 38 (November 1, 1980), p. 3289.

16. J. Leonard Reinsch, *Getting Elected: From Roosevelt and Radio to Television and Reagan* (New York: Hippocrene Books, 1988), p. 238.

17. Harold W. Stanley and Richard G. Niemi, eds., *Vital Statistics on American Politics* (Washington, DC: Congressional Quarterly Press, 1988), p. 83.

18. Charles E. Jacob, "The Congressional Elections," in Gerald Pomper, et al., eds., *The Election of 1980* (Chatham, NJ: Chatham House, 1981), p. 119.

19. Asher, *Presidential Elections,* p. 186. See also Paul R. Abramson, John H. Aldrich, and David W. Rohde, *Change and Continuity in the 1980 Elections* (Washington, DC: Congressional Quarterly Press, 1982); Douglas A. Hibbs, Jr., "President Reagan's Mandate from the 1980 Elections: A Shift to the Right?" *American Politics Quarterly* 10 (October 1982), pp. 387–420; Everett Carll Ladd, Jr., "The Brittle Mandate: Electoral Dealignment and the 1980 Presidential Election," *Political Science Quarterly* 96 (Spring 1981), pp. 1–25; Warren E. Miller and J. Merrill Shanks, "Policy Directions and Presidential Leadership: Alternative Interpretation of the 1980 Presidential Election," *British Journal of Political Science* 12 (1982), pp. 299–356; Arthur H. Miller and Martin P. Wattenberg, "Throwing the Rascals Out: Retrospective Political Thinking in the American Public 1952–1980."

Paper presented at the annual meeting of the Midwest Political Science Association, Chicago, April 21-23, 1983; William Schneider, "The November 4 Vote for President: What Did It Mean?" in Austin Ranney, ed., *The American Elections of 1980* (Washington, DC: American-Enterprise Institute for Public Policy Research, 1981).

20. "Modern Presidential Elections," *Elections '88,* p. 12.

21. Asher, *Presidential Elections,* p. 195.

22. Ibid., p. 193.

23. Ibid., p. 192.

24. Henry A. Plotkin, "Issues in the Campaign," in Gerald Pomper, et al., eds., *The Election of 1984* (Chatham, NJ: Chatham House, 1985), p. 49.

25. Ibid., p. 49.

26. Asher, *Presidential Elections,* pp. 191, 193.

27. Ibid., p. 194.

28. Sorauf, *Money in American,* pp. 209, 210, 113.

29. Herbert E. Alexander and Brian A. Haggerty, *Financing the 1984 Election* (Lexington, MA: Lexington Books, 1987), p 331.

30. Herb Asher, "The Three Campaigns for President," in Alexander Heard and Michael Nelson, eds., *Presidential Selection* (Durham, NC: Duke University Press, 1987), pp. 216-246.

31. Ibid., p. 243.

32. William C. Adams, "Media Coverage of Campaign '84: A Preliminary Report," in Michael J. Robinson and Austin Ranney, eds., *The Mass Media in Campaign '84* (Washington, DC: American Enterprise Institute, 1985), pp. 10-14.

33. Reinsch, *Getting Elected,* p. 256.

34. Ibid., p. 262.

35. "Modern Presidential Elections," *Elections '88,* p. 12.

36. Reinsch, *Getting Elected,* p. 294.

37. "Modern Presidential Elections," *Elections '88,* pp. 12, 13.

38. Asher, *Presdential Elections,* p. 188.

39. Adam Clymer, "Religion and Politics Mix Poorly for Democrats," *The New York Times,* November 25, 1984, p. 2E, as noted in Asher, *Presidential Elections,* p. 194.

40. Scott Keeter, "Public Opinion in 1984," in Gerald Pomper, et al., eds., *The Election of 1984* (Chatham, NJ: Chatham House, 1985), p. 105.

41. Thomas E. Cronin, "The Presidential Election of 1984," in Ellis Sandoz and Cecil V. Crabb, Jr., eds., *Election '84* (New York: New American Library, 1985), p. 52.

42. See "Don't Worry, Be Happy," *Newsweek* 112 (November 21, 1988), p. 85.

43. Rhodes Cook with Dave Kaplan, "In 1988, Caucuses Have Been the Place for Political Passion," *Congressional Quarterly Weekly Report* 46 (June 4, 1988), pp. 1523–1527.

44. Thomas B. Edsall and Richard Marin, "Super Tuesday's Showing," *The Washington Post National Weekly Edition* 5 (March 14-20, 1988), p. 37.

45. Rhodes Cook, "Current Democratic Advantage Could Evaporate by November," *Congressional Quarterly Weekly Report* 46 (June 11, 1988), p. 1579, and Rhodes Cook with Dave Kaplan, "In 1988, Caucuses Have Been the Place for Political Passion," *Congressional Quarterly Weekly Report* 46 (June 4, 1988), p. 1525.

46. Rhodes Cook, "Pressed by Jackson Demands, Dukakis Yields on Party Rules," *Congressional Quarterly Weekly Report* 46 (July 2, 1988), p. 1799.

47. "Opinion Roundup," *Public Opinion* 11 (July/August 1988), p. 35.

48. E. J. Dionne, Jr., "Issues, or Their Lack, Reflect Voter Concern, or Its Lack," *The New York Times,* September 18, 1988, p. 18.

49. E. J. Dionne, Jr., "If Nonvoters Had Voted: Same Winner, But Bigger," *The New York Times,* November 21, 1988, p. 10.

50. E. J. Dionne, Jr., "Poll Shows Bush Sets Agenda For Principal Election Issues," *The New York Times,* September 14, 1988, p. 17.

51. Richard Morin, "For Dukakis, It's Going, Going, But Not Yet Gone," *The Washington Post National Weekly Edition* 5 (October 24-30, 1988), p. 38.

52. Richard L. Berke, "Parties Ask Outside Groups to Stop Raising Money," *The New York Times,* October 8, 1988, p. 8.

53. Richard L. Berke, "Independent Groups Putting 11th-Hour Millions in Races," *The New York Times,* October 26, 1988, p. 11.

54. Richard L. Berke, "In Election Spending: Watch the Ceiling, Use a Loophole," *The New York Times,* October 3, 1988, pp. 1, 13.

55. Ibid., p. 13.

56. "Soft Money? No—Sewer Money," *The New York Times,* October 21, 1988, p. 24.

57. Andrew Rosenthal, "As Jackson Rises, Newspapers and Television Search for a Proper Balance," *The New York Times,* April 8, 1988, p. 11.

58. Laurence Zuckerman, "The Made-for-TV Campaign," *Time* 132 (November 14, 1988), p. 71.

59. Jill Lawrence, "Bush's Aggressive Advertising Sways Voters to His Side," *Pittsburgh Post-Gazette,* October 24, 1988, p. 3.

60. B. Drummond Ayres, Jr., "Electoral College's Stately Landslide Sends Bush and Quayle Into History," *The New York Times,* December 20, 1988, p. 13; and Richard L. Berke, "50.16% Voter Turnout Is 64-Year Low," *The New York Times,* December 18, 1988, Section 1, p. 18.

61. "Dismal Turnout Trend Examined," *The Pittsburgh Press,* November 10, 1988, p. A21.

62. E. J. Dionne, Jr., "If Nonvoters Had Voted," p. 10.

63. "Dukakis Hurt by Drop in Black Voter Turnout," *The Pittsburgh Press,* November 10, 1988, p. 1.

64. Robert W. Merry, "Status Quo May Really Be Calm Before Storm," *Congressional Quarterly Weekly Report* 46 (November 12, 1988), p. 3239.

65. Larry J. Sabato, *The Rise of Political Consultants* (New York: Basic Books, 1981), p. 8.

66. Ibid., p. 13.

67. Seymour Martin Lipset, "Vote For the Other Guy," *Public Opinion* 11 (July/August 1988), p. 5.

68. Sabato, *The Rise of Political Consultants,* p. 29.

69. Ibid., pp. 33, 34.

70. "The Business of Politics," *Elections '88,* p. 134.

71. Gregory Markus, "The Impact of Personal and National Economic Conditions on the Presidential Vote: A Pooled Cross-Sectional Analysis," *American Journal of Political Science* 32 (February 1988), pp. 137–154.

72. David P. Glass, "Evaluating Presidential Candidates: Who Focuses on Their Personal Attributes?" *Public Opinion Quarterly* 49 (Winter 1985), pp. 517–534.

73. Eugene Declercq, Thomas J. Hurley, and Norman R. Luttbeg, "Voting in American Presidential Elections 1956–1972," *American Politics Quarterly* 3 (July 1975), pp. 222–246. Quotation is from pp. 239–240.

74. James E. Campbell, "The Electoral Consequences of Issue Ambiguity: An Examination of the Presidential Candidates' Issue Positions from 1968 to 1980," *Political Behavior* 5 (1983), pp. 277–291.

75. Anne N. Costain, "An Analysis of Voting in American National Nominating Conventions, 1940–1976," *American Politics Quarterly* 6 (January 1978), pp. 95–111.

76. Arthur H. Miller and Martin P. Wattenberg, "Throwing the Rascals Out: Policy and Performance Evaluations of Presidential Candidates, 1952–1980," pp. 359–372.

77. Gary R. Orren, "The Linkage of Policy to Participation," in Alexander Heard and Michael Nelson, eds., *Presidential Selection* (Durham, NC: Duke University Press, 1987), pp. 77–79.

78. Ibid., p. 75.

79. See Arthur H. Miller, "Political Issues and Trust in Government: 1964–1970," *American Political Science Review* 68 (September 1974), pp. 951–972; and Rich E. Rollenhagen, "Explaining Variation in Concern About the Outcome of Presidential Elections, 1960–1980," *Political Behavior* 6 (1984), pp. 147–157.

7

Congressional Elections

INTRODUCTION

Until recently, congressional contests were the orphans of U.S. election research. Data were plentiful on presidential elections, and more readily available. Presidential elections are strictly national campaigns, whereas congressional elections involve federal, state, and local considerations.

Clearly, congressional elections have a tremendous impact on politics in the United States. When we think of representative democracy, we think of legislators. These congressional contests affect the careers of many party politicians, help determine who our national leaders will be, decide which party will have a majority in each chamber of Congress, and affect the ability of presidents to pass their programs by determining the size of their party in each chamber.[1] In 1978, the Center for Political Studies at the University of Michigan created the Committee for Congressional Election Research and began conducting National Election Studies in midterm congressional election years. The fruits of this research have broadened our understanding of these contests considerably. However, there are still many questions to be answered. This chapter explores the nature of candidates, campaigns, and voters at the congressional level.

CONGRESSIONAL CANDIDATES

Where do congressional candidates come from? The recruitment process varies a good deal from state to state, but it always performs the crucial function of channeling individuals toward leadership positions. Unfortunately, this process has not received a great deal of attention from scholars. We know that most successful candidates are "WASPs" (white, Anglo-Saxon, Protestants), and lawyers, high on the socioeconomic scale. Most have held state or local office prior to their successful bid for Congress. We also know that some candidates are self-starters, whereas others are draftees. Several factors seem to greatly affect their decision to run. These include whether or not the seat is held by an incumbent, a retiring incumbent, or is open. Other factors include the candidate's personal and family considerations, and the candidate's financial situation. The main concern underlying all these factors is the likelihood of winning.[2]

While most candidates are self-starters, state party organizations help recruit candidates, as do the House and Senate campaign committees of each party. The Republican party has been particularly active in recruiting and training promising candidates.[3] The national political climate, and who holds the White House, affect the ability of the parties to recruit good candidates. Republicans had a relatively easy time encouraging people to run in 1981 because of Reagan's big win over Carter in 1980. By 1982, the economy was faltering and Republicans lost twenty-six House seats. But the losses might have been greater if the party had not been able to attract good candidates in 1981. The candidates recruited for the 1984 races were chosen in 1983, when the country and the party were still feeling the effects of the recession. Republicans had a harder time finding candidates who could wage good campaigns.

Local parties, as well as both the Democratic Congressional Campaign Committee and the National Republican Congressional Committee sought challengers to incumbents perceived as vulnerable in the 1986 election.[4] But parties, for the most part, have taken a back seat to individual drive. Roger H. Davidson and Walter J. Oleszek describe what they call a case of "wide-open recruitment":

> An extreme version of today's wide-open recruitment is the story of Ron Packard, a dentist who ran in a field of eighteen candidates for the 1982 Republican nomination in California's 43rd District. Packard lost the primary by ninety-two votes to another contender, a political novice who poured nearly one million dollars of his personal fortune into an aggressive campaign. Although the primary winner gained support from most GOP leaders, his costly campaign angered many voters. Packard ran as a write-in candidate in the general election and won. His campaign produced 350,000 pieces of mail proclaiming him the legitimate Republican alternative; his workers patrolled every polling place, handing out pencils imprinted with his name and urging that they be used to mark the ballot. It was a stunning example of open recruitment.[5]

In most congressional contests, incumbents will be running, and more than 90 percent of the House incumbents who run for reelection win. About 75 percent of the Senate incumbents who run will be successful.[6] Incumbents have many factors in their favor: name recognition (familiarity among the voters), franking privileges (which provide them with free advertising), travel privileges (which allow trips abroad and back home), a forum for their views (the congressional committees and the floor of the Congress), the ability to garner favor through constituency service, and the ability to attract political action committee (PAC) money. These advantages often frighten away qualified challengers. In fact, one reason why House members are so successful is because their challengers tend to be unknowns. (We will return to this subject in our discussion of voters.) Political scientists do not share a consensus on the precise role that each of these factors plays, but, at any rate, the decision to challenge an incumbent is a weighty one. Of course, incumbency can be a liability under some circumstances. Incumbents have records that are visible and occasionally vulnerable to attack.

Personal considerations also play a role in decisions to run. Not everyone can afford to take time away from his or her job or career in order to campaign. One reason for the prevalence of lawyers in Congress, for example, is that lawyers have flexible work schedules. The health of the would-be candidate, or that of his family, may be important. Past scandals or secrets may make a person resist recruitment efforts. Even those with nothing to hide may dislike the invasion of privacy that comes with a candidacy. Personal traits such as stamina and ambition make a difference also.[7] Some individuals feel a need to perform public service, perhaps out of selflessness, perhaps as a result of valuing nonmaterial goods, or perhaps because it fulfills a particular psychological need.

Finally, congressional elections are very expensive enterprises. About $400 million was spent on congressional races in 1984 and 1986.[8] (See Table 7–1 for expenditures from 1976 to 1986.) In 1986, $97 million was spent by congressional candidates in the general election to buy radio and television advertising alone.[9] Competitive races are especially expensive. Incumbents tend to attract more campaign contributions than challengers; they are considered better risks.[10] The money comes from individuals, PACs, and parties. Most will come from individuals. As far as direct contributions go, the party will not help much. In 1982 such contributions made up only 6 percent of the contributions in the average House race and 1 percent in the average Senate race.[11] The Republican party usually can afford to provide more money to candidates, and Republican House candidates now get 10 percent of their funds from the party. Republican Senate candidates receive about 15 percent of their funds from the party.[12]

Congress mandates public funding for presidential elections, but not for its own elections. Why rock the boat, when incumbents are so successful? Would-be candidates, particularly would-be challengers, must be prepared to spend much time and effort raising money. It's not easy, though. Between

TABLE 7-1   Mean Congressional Campaign Expenditures, 1976–1986

CHAMBER	1976	1978	1980	1982	1984	1986
House	$ 73,316 (N = 819)	$ 109,440 (N = 787)	$ 153,221 (N = 752)	$ 228,060 (N = 767)	$ 241,313 (N = 733)	$ 260,032 (N = 810)
Senate	595,449 (N = 64)	951,405 (N = 68)	1,106,920 (N = 67)	1,781,815 (N = 64)	2,327,250 (N = 61)	2,578,016 (N = 71)

SOURCE: Norman J. Ornstein, Thomas E. Mann, and Michael J. Malbin, eds., *Vital Statistics on Congress, 1987–1988* (Washington, DC: Congressional Quarterly Press, 1987), pp. 72, 77. Reprinted with permission.

campaign events and fund-raising events, candidates have little time left over for any kind of private life. House members, with two-year terms, never really stop running for reelection.

CAMPAIGNS

Reapportionment

The reapportionment process in the states helps define the political environment in which House elections take place. After each decennial U.S. Census, state legislatures are charged with making any adjustments required by population migration in or out of the state. District lines may be drawn in such a way as to pit two incumbents against each other, or to create a district with no incumbent. The districts of incumbents can be made safer, or more competitive, depending on what types of voters are included and excluded in the district. The party dominating the state legislature will try to draw the lines in ways that benefit that party, while honoring the directive that districts be equal in population. What usually happens is incumbent protection. All of these decisions have an impact on the willingness of challengers and incumbents to stand for election.

The Republican party has anticipated gains in the South and West, due to migration into these traditionally conservative states, and to changing attitudes in the South toward the two major parties. Their first opportunity to capitalize on this development came after the 1980 census, but things did not work out the way the party hoped. Republicans won only seven of the seventeen new House districts created in the Sun Belt.[13] Democratic influence in state legislatures and federal courts helped that party hang on, even in the Northeast and Midwest. In the ten northern states that lost districts, Republicans ended up with eighteen fewer seats than they possessed before the election.[14] Republicans were particularly hard hit in California, where Democratic Representative Phillip Burton "masterminded a remap that dissolved three GOP-held seats and diluted a fourth enough to fatally weaken the incumbent."[15] Burton squeezed five new seats for Democrats out of the two new districts California received due to population gains. Burton's plan, passed by the state legislature, was, for the most part, upheld by federal courts.

Campaign decisions by future Democrats and Republicans will be affected by this past reapportionment. And both parties will be waiting to see whether or not the same pattern will hold for the post-1990 census redistricting. President Reagan was able to appoint many federal judges during his tenure (almost half the sitting judges), and this may help the Republicans on the legal end of this battle.

Strategies of Incumbents and Challengers

The strategies of incumbents and challengers will vary in several ways. Incumbents possess name recognition. As Richard F. Fenno, Jr., has noted, they can use their opportunities to address voters to explain and defend their records, and to claim credit for policies that have benefited their districts.[16] Incumbents often refrain from mentioning their challengers' names, reluctant to give them any publicity. Challengers, especially House challengers, have to work very hard to become known to the voters. (The type of person who gets nominated for a Senate seat tends to be someone who already possesses a statewide reputation.) The challenger's lack of record may help or hurt, depending on the attitude of the constituents. Challengers try to demonstrate their virtues as candidates, but often attack the incumbents as well. While incumbents are not likely to have voting records that are vulnerable, they might have weaknesses in terms of excessive absences from Congress or excessive junketing, or personal failings that can be exploited (a messy divorce, a problem with alcohol, and so forth).

Strategic campaign questions essentially involve the allocation of money, time, and personnel.[17] The answers to these questions depend not only on incumbent or challenger status, but also on majority or minority party status and the type of constituency involved.

About 60 percent of us identify with one of the two major parties and use that identification when we vote—at least some of the time.[18] Tickets may be split more often than in the past, and there may be more independents, but party is still an important influence on many voters. Party identification colors our perceptions of candidates and issues. Barbara Hinckley found that

> partisanship affects the ability to recall the name of the candidate and to make comments about the candidate. . . . Visibility may not produce positive effects, but the lack of visibility can reduce the likelihood that a candidate is voted for. Independently of visibility, partisanship also affects the evaluation of candidates and the rating of the incumbent's job performance. Finally, as might be expected from the effects on visibility and evaluations, partisanship affects the vote.[19]

Representing the party which holds the majority in the state will usually help a candidate considerably, but party is not the only factor in the equation. Remember that incumbents have very high reelection rates. While many voters will stand by their party, some will abandon it to support incumbents.[20] This is likely to happen when the incumbent stresses constituency service, and the voters are happy with that service.

Campaigns and Advertising

Type of constituency also affects campaigners. Compact, homogeneous districts make for easier campaigns. Senate candidates, for example, usually have more territory to cover (and more constituents to represent) than do House candidates. Senators have an important tool to help them overcome this problem: television. Because media markets rarely coincide with House districts, it is less efficient for House candidates to use television advertising in their campaigns (although some do). But television time is not cheap, and its cost is a major reason why Senate races are more expensive than House races.

Lately, candidates and their consultants have adopted the negative approach with television ads, attacking their opponents rather than promoting themselves. Just a few years ago, negative ads were avoided because of the fear that they might backfire. In addition, it was perceived that negative ads demeaned the office. At that time, negative ads for commercial products were also avoided. But advances in technology and campaign polling have allowed those with enough money to mount sophisticated advertising strategies. Alan Ehrenhalt of the *Congressional Quarterly* quotes Robert Squier, a Democratic media consultant, on how the process works:

> In the 1970s . . . you took a poll, analyzed yourself and your opponent, devised a strategy, and produced commercials. Three weeks before the election, you dropped everything on the voter. And your opponent did the same thing. Now, that whole process can take place in three days—and be repeated over and over during the campaign.[21]

The 1984 Senate campaign witnessed the use of negative ads in the Paul Simon–Charles Percy race in Illinois, the Mitch McConnell–Walter Huddleston race in Kentucky, and the Jesse Helms-James B. Hunt, Jr., race in North Carolina. While House candidates usually cannot afford to emphasize television ads, Ehrenhalt writes that new campaign techniques usually do filter down to "competitive House districts where both parties are well funded."[22] The bill can be very high: Jesse Helms spent almost $17 million in his hotly contested and successful 1984 race. Senator Paula Hawkins (R-Florida) spent $750,000 on media in 1985—a year *before* she was up for reelection. Still, she lost the race.

Since television ads are prohibitively expensive and inefficient for most House candidates, they rely instead on canvassing, billboards, and radio and newspaper advertisements. Straight news coverage is very helpful to House candidates on a tight budget—it's free. Unfortunately, though, House districts rarely parallel newspaper markets either. Since most papers have circulation areas covering more than one district, and a shortage of both reporters and space on their pages, House races usually get sparse coverage. This is even more likely in the many races where the incumbent is safe. Editors will decide there is no sense spending a lot of effort covering a story when everyone knows the ending. Of course, this lack of coverage poses no problem for the incumbent, who has had two or more years to utilize the in-house media such as the Cable Satellite Public Affairs Network (C-SPAN), the franking privilege, press releases, and so forth, to get messages to the public. But the challenger lacks these tools. Taxpayers, in effect, subsidize the reelection campaigns of incumbents.

CAMPAIGN FINANCING

The procedure by which money is raised and spent for congressional elections is both important and a matter of continuing controversy. It is unseemly in a democracy for campaign money to come from only a few wealthy people in the district, or from people residing outside the district or state. Small fortunes are spent these days to win offices that pay relatively low salaries. The public is often skeptical regarding the election system, and voters often suspect that corruption exists in the system. In this section, we will examine where the money comes from, where it goes, and the controversy over the role of political action committees (PACs).

Where the Money Comes From and Where it Goes

The 1971 Federal Election Campaign Act (FECA) and the amendments to that law mandate the reporting of the name, address, occupation, and principal place of business of each contributor to a campaign.[23] Contributions for congressional campaigns come from individuals (including the candidates themselves), PACs, and political parties. In 1986, House candidates received 60 percent of their funds from individuals, 36 percent from PACs, and 4 percent from parties. Senate candidates got 70 percent from individuals, 22 percent from PACs, and 8 percent from parties.[24] In both the House and the Senate campaigns, contributions from corporate PACs outnumbered contributions from labor, trade/membership/health, or nonconnected PACs (PACs that are not affiliated with unions or particular businesses).[25] In 1974, PACs contributed $11.6 million, or 15.7 percent of the total amount of campaign funds raised for that year. In 1980, the figures were $55.2 million and 27.4 percent. By 1982, the numbers were $83.1 million and 27.6 percent.[26]

The FECA limits individual contributions to $1,000 per person in a primary, and to $1,000 per person in a general election.[27] But candidates are free to use their own personal wealth, either as contributions or loans to their campaigns. The FECA originally restricted candidates' use of their own money, but in the case of *Buckley* versus *Valeo* (424 U.S. 1, 1976), these limitations were declared an unconstitutional infringement of freedom of speech by the U.S. Supreme Court. Since congressional candidates do not receive public funding, the court reasoned, the government lacks the right to restrict such spending.

Candidates for the Senate are more likely to spend their own money than are House candidates.[28] According to Glen Craney, by 1988 one out of every ten dollars raised for Senate races now comes from loans made by candidates to their own campaigns.[29] When wealthy Republican John Heinz campaigned against Arlen Specter in Pennsylvania for a Senate nomination in 1976, he financed almost 90 percent of the campaign with loans from his own wealth ($585,765 out of $673,869). When loans to fund the general election are also included, the total amount Heinz lent to his campaign was $2,465,500.[30] In 1982 a number of candidates made very large contributions to their own campaigns. In New Jersey, Democrat Frank Lautenberg gave or lent $5.1 million to his Senate campaign, and defeated Republican Millicent Fenwick, who gave or lent $877,000 to hers.[31] The ability to make such contributions does not ensure success. Also in 1982, Minnesota Democrat Mark Dayton spent $6.9 million of his own money against Republican Senator David Durenberger, and he still lost the election.[32] In 1986, Republican Senate candidates raised $28 million more than Democratic candidates, yet they still lost the Senate.[33]

Political parties support candidates in several ways, including direct cash contributions, coordinated expenditures made on behalf of candidates, and in-kind contributions (that is, contributions of services). In-kind contributions can involve the services of pollsters, media specialists, direct mail outfits, workers to conduct voter registration drives, trainers of campaign workers, and so forth. Gary C. Jacobson explains the rules on this kind of campaign support:

> Direct party contributions are limited to $5,000 per candidate per election for House candidates. This means that any party committee can give, at most, $10,000 to a candidate in an election year ($15,000 if there is a primary runoff). Both the national committees and the congressional campaign committees of each party can contribute this amount, so direct national party contributions can amount to $20,000 in House campaigns, which is less than 10 percent of what it costs to run a minimally serious campaign. The maximum allowable contribution to Senate candidates from all national party sources is even smaller: $17,500. Parties cannot be a major source of direct campaign contributions because the FECA will not allow it.[34]

In 1984, House candidates could receive as much as $70,400 in direct or indirect assistance from national party sources, while Senate candidates could receive from $108,300 to $1.5 million.[35] As stated, direct party contributions to Senate candidates are limited to a maximum of $17,500 per candidate for all national committees, but the limits on coordinated expenditures are much higher. In 1986, this limit was $21,810 for the House. The Senate limit is based on population, and it ranged from $43,620 to $851,681 in 1986.[36] Coordinated expenditures are defined as ones where the party as well as the candidate has some control over how the money is spent. Normally this money helps pay for conducting polls, producing ads, buying media time, and so forth. Most coordinated expenditures in both parties are for Senate campaigns, where the law allows more party activity.[37] Of the two major parties, the Republicans are in a better position to help candidates. Their national committees have mastered the art of raising money through organized appeals and then redistributing it to their congressional candidates. By 1981–1982, the Republicans were contributing more than three times as much money to their candidates as the Democrats ($5.2 million to $1.6 million); Republicans also were spending almost five times as much as the Democrats on behalf of their candidates ($14.0 million to $2.9 million).[38]

Candidates and their staffs spend an enormous amount of time at fundraising events, and also devote much time to courting PACs. PACs may directly contribute $5,000 per candidate per election ($5,000 for a primary and another $5,000 for the general election).[39] There is no limitation on the amount of money that PACs independent of the candidate may spend on that candidate's behalf. Even those assured of reelection may raise an impressive war chest to discourage opponents. Challengers have the toughest job, though, when it comes to PAC contributions. Most PAC money goes to incumbents (with some exceptions in 1980). According to a Common Cause study of the 1984 elections, House challengers on average received $1.00 for every $4.60 that incumbents got from PACs.[40] A study of the 1986 election by the same group showed that more than one-third of the money raised by House candidates came from PACs. The same study showed that PACs favored incumbents over challengers by a six-to-one ratio that year.[41] We will return to this incumbent favoritism in a discussion of PAC controversies.

The money that candidates spend so much time raising is spent on predictable activities. Money that comes in early is used as seed money to raise more. Often this early money is used on direct mail appeals. These are not cheap, because they require the development of the mailing list, the production of mailing labels, and the administration and coordination of the mailing. Money also goes for traditional fund-raising events (dinners, speakers, barbecues, and so forth). Advertisements and promotions demand a large chunk of the campaign treasury. These can range from potholders or rulers imprinted with the candidate's name, to billboards, to ads in print, or on radio and television. It is, of course, the mass media ads that are the most costly. Some money is spent on polling and research and on otherwise maintaining the campaign organization. Intense campaigns can activate voters, getting them to come to the polls on election day.[42]

Nonincumbents, especially in House races, must spend an enormous amount of money in order to become known to the voters. Studies have shown that nonincumbent campaign expenditures are directly related to the proportion of votes that these candidates receive. For incumbents, the situation is different.[43] It is an irony that those in the best position to raise money—incumbents—are also the least well served by that money. Incumbents have had several years in office and all the associated perquisites of their office to advertise themselves and their positions. Money cannot really improve on this. Therefore, when incumbents spend heavily it is a sign that they are facing fierce opposition, fighting for their political lives. Such high spending is a sign of incumbent weakness.

Incumbent expenditures also may be affected by motives correlated with one of two congressional career phases. Fenno has determined that most members of Congress go through an expansionist and a protectionist phase.[44] During the expansionist phase, new members seek to build on the coalition that put them in office. Such expansion can require expensive advertisements. Fenno argues that members reach a point, though, where they cannot realistically broaden this coalition any further. During the protectionist phase, members concentrate on keeping their supporters happy, not on adding to their numbers. The key to this phase is often constituency service—finding lost Social Security checks, helping constituents contact children in the armed forces, and so forth. These activities are performed by staffers whose salaries are paid for by the taxpayers.

However, incumbents will still raise enormous campaign chests when they can. Under the circumstances, their best strategy is to discourage strong opponents (from within their own party and from outside) in the first place. As stated previously, a hefty bank account is one effective method for doing just that. By February 1984, Senator Alfonse D'Amato of New York had raised $1.3 million for his 1986 race.[45] He easily won reelection.

The Controversy Over PACs

The development and growth of political action committees is outlined in Chapter 4. Here we are concerned with how PACs have affected congressional elections. It has already been shown that PACs provide a significant, if not major, proportion of campaign funds in these races. It is perfectly legal and, due to the disclosure requirements of federal law, we now know much more than in the past about who is donating what to whom. Yet the role of PACs has sparked a continuing controversy, especially in terms of congressional elections. No part of the congressional election process is publicly funded, as are the presidential elections.

Several elements contribute to the controversy over PACs. Some resent the way many PACs require candidates seeking donations to fill out detailed questionnaires. The PACs are looking for pledges of support for or opposition to certain policies. A 1982 article in *Time* magazine described how this can work:

> Candidates seeking the Realtors' [National Association of Realtors PAC] money must submit answers to a six-page questionnaire. In some cases the "correct" answers are all too obvious. "Do you agree or disagree [that] trade associations

have a right and a responsibility to hold members of Congress accountable for their votes?'' Others are trickier. One asks candidates to rank what contributes most to high interest rates: record deficits, restrictive monetary policy, excessive tax cuts, etc. (A: The Realtors have fought strongly against high deficits.) ''Sometimes candidates plead with me to give them the correct answers,'' says Political Resources Director Randall Moorhead.[46]

Particularly problematic are the "single-issue" groups that threaten to withdraw support over a single "wrong" vote. Critics of these practices believe legislators should have more leeway in their voting decisions and room to bargain and maneuver without worries about the withdrawal of campaign support. These critics argue that members of Congress should not be made to feel like commodities that have been bought and paid for.

As mentioned earlier, incumbents receive the lion's share of PAC money. Table 7–2 allows us to compare the difference between the total receipts and PAC contributions for House incumbents, for challengers, and for open seats, broken down by party. Incumbents tend to get more money than challengers in both total receipts and PAC contributions.

Another practice that causes controversy is the way some PACs "target" candidates to support or oppose. Committee chairs and members of prominent committees often get substantial financial support from groups with a vested interest in legislation emanating from the committees. Critics argue that it smacks of bribery when such committees subsequently vote in ways that please these donors. Members of committees such as the House Judiciary Committee and the House Foreign Affairs Committee receive relatively little from PACs, whereas the House Ways and Means Committee, and the Energy and Commerce Committee get quite a lot.[47] While interest groups do not always get their

TABLE 7–2 Campaign Contributions, House Incumbents and Challengers, 1986

	Total Receipts	PAC Contributions
Incumbents		
Democrats	$84.3 million	$48.6 million
Republicans	67.0	37.1
Challengers		
Democrats	22.1	30.1
Republicans	21.5	11.3
Open Seats		
Democrats	19.6	35.8
Republicans	20.4	25.5

SOURCE: Norman J. Ornstein, Thomas E. Mann, and Michael J. Malbin, eds., *Vital Statistics on Congress, 1987–1988* (Washington, DC: Congressional Quarterly Press, 1987), p. 97. Reprinted with permission.

way, more and more examples like these surface each year. Members of Congress (and many political scientists) argue that acceptance of these contributions in no way constitutes a bribe. They contend that the votes in situations like these would have been the same with or without the donations. Nonetheless, such practices contribute to the image of a Congress that is up for sale. A few members refuse to accept PAC campaign donations; other members look for other ways to demonstrate their independence:

> The U.A.W. PAC in New Jersey has long backed Congressman Peter Rodino. But last month [September 1982] Rodino was informed that future support would be contingent on his agreeing to co-sponsor the domestic content bill. When his office said he would, the union publicly announced that its endorsement came "following Rodino's decision to sign on as a co-sponsor" of the bill. The appearance of coercion annoyed Rodino. Said an aide: "He thought it was the most heavy-handed thing he had seen during his career." Rodino withdrew as a co-sponsor, although he is still backing the bill.[48]

Defenders of PACs respond to these criticisms by pointing out that PACs contribute to many different candidates. Labor PACs may focus their support on Democrats, but corporate PACs donate to both Democrats and Republicans (helping the Democrats to counteract the additional money that the Republican party has to give to its candidates). PACs are incredibly diverse in outlook. Incumbents usually receive most PAC money, but not always. And what is wrong with rewarding members who support your interests? Targeting candidates, PAC supporters argue, is merely smart strategy. Why waste money when you can put it where it can do the most good? PACs provided one-third of the funding for the House candidates in 1987 and 21 percent for the Senate candidates; the majority of candidate funds came from other sources.[49] Finally, PAC defenders would remind us that PAC money comes from many individual contributors, people who are able to pool their small contributions into large ones that carry clout. In this sense, the PAC system under current law encourages wide-ranging citizen involvement in financing campaigns. Do we wish to return to the system of old, dominated by a few "fat cats"?

> Defenders of the PAC system say that contributions are an effect, not a cause; and that they are given to those who are already known to be supportive of a PAC's position. "The idea that there's a *quid pro quo* is balderdash," says Republican Congressman Bill Frenzel of Minnesota. Argues BIPAC's [Business Industry PAC] [Bernadette] Budde: "PACs are not buying anyone. They're rewarding." Because a single PAC is limited to $5,000 a race, the power it can command, while large, is not overwhelming. The most you can purchase, proponents claim, is access. Says Grumman PAC Chairman [Dave] Walsh: "We don't expect contracts because we gave someone $5,000. But the likelihood of us getting in to see the Congressman is much higher."[50]

PAC Reform

Obviously, PACs are here to stay. But reformers are backing bills that would either alter current regulations or institute some form of public financing for congressional candidates. HR 2490, for example, limited the amount a candidate could accept from PACs; limited the amount candidates could spend of their personal wealth; provided House candidates with optional partial public financing; and limited total spending by House candidates in the general election to $200,000 each.[51] Proposed by co-sponsors David R. Obey (D-Wisconsin) and Jim Leach (R-Iowa) in the Ninety-eighth Congress, the bill was not passed. Opponents believed that public funding would help incumbents and undermine the two-party system. A compromise proposal substituted tax credits for campaign contributions instead of public funding, but no action was taken on this bill.

Senators, too, have proposed changes. The Senate bill S2, sponsored in 1987 by David Boren (D-Oklahoma), would set voluntary spending limits on Senate elections and provide some public funding for Senate candidates. The bill would limit the amount of money House and Senate candidates could receive from PACs.[52] Given that Democrat incumbents, on average, received

SOURCE: Brookins, Richmond Times-Dispatch, Field Enterprises, Inc. Copyright 1983. Reprinted with permission.

more PAC money in 1984 than Republican incumbents, these proposals could hurt Democrats more than Republicans.[53] But Republicans feel that voluntary spending limits threaten them, since Republican candidates often challenge Democratic incumbents. (Recall that challengers generally must spend high amounts to compete effectively against the advantages of incumbency.) The bill was set aside in February 1988 after a Republican filibuster.

Other proposals seek to strengthen the role of parties by increasing the amount they can give to candidates. Public funding is perhaps the most controversial of the suggested reforms. Many feel that it is one thing for the public to help pay for presidential campaigns, which occur just once every four years and involve relatively few candidates, but public funding for the enormous number of House and Senate candidates is another matter. There is the important question of how public funding will affect the desire of individuals to run as third-party or independent candidates. As discussed in Chapter 6, the FECA discriminates against third-party candidates in presidential elections. Would this be imitated at the congressional level? What form would public funding take? Would the money go to parties or candidates? If identical spending limits are put on challengers and incumbents, incumbents normally will have a huge advantage. The challenger must spend money to become known. The incumbent already is known, and has the advantage of office perquisites as well.

The climate for reform appears to be changing in light of the 1988 elections. Republicans were particularly unhappy with what they saw as their lack of PAC support that year. Republicans felt almost shut out by PAC support for incumbents, who are mostly Democrats. As a result, GOP members of Congress seem more supportive of PAC reform.[54] Sitting members of Congress are not likely to pass legislation giving challengers more to spend than they themselves will have. As a matter of fact, public financing is probably doomed. Recall that incumbents have a very high reelection rate now. Why rock the boat? Of one thing we can be absolutely certain: Money has *always* been important in elections, one way or another.

VOTERS IN CONGRESSIONAL ELECTIONS

Generally speaking, voter interest in congressional elections is dramatically lower than their interest in presidential elections.[55] This has been true for many years and is related to lower voter turnout levels for congressional races. (See Table 7–4.) About half those surveyed can name their House member; fewer than this can claim to have read or heard something about their representative, and they are unsure of the content of this information.[56] (Higher percentages of people *are* able to recognize their representative's name when they see it, which helps incumbents get reelected.) Here, as well as in presidential elections, voter interest in and information known about congressional elections varies with the voter's educational level, socioeconomic status, self-esteem, and sense of political efficacy.[57] Obviously, though, many lose interest in the ballot once they get past the presidential candidates.

What is on the minds of those who *do* bother to vote for congressional candidates? Naturally, voters expect to nominate and elect candidates who share their basic orientation toward politics. A candidate's position on major issues *can* matter.[58] Beyond this, though, voters are not strict about ideology. According to Davidson and Oleszek,

> When they enter the polling booth, America's voters do not, in general, carry a lot of ideological or even issue-specific baggage. In other words, they do not usually make detailed calculations about which party actually controls Congress, which party ought to control Congress, or which party favors what policies. As a general rule, voters reach their decisions on the basis of three factors: (1) party loyalties, which are declining in saliency; (2) candidate loyalties, growing in saliency and heavily weighted toward incumbents; and (3) overall judgments about the state of the nation and the economy.[59]

When the forces of party affiliation and incumbency are operating in tandem, they are "an almost unbeatable combination."[60] One study found that even candidates accused of corruption usually are reelected, although they appear to win by smaller margins than they would have without the charge against them. (Charges of bad moral conduct are taken more seriously by voters than are charges of campaign violations or conflicts of interest.)[61]

A big part of the advantage incumbents possess is because voters tend to know more about incumbents, particularly House members, than about challengers. This knowledge is strongly linked to voting choices.[62] Jacobson describes the relationship between party affiliation and voter knowledge of the candidate in House and Senate elections:

> Very few partisans defect if they remember the name of their own party's candidate but not that of the opponent; more than half usually defect if they remember only the name of the other party's candidate; defection rates of voters who know both or neither fall in between.[63]

Jacobson discovered that, in House elections, about 50 to 60 percent of voters can remember the incumbent's name, while 20 to 30 percent can recall the challenger's name. If voters remembered only one of the two candidates, 95 percent of the time it was the incumbent they remembered.[64] And it is of no small consequence that many who cannot recall the incumbent's name on their own can recognize it when they see it on the ballot. Jacobson also found that independents vote for the better-known candidate—usually the incumbent—more than 80 percent of the time.[65] The knowledge that voters possess about

House candidates does not always produce favorable evaluations. Yet incumbents are also far more likely to be liked than challengers.[66]

Jacobson makes further distinctions based on the type of candidate involved. He found that candidates for open seats are better known than challengers, but are not as well known as incumbents. Senate candidates are better known than House candidates. Senate incumbents are also better known than their challengers, but the distance between the two is not nearly as wide as it is on the House side.[67]

Other research suggests that House candidates are better able than Senate candidates to avoid divisive national issues. House candidates—particularly incumbents—can focus on their personal qualities and constituency service.[68] This is because House members also are better able to control the information voters receive about them. House incumbents can build trust with voters through personal contacts and constituency service. Senators have too many constituents to do this effectively. Their contact with voters comes through paid television ads.[69] And the media examine Senate campaigns much more closely than House ones.

In spite of the low voter turnout in congressional elections, many voters can and do evaluate the job performance of incumbents. Voters do not merely cast automatic votes for incumbents; they *like* what incumbents are doing in office. Along with the very favorable image that House members have is "the relatively negative images—if any—projected by their opponents."[70] This point must be stressed—usually House challengers are virtually invisible. Senate challengers are not, and this helps explain the difference in the success rate of House and Senate incumbents.

MIDTERM ELECTIONS

Political scientists use a concept known as the *normal vote* to help put elections in perspective. The normal vote represents the way we would expect people to vote if they all followed their party identification. This rarely, if ever, occurs; short-term forces (candidate evaluations, the issues, and campaign events) often interfere with the long-term influence of party identification. Examination of how much an election deviates from the normal vote informs us about the electorate and its attitudes toward parties and candidates.

A curious thing happens in congressional elections that are held in the middle of a president's term ("midterm" elections): The vote deviates a great deal from the normal vote, and in every twentieth century midterm election (except the election of 1934), it has deviated in a direction that costs the president's party seats.[71] (See Table 7–3 for these figures, and for House-Senate comparisons.)

Even if it is conceded that some voters will be swayed by short-term forces, it is difficult to explain this consistency in what appears to be a punish-

TABLE 7–3 Losses By President's Party in Midterm Elections, 1862–1986

Year	Party Holding Presidency	President's Party Gain/Loss of Seats in House	President's Party Gain/Loss of Seats in Senate
1862	R	- 3	8
1866	R	- 2	0
1870	R	- 31	- 4
1874	R	- 96	- 8
1878	R	- 9	- 6
1882	R	- 33	3
1886	D	- 12	3
1890	R	- 85	0
1894	D	-116	- 5
1898	R	- 21	7
1902	R	9	2
1906	R	- 28	3
1910	R	- 57	-10
1914	D	- 59	5
1918	D	- 19	- 6
1922	R	- 75	- 8
1926	R	- 10	- 6
1930	R	- 49	- 8
1934	D	9	10
1938	D	- 71	- 6
1942	D	- 55	- 9
1946	D	- 55	-12
1950	D	- 29	- 6
1954	R	- 18	- 1
1958	R	- 48	-13
1962	D	- 4	3
1966	D	- 47	- 4
1970	R	- 12	2
1974	R	- 48	- 5
1978	D	- 15	- 3
1982	R	- 26	1
1986	R	- 5	- 8

NOTE: Negative numbers reflect seats lost by the president's party in that midterm election and positive numbers seats won by that party in the preceding general election. Because of changes in the overall number of seats in the Senate and House, in the number of seats won by third parties, and in the number of vacancies, a Republican loss is not always matched precisely by a Democratic gain, or vice versa.
SOURCE: Norman J. Ornstein, Thomas E. Mann, Michael J. Malbin, Allen Schick, and John Bibby, eds., *Vital Statistics on Congress, 1984–85* (Washington, DC: American Enterprise Institute, 1984), p. 44. Reprinted with permission.

ment of the president's party. And the House figures get worse the longer the party holds on to the White House. (Observe the figures for 1938, 1942, 1946, 1958, 1966, and 1974.) Part of this phenomenon is explained by the number of seats the party holds in the chamber in the first place. Many new Democrats were elected to the House in the 1932–1934 realignment and in 1964 with the election of Lyndon Johnson. The party thus had more seats to defend, and more to lose, in 1938 and 1966. But this explanation does not apply in all cases.

What goes on here? Much research has attempted to answer this question, but no consensus has been reached among political scientists.[72] It is an important phenomenon. Obviously, a president who loses party members is going to have less support from the new Congress, and his ability to advance his program is hindered. The research completed so far has led to two major, but less than satisfactory, explanations: (1) the effect of presidential coattails, and (2) negative voting against the president's party.

Presidential Coattails

This hypothesis looks to the notion that a strong candidate at the top of the ticket has *coattails,* that is, the ability to attract votes for other candidates of the same party further down the ballot. In a midterm election, the president is not on the ballot, and even a popular president is thus unable to directly stimulate votes for other candidates. This is known as the "surge and decline" theory. Aggregate studies support this theory, but as Jacobson points out, it ultimately fails as an explanation because studies of individual voting behavior fail to bear it out. The theory also "failed to explain the *size* of the midterm loss of the president's party, which has varied from one to fifty-six House seats in postwar elections."[73] Besides, recall the high reelection rate of incumbent House members and the small number of competitive seats. Many of these incumbents are extremely popular and hardly need any help from their party's president. With increasing numbers of people splitting their tickets, the validity of presidential coattails is easily questioned. Some scholars believe that Reagan exhibited coattails in 1980, but he certainly did not in 1984, when the Republicans made few inroads in Congress.[74] Also, eleven of the seventeen victorious Republican Senate candidates in 1984 won by margins *greater* than Reagan's.[75] There were also no coattails in 1988.

A second approach to this presidential coattails explanation posits that the pool of voters changes significantly from presidential election years to midterm election years. We know that voter turnout is much lower in midterm elections. (See Table 7-4.) Even in presidential election years, not everyone who votes for a presidential candidate votes for a House candidate. Is it possible that the smaller group of voters in midterm elections is different in some significant way—politically, economically, demographically—from the larger group that votes in presidential elections? According to Angus Campbell's 1960 study, midterm election voters are more partisan, more interested in elections, and more habitual as voters.[76] Campbell's work used aggregate data. More recent work on this question, based on survey results, does not support this contention.[77] Midterm voters were not markedly different from presidential voters.

TABLE 7-4   Turnout in Presidential and House Elections, 1960–1986 (percentage of voting age population)

Year	Presidential Elections	House Elections
1960	62.6	58.5
1962	——	45.4
1964	61.9	57.8
1966	——	45.4
1968	60.9	55.1
1970	——	43.5
1972	55.4	50.9
1974	——	36.1
1976	54.4	49.5
1978	——	35.1
1980	53.4	48.1
1982	——	37.7
1984	53.3	47.4
1986	——	33.4

SOURCE: Norman J. Ornstein, Thomas E. Mann, and Michael J. Malbin, eds., *Vital Statistics on Congress, 1987–1988* (Washington, DC: Congressional Quarterly Press, 1987), p. 46. Reprinted with permission.

Negative Voting

The second major explanation of the midterm phenomena is what Barbara Hinckley calls *negative voting,* that is, voter disapproval of the president and his policies even though he is not on the ballot. Voter attitudes toward economic policies, in particular, have received much attention from scholars. Edward Tufte views midterm elections as presidential referenda, and uses the president's popularity and the voter's economic well-being (their real disposable personal income) to explain the size of the midterm loss for the president's party. Tufte used aggregate data from eight midterm elections.[78] Given that voters know little information about congressional candidates and issues, voters are using something else on which to base their congressional vote.

Other studies concur with the notion that, at the aggregate level, there is a relationship between economic well-being and support for the president's party. But studies at the individual level, based on survey responses, do not support this idea. People do seem to make judgments about the economy, in general, and about the parties' ability to run the economy, but these judgments do not seem to play a major role in their voting decisions in congressional elections.[79]

Hinckley argues that the evidence for negative voting is "highly speculative," citing methodological problems with the relevant studies.[80] Aside from those problems (important as they are), it is intuitively difficult to believe that local, congressional factors are unimportant in midterm elections. Certainly presidential evaluations can affect the congressional vote in indirect ways, but to assume that midterm elections are presidential referenda is to assume that voters are ignoring congressional candidate quality, local issues, congressional campaigns, and so forth. Jacobson believes that

> for the most part the congressional vote is determined by evaluations of candidates as individuals, with little reference to national politics or personalities. The choice offered locally between a pair of candidates is what matters most, and the relative political talents and campaign resources of congressional challengers have the most to do with framing that choice.[81]

National politics *can* influence the choice that is offered to voters in midterm elections. Potential candidates of high quality may feel that it is a bad year for their party, and choose not to run (some Republicans in 1974 after the Watergate scandal, for example). That party's incumbents may even choose to retire rather than face a tough reelection battle. The reverse would happen in a year deemed good for the party (for example, the Democrats felt confident in 1974).[82] Had the Iran-contra scandal been revealed prior to the 1986 elections, the Republican party no doubt would have suffered greater losses.

But voters *are* capable of evaluating the candidates presented to them. Clearly they are not merely following party identification. And just as clearly, many are splitting their tickets to support incumbents. Votes in House districts usually show a "sophomore surge" and "retirement slump." This means that freshmen usually improve on their winning vote margins in their second elections (reflecting the advantages of incumbency). Since 1966, the sophomore surge has averaged around 6 percent of the vote.[83] When an incumbent retires, the same party may hold onto the seat, but the winning margin is usually lower than it would have been with the incumbent running. We may be unsure of much that is going on in congressional elections, but there can be no doubt of incumbent advantage.

THE IMPACT OF ELECTIONS ON CONGRESS

What is the end result of all the hoopla and campaign activity? What impact do elections have on Congress as an institution, or on policies? We will examine these questions in terms of four factors: majority party status, the internal structure of Congress, voter control over policy, and the kind of representation citizens receive.

Congressional elections have the important function of determining which party holds the majority in the House and Senate, as mentioned at the outset of this chapter. This is of crucial significance, since the majority party is allowed to run the chamber, obtaining the meaningful leadership posts and all the committee chairs. David Brady has studied the effects of historical partisan realignments on policies endorsed by Congress. He found that members of "new" majority parties do indeed support and enact policy changes.[84] Presidents can anticipate support from Congress more than four times out of five when their party controls Congress.[85] It *does* make a difference whether Republicans or Democrats control the House or the Senate or the whole Congress. According to Charles E. Jacob,

> In Congress, granting the exceptions that always exist, liberals *tend* to be more open to social and political experimentation than their conservative counterparts. They *tend* to favor domestic social welfare and economically redistributive programs as against the normal conservative suspicion of such thrusts. Historically, liberals tend to tolerate a larger role for the federal government and freer government spending. Conservatives have an ingrained skepticism about big government and usually advocate a tighter rein on the public treasury.[86]

Consider the difference in the response of the Republican Senate as compared with the response of the Democratic House to President Reagan's proposals.

Less obviously, elections, through their impact on congressional and senatorial membership turnover, affect the internal structure of Congress. According to Thomas E. Mann, the type of individuals recruited and elected "determines what legislative styles will predominate in each chamber."[87] Mann writes that "elections register the relative importance of national and local forces."[88] For example, in 1974 many Democrats were elected to the House from normally Republican districts. These "Watergate babies," as they are called, have stressed constituency service in their districts at the expense of dealing with issues. They tend to be more comfortable with new campaign styles. Indiana Representative Phillip R. Sharp of the 2nd District has survived massive partisan gerrymandering of his district through his service-engendered popularity. The more members elected in such an environment, the more the House will stress constituency service. "Watergate babies" have also helped Congress focus on government reform issues, leading to a democratized House and federal campaign finance reform. It was largely this class of Democrats that modified the seniority system (committee chairs are now voted on by secret ballot), limited the number of chairs an individual could hold, and expanded the powers of the subcommittee chairs. They also were a force behind the amendments to the Federal Election Campaign Act.

Fifty-seven Democrats were elected to the House in 1982, an election year strengthened for that party by a recession. This was the third-largest party freshman class in thirty years.[89] Their focus is on deficit reduction. Their bloc is a loose one, lacking regular class meetings, but many from this group attend weekly meetings of the Democratic Budget Group. The class introduced the idea of a budget freeze, and helped pass the Gramm-Rudman-Hollings deficit reduction law (parts of which were declared unconstitutional by the Supreme Court in 1986).[90]

In April 1986, the group forced the House to take a second vote on a resolution that raised the limit on members' outside earnings (largely from speeches to outside groups). According to the *Congressional Quarterly Weekly*

Report, "Junior members objected that the vote had been sneaked through to benefit senior members, who are most in demand to speak before interest groups, and at considerable political risk to themselves."[91] The increase was defeated on the second vote.

The 1982 class is not as conservative as some thought it would be. (Of the fifty-seven members, twenty-three are from the South or Southwest, conservative territory.) Many opposed funds for the MX missile and for the Strategic Defense Initiative (the space weapons program commonly known as "Star Wars"). Given their interest in reducing the deficit, they attacked wasteful Pentagon spending. But they were equally wary of the "antidefense" image of the Democratic party, and worked to dispel it by adopting what they consider to be a pragmatic approach to defense policies.[92]

These two groups—the "Watergate babies" and the class of 1982— illustrate the impact that conditions existing during the year they are first elected can have on House members, and on the Congress. Other forces and issues will come to bear as time passes, but the general orientation of these new members may never change.

Do elections give voters what they want? This question is not answered easily. For one thing, it is not always clear what voters want. Opinion in the district or state may be divided. Many issues today are ones that cannot be easily resolved. The conditions for the popular control of policies mandated by democratic theory are the following:

1. Voters must identify the issue positions of the candidates.
2. Voters must vote with reference to these candidate positions.
3. Candidates must differ in their issue positions.
4. Winners must vote consistently with their stated preelection positions.

These conditions, unfortunately, are often unmet.[93]

Jacobson takes a broad view in assessing the impact of elections on Congress. He points out the tension between individual and collective pursuits. (What it takes to reach an individual goal, such as reelection, may be the opposite of what is needed to reach a collective goal, such as deficit reduction.) Jacobson writes of a "fundamental flaw" in the representation resulting from the electoral process that produces:

> great individual *responsiveness,* equally great collective *irresponsibility.* Emphasis on constituency service becomes more attractive as policy matters become more divisive and threatening. Beyond that, the safest way to cope with contradictory policy demands is to be acutely sensitive to what constituent and other politically important groups want in taking positions but to avoid responsibility for the costs they would impose. Voting for Gramm-Rudman-Hollings [the deficit reduction bill] but against cuts in all of a member's favorite programs is the paradigmatic strategy.[94]

Jacobson laments "responsiveness without responsibility," arguing that it deprives citizens of a "crucial form of representation."[95] He suggests that strengthening the parties would help foster collective action, and there is great truth in this. Citizens, however, should not be let off the hook. Much of the blame rests with voters who fail to hold individual members accountable for what Congress does as an institution. We end up supporting and reelecting our individual Representatives and Senators, and hating Congress as an institution. If we choose to allow ourselves to be "bought off" with constituency service, we get the representation we deserve.

SUMMARY

Many changes have occurred in the congressional electoral environment in the past twenty years. While there is plenty of wide-open recruitment, national party organizations are becoming somewhat more important in attracting candidates and providing campaign aid. PACs are important too, and these two developments may be enhancing the national aspects of these campaigns over state and local concerns. This nationalization threatens to limit the autonomy that congressional candidates have been used to.[96] The old style of lobbying was done by insiders with an inside focus; lobbyists encouraged members to back projects they were already inclined to pursue by providing organizational backup. Lobbyists virtually ignored their opponents. Today's PACs operate in a very different fashion; they have an outside focus, and bring external demands to members of Congress.[97] House members have retained a high reelection rate, but they work much harder than they used to, particularly in terms of constituency service. Congressional elections will continue to be important due to their impact on personnel and policies, and money most definitely will continue to be important in congressional elections.

The tension between individual responsiveness and collective irresponsibility will continue to plague us. As long as we are a heterogeneous society, members of Congress will reflect the differences that exist. Is this not the role of a representative institution?

SUGGESTED READINGS

BERNSTEIN, ROBERT A., *Elections, Representation, and Congressional Voting Behavior.* Englewood Cliffs, NJ: Prentice-Hall, 1989.

FIORINA, MORRIS P., *Congress: Keystone of the Washington Establishment.* New Haven, CT: Yale University Press, 1977.

HINCKLEY, BARBARA, "The American Voter in Congressional Elections," *American Political Science Review* 74 (1980), pp. 641–650.

———, *Congressional Elections.* Washington, DC: Congressional Quarterly Press, 1981.

JACOBSON, GARY C., *Money in Congressional Elections.* New Haven, CT: Yale University Press, 1980.

———, *The Politics of Congressional Elections* (2nd ed.). Boston: Little, Brown, 1987.

——— AND SAMUEL KERNELL, *Strategy and Choice in Congressional Elections* (2nd ed.). New Haven, CT: Yale University Press, 1983.
MAYHEW, DAVID R., "Congressional Elections: The Case of the Vanishing Marginals," *Polity* 6 (1974), pp. 295–317.

DISCUSSION QUESTIONS

1. What are the advantages and disadvantages of reelecting incumbents?
2. What is your opinion about the use of negative ads in campaigns?
3. Should congressional campaigns be publicly financed?
4. What are the pros and cons of allowing congressional candidates to contribute unlimited amounts of their own money to their campaigns? Do you agree or disagree with the Supreme Court decision (*Buckley* versus *Valeo*) on this issue?
5. What are the advantages and disadvantages of the nationalization of fund-raising brought on by PACs and, to some extent, the party national committees for (1) candidates and (2) donors?
6. How do you feel about the low voter turnout in congressional elections? If it disturbs you, what steps would you suggest to try to increase turnout in these elections?
7. Is there a way to reconcile individual responsiveness with collective responsibility?

NOTES

1. Robert L. Peabody in his introduction to Barbara Hinckley, *Congressional Elections* (Washington, DC: Congressional Quarterly Press, 1981), pp. v, vi.

2. Roger H. Davidson and Walter J. Oleszek, *Congress and Its Members,* 2nd ed. (Washington, DC: Congressional Quarterly Press, 1985), Chapter 3, pp. 51–79.

3. Ibid., p. 60.

4. "Freshmen Find It Easier to Run as Incumbents," *Elections '86* (Washington, DC: Congressional Quarterly Press, 1986), p. 19.

5. Davidson and Oleszek, *Congress and Its Members,* p. 61.

6. Ibid., pp. 61, 62.

7. Ibid., p. 64.

8. Ibid., p. 66; see also Andrew Rosenthal, "On the Air: $97 Million Spent in '86," *The New York Times,* July 14, 1987, p. 10.

9. Rosenthal, "On the Air," p. 10.

10. Davidson and Oleszek, *Congress and Its Members,* p. 68.

11. Ibid., p. 70.

12. Gary C. Jacobson, "Parties and PACs in Congressional Elections," in Lawrence C. Dodd and Bruce I. Oppenheimer, eds., *Congress Re-*

considered, 3rd ed., (Washington, DC: Congressional Quarterly Press, 1985), p. 136.

13. *Congressional Quarterly Almanac, 1983* 39 (Washington, DC: Congressional Quarterly Press, 1984), p. 12B.

14. Ibid.

15. Ibid.

16. Richard F. Fenno, Jr., *Home Style: House Members in Their Districts* (Boston: Little, Brown, 1978).

17. Davidson and Oleszek, *Congress and Its Members,* p. 82.

18. Barbara Hinckley, *Congressional Elections* (Washington, DC: Congressional Quarterly Press, 1981), p. 61.

19. Ibid., p. 64.

20. Albert Cover, "One Good Term Deserves Another," *American Journal of Political Science* 27 (August 1977), pp. 535, 536.

21. Alan Ehrenhalt, "Technology, Strategy Bring New Campaign Era," *Congressional Quarterly Weekly Report* 43 (December 7, 1985), p. 2559.

22. Ibid., p. 2564.

23. Ibid.

24. Norman J. Ornstein, Thomas E. Mann, and Michael J. Malbin, eds., *Vital Statistics on Congress, 1987-1988* (Washington, DC: Congressional Quarterly Press, 1987), pp. 92, 93.

25. Table 3-8, Campaign Funding Sources for General Election Candidates in House and Senate Elections, 1982, in Norman Ornstein, et al., eds., *Vital Statistics on Congress* (Washington, DC: American Enterprise Institute, 1984), pp. 80, 81.

26. Larry Sabato, "Parties, PACs, and Independent Groups," in Thomas E. Mann and Norman J. Ornstein, eds., *The American Elections of 1982* (Washington, DC: American Enterprise Institute, 1983), p. 87.

27. Edie N. Goldenberg and Michael W. Traugott, *Campaigning for Congress* (Washington, DC: Congressional Quarterly Press, 1984), p. 62.

28. Ibid, p. 64.

29. Glen Craney, "PACs Step Up Contributions, Particularly to Incumbents," *Congressional Quarterly Weekly Report* 46 (May 7, 1988), p. 1205.

30. Herbert E. Alexander, *Financing Politics,* 3rd ed. (Washington, DC: Congressional Quarterly Press, 1984) p. 27.

31. Ibid.

32. Ibid.

33. Richard L. Berke, "G.O.P. Lost Senate With $107 Million," *The New York Times,* February 8, 1987, Section 1, p. 13.

34. Gary C. Jacobson, *The Politics of Congressional Elections,* 2nd ed. (Boston: Little, Brown, 1987), p. 68.

35. Jacobson, "Parties and PACs," p. 133.

36. Jacobson, *Politics of Congressional Elections,* p. 68.

37. Ibid., p. 71.

38. Goldenberg and Traugott, *Campaigning,* p. 64.

39. Jacobson, *Politics of Congressional Elections,* p. 62.

40. "Freshmen Find It Easier," *Elections '86,* p. 20.

41. Richard L. Berke, "Study Says PACs Play Growing Elections Role," *The New York Times,* April 8, 1987, p. 13.

42. Gary W. Copeland, "Activating Voters in Congressional Elections," *Political Behavior* 5 (1983), pp. 391-401.

43. Jacobson, *Politics of Congressional Elections,* p. 49, 52.

44. Fenno, Jr., *Home Style,* pp. 171-176.

45. Stephen A. Salmore and Barbara G. Salmore, *Candidates, Parties, and Campaigns* (Washington, DC: Congressional Quarterly Press, 1985), p. 68.

46. Walter Isaacson, "Running With the PACs," *Time* 120 (October 25, 1982), p. 21.

47. Salmore and Salmore, *Candidates, Parties,* p. 69.

48. Isaacson, "Running With the PACs," p. 24.

49. Robert J. Samuelson, "The Campaign Reform Fraud," *Newsweek* 110 (July 13, 1987), p. 43.

50. Isaacson, "Running With the PACs," p. 24.

51. "Controls on Political Spending," *Elections '86,* p. 41.

52. David S. Cloud, "Campaign-Finance Bill Snagged on Partisanship," *Congressional Quarterly Weekly Report* 46 (March 12, 1988), pp. 669, 670.

53. "Controls on Political Spending," *Election '86,* pp. 44, 45.

54. Chuck Alston, "Campaign-Finance Gridlock Likely to Persist," *Congressional Quarterly Weekly Report* 46 (December 17, 1988), pp. 3525-3529.

55. Hinckley, *Congressional Elections,* p. 18.

56. Robert S. Erikson and Gerald C. Wright, "Voters, Candidates, and Issues in Congressional Elections," in Dodd and Oppenheimer, eds., *Congress Reconsidered,* 3rd ed., p. 96.

57. Hinckley, *Congressional Elections,* p. 17.

58. Erikson and Wright, "Voters, Candidates and Issues," p. 105.

59. Davidson and Oleszek, *Congress and Its Members,* p. 92. For an opposing view, see Amihai Glazer and Marc Robbins, "Voters and Roll Call Voting: The Effect on Congressional Elections," *Political Behavior* 5 (1983), pp. 377-389; Jacobson, *Politics of Congressional Elections,* p. 138; and Alan I. Abramowitz, "A Comparison of Voting for U.S. Senator and Representative in 1978," *American Political Science Review* 74 (September 1980), pp. 633-640.

60. Ibid., p. 96.

61. John G. Peters and Susan Welch, "The Effect of Charges of Corruption on Voting Behavior in Congressional Elections," *American Political Science Review* 74 (September 1980), pp. 697-708.

62. Jacobson, *Politics of Congressional Elections,* pp. 108, 109.

63. Ibid., p. 109.

64. Ibid., p. 110.

65. Ibid., p. 112.

66. Ibid., p. 114.

67. Ibid., p. 112.

68. Davidson and Oleszek, *Congress and Its Members,* p. 100.

69. Jacobson, *Politics of Congressional Elections,* p. 117.

70. Ibid., p. 128.

71. Hinckley, *Congressional Elections,* p. 113.

72. See, among others, Angus Campbell, "Surge and Decline: A Study of Electoral Change," *Public Opinion Quarterly* 24 (Fall 1960), pp. 397–418; George Edwards, "The Impact of Presidential Coattails on Outcomes of Congressional Elections," *American Politics Quarterly* 7 (January 1979), pp. 94–108; Gary C. Jacobson, "Presidential Coattails in 1972," *Public Opinion Quarterly* 40 (Summer 1976), pp. 194–200; Donald Kinder and D. Roderick Kiewiet, "Economic Discontent and Political Behavior: The Role of Personal Grievances and Collective Economic Judgments in Congressional Voting," *American Journal of Political Science* 23 (August 1979), pp. 495–527; Samuel Kernell, "Presidential Popularity and Negative Voting: An Alternative Explanation of the Midterm Congressional Decline of the President's Party," *American Political Science Review* 71 (March 1977), pp. 44–66; Herbert Kritzer and Robert Eubank, "Presidential Coattails Revisited: Partisanship and Incumbency Effects," *American Journal of Political Science* 23 (August 1979), pp. 615–626; Edward Tufte, "Determinants of the Outcomes of Midterm Congressional Elections," *American Political Science Review* 69 (September 1975), pp. 812–826.

73. Jacobson, *Politics of Congressional Elections,* p. 144.

74. John A. Ferejohn and Morris P. Fiorina, "Incumbency and Realignment in Congressional Elections," in John E. Chubb and Paul E. Peterson, eds., *The New Direction in American Politics* (Washington, DC: The Brookings Institution, 1985), p. 111.

75. Charles E. Jacob, "The Congressional Elections," in Gerald Pomper, et al., eds., *The Election of 1984, Reports and Interpretations* (Chatham, NJ: Chatham House, 1985), p. 117.

76. Angus Campbell, "Surge and Decline: A Study of Electoral Change," *Public Opinion Quarterly* 24 (Fall 1960), pp. 397–418.

77. Hinckley, *Congressional Elections,* p. 116.

78. Edward Tufte, "Determinants of the Outcomes of Midterm Congressional Elections," *American Political Science Review* 69 (September 1975), pp. 812–826.

79. Hinckley, *Congressional Elections,* p. 117.

80. Ibid., pp. 117, 118.

81. Jacobson, *Politics of Congressional Elections,* p. 155.

82. Gary C. Jacobson and Samuel Kernell, *Strategy and Choice in Congressional Elections* (New Haven, CT: Yale University Press, 1981).

83. Erikson and Wright, "Voters, Candidates, and Issues," p. 99.

84. David Brady, "Congressional Party Realignment and Transformations of Public Policy in Three Realignment Eras," *American Journal of Political Science* 26 (May 1982), pp. 333–360.

85. Charles E. Jacob, "The Congressional Elections," p. 124.

86. Ibid., p. 121.

87. Thomas E. Mann, "Elections and Change in Congress," in Thomas E. Mann and Norman J. Ornstein, eds., *The New Congress* (Washington, DC: American Enterprise Institute, 1981), p. 33.

88. Ibid.

89. Jacqueline Calmes, "Class of '82: Redefining Democratic Values," *Congressional Quarterly Weekly Report* 44 (June 7, 1986), p. 1269.

90. Ibid., p. 1271.

91. Ibid., p. 1272.

92. Ibid.

93. Davidson and Oleszek, *Congress and Its Members,* p. 103.

94. Jacobson, *Politics of Congressional Elections,* pp. 216, 217.

95. Ibid., p. 217.

96. Ibid., pp. 131–158.

97. Jacobson, "Parties and PACs in Congressional Elections," p. 153.

8

State and Local Elections

INTRODUCTION

When we think of democracy, we often think in terms of the grass-roots level, in terms of citizens addressing problems of local concern. Yet elections at the state and local level get sporadic attention from electoral experts. One problem is that we have fifty states and thousands of localities, with different political environments and electoral rules. Generalizations are difficult to come by, thanks to the diversity afforded by federalism. Another problem is that national candidates, issues, and elections are often (wrongly) perceived as being more important and more interesting than other contests. The fact is that most of the governmental rules that have a daily impact on us arise from local, not national, government. Broad questions such as whether or not to go to war are undoubtedly of prime importance, but how often are we faced with such momentous decisions? More commonly, our immediate concerns center around issues such as education, roads, and safety—local issues. States today are large enterprises; thirty-one have revenues equal to or greater than the top 100 companies in the *Fortune* ''500'' listing.[1] As the national government has been scaled down, states have had to take on a greater share of the domestic policy burden, managing water distribution, prisons, schools, welfare programs, and job training centers. As far as the candidates go, state and local elections are full of talented, fascinating, eccentric figures that are at least as interesting as the presidential candidates.

Unfortunately, the public seems to share many of the same biases that afflict scholars. Voter turnout in state and local elections is low, and apathy is a problem, as it is at the national level. There is also the perception that these contests are less glamorous than the national ones. Still another factor is that state and local races often are uncontested. States with long, complicated ballots discourage some would-be voters. States and local communities also often insist on holding their elections in "off-years," years when there is no presidential election. This can focus the local contests on local issues, but without the excitement of the national election fight, many citizens stay at home on election day. On top of that, some contests for specific posts (judgeships, most commonly) are held separately from other local elections as well as from the national elections. Many local elections are also nonpartisan, and voter turnout in such elections is lower than in partisan ones. Without a contest, interest declines.

It once was fair to argue that state and local elections featured candidates chosen by cliques of party leaders, and that nominations often rewarded party loyalists who were not always qualified for such posts.[2] In the days of machine politics, when power brokers might put people in office simply because they knew they could control them, there was some truth to this. But today, noting the odd exception, these charges are not fair. Governors, state legislators, and mayors are well-educated individuals facing difficult tasks. Citizens want more services but lower taxes, and in the face of federal cutbacks, the pressure is on state and local officials to solve policy problems. What is astounding is the number of such officials who are up to the task. (Reuben Askew in Florida, Bruce Babbitt in Arizona, and Gerald L. Baliles in Virginia are just some examples of competent state officials.)

In part, this is the result of state legislatures gradually granting more formal authority to governors in the past thirty years. Almost all of the states have given governors four-year terms, and have lifted one-term restrictions. Cuts in federal funds, reinforced by Reagan administration rhetoric about the need for states to do more and the federal government less, have given governors an opportunity to set the agenda in their states. These developments have made the governor's spot more attractive, to the point where it is getting more difficult to find people willing to run for the U.S. Senate. Strong candidates would rather run for governor.[3]

State legislatures also have changed. Writing about state legislators, Alan Ehrenhalt provides an apt description of how power is changing hands throughout the United States:

> L. Marion Gressette is the symbol of legislators past. President pro tempore of the South Carolina Senate, he has served in it as a Democrat since 1937, but did not become its presiding officer until 1972, when he was more than seventy years old. A lifelong resident of rural Calhoun County, he goes home to practice law there

between legislative sessions. Thomas A. Loftus is the symbol of legislators to come. After taking a political science degree and studying public administration in graduate school, he went to work for the Democrats in the Wisconsin Assembly, and served as an aide to its Speaker. He became a member of the Assembly in 1977; six years later, at age thirty-seven, he became Speaker himself. Loftus is a full-time legislator—he has done nothing but political work since he left the University of Wisconsin.[4]

The power of rural areas has declined, the issues are more complex, and the pace of political life has quickened. Ehrenhalt points out that George C. Wallace, once elected to the Alabama governorship from a rural base, won again in the 1980s as the head of a coalition made up of blacks, teachers, and labor. In the East and Midwest, power is changing hands in the Democratic party, going from urban labor interests to youthful, independent, full-time legislators who win their seats through personal campaigning with little party assistance. These younger legislators are liberal on social issues, but often part with veteran Democrats in other areas.

In examining state elections, it is important to understand that each locality has a political culture that is at least slightly different from the areas around it, and often very different from distant areas. All localities feel the effects of national events, but to different degrees. Daniel J. Elazar has studied these political cultures, calling them "particularly important as the historical source of differences in habits, perspectives, and attitudes that influence life in the various states."[5] Elazar identifies three kinds of political cultures (or subcultures) found at the local level in the United States: individualistic, moralistic, and traditionalistic.

The *individualistic* culture defines democracy as a marketplace. Government is created for utilitarian purposes in order to provide those services demanded by the people. Private concerns are of prime importance, so community or government intervention into private activities is strictly limited. Political participation is seen as merely one option among many for improving oneself, and political careers are viewed much the same as business careers. Political life is anchored in mutual obligations based on personal relationships. Since states are large, complex political entities, these relationships occur through political parties rather than face to face. Politics is seen as a specialized, businesslike activity with which the masses need not concern themselves. The public is likely to view politics as a dirty business best left to others. This attitude leads to a certain degree of tolerance for perquisites and corruption in politics. An ambivalent attitude prevails toward bureaucracy; bureaucracies are the opposite of an individualistic process, yet they also bring efficiency, much valued in this businesslike approach to politics.

The *moralistic* political culture considers politics "one of the great activities of humanity in its search for the good society."[6] Government is defined as a commonwealth, advancing the public interest, and good government is government that does so in an honest and selfless way. Individualism is valued, but intervention into private activities is allowed when necessary to protect the good of the whole. Discussion and pursuit of the public interest is centered around issues, and these activities are seen as the concern of all citizens, not just a few. Participation is a duty. Because of the emphasis on the public interest, public service is characterized as involving moral obligations that are more demanding than those of the business world. Private gain from politics is not appreciated. Service to the community takes precedence over party loyalty. Moralistic cultures lead to less corruption and more amateur participation. Merit-based bureaucracies fit in well with moralistic political cultures.

The *traditionalistic* culture has what Elazar calls a "preindustrial" political culture, with a paternalistic and elitist conception of the commonwealth.[7] This culture perceives society as a hierarchy, with those at the top expected to take a more active role in politics than those at the bottom. It sees government as a positive element in the community, but nonetheless tries to limit political power to a small, elite group. Social and family relationships become extremely important in the transfer of political power. Those outside the elite circle are not expected to play any role in politics; they are not even expected to vote. Political parties are downplayed, as they are too open for this closed approach to politics. Traditionalistic states tend to be one-party systems, with factional divisions more important than party divisions. The approach to governance is custodial, conserving that which exists while not attempting to increase or to expand the role of government. Such systems tend to be antibureaucratic, relying as they do on interpersonal relationships.

Elazar finds that all three political cultures are evident in different parts of some states, and he attributes the distribution of these cultures across the fifty states to migrational patterns and events such as depressions and wars. Racial, religious, ethnic, regional, urban, and rural factors help define an area's political culture. However these subcultures developed, what is important here is that they exist. Generalizations that might be attempted about state and local political activity must be absorbed with these subcultures in mind. They can account for a variety of differences in state and local political behavior.

Robert S. Erikson and his associates, using a different approach to political culture than Elazar, found that state cultures have an impact on the partisanship and ideology of their citizens. They discovered that demographic factors are important in explaining how individuals behave, but these factors are not important in explaining differences among states. Erikson and his colleagues decided that they were measuring something different from Elazar, but their work nonetheless again demonstrates the importance of state differences on political behavior.[8]

State constitutions reflect these political cultures, with some promoting the political marketplace (featuring unhindered competition) and others facilitating government intervention into private affairs. These constitutions are extremely important factors in electoral politics, since they contain provisions on referenda, initiatives, and recalls; on the eligibility to vote; on terms of office; on getting on the ballot; on legislative apportionment; and on political parties. The political culture also affects the kinds of laws that are or are not passed dealing with the timing of elections; voter registration; campaign finances; governance of political parties; nomination procedures; and interest groups. (For example, a few states allow party endorsements in primary elections, whereas others forbid them.)

National factors and trends do influence state decisions, and lead to some commonalities.[9] For example, with one exception (Nebraska), all the states have bicameral legislatures. Most lower house legislators have two-year terms, and most state senators have staggered four-year terms. All states are bound by amendments to the U.S. Constitution, which provide for the popular election of U.S. senators, women's suffrage, and the enfranchisement of eighteen-year-olds. Federal legislation, particularly the Voting Rights Act of 1965, affects the states, as do the U.S. Supreme Court decisions on reapportionment. State elections can be affected by national trends favoring one party over another. The national media are also received in all the states, and can affect state agenda-setting. Population mobility also erodes the differences among the states, to some extent.

Voting behavior at the state level, trends in ballot initiatives, and state parties will be examined in this chapter. Important considerations include the level of party competition in states and whether elections are partisan or nonpartisan. The consequences of nonpartisan politics will be closely examined. The reader is reminded that generalizations can hide a great deal of variation. Some states require the collection and publication of useful data, whereas others do not; thus we operate under less-than-perfect research conditions.

STATE VOTING BEHAVIOR

Voter Turnout

Voter turnout in presidential elections averages about 55 percent; in gubernatorial elections, about 45 percent; in mayoral elections, about 25 percent.[10] Turnout in state and local elections is quite low for many of the same reasons that turnout in national elections is low: socialization processes have changed, registration laws inhibit some, feelings of apathy and low political efficacy exist, fewer people identify with a political party, and interest in these elections is often low. In addition, many local elections are nonpartisan, and, as previously stated, nonpartisanship is associated with low turnout. (Nonpartisanship will be discussed in more detail later.)

Significant regional differences exist in voter turnout. The South tends to be an area of low turnout, largely because of lower educational levels. Table 8–1 illustrates both the decline in turnout when presidential candidates are not on the ballot and the regional differences in voting in congressional elections.

TABLE 8–1   Percentage of Voting Age Population Casting Votes, Region

REGION	1982 CONGRESSIONAL ELECTION	1984 PRESIDENTIAL ELECTION
Northeast	39.6%	50.9%
Midwest	44.7	56.0
South	29.5	38.6
West	42.3	49.4

SOURCE: *Statistical Abstract of the United States, 1987*, 107th ed. (Washington, DC: U.S. Bureau of the Census, 1986), p. 243. Reprinted with permission.

The low turnout levels of the South are clear at both the presidential and congressional levels. In both categories, the Midwest had the highest turnout.

While voter turnout is higher when elections are held in presidential election years, even then there is a "roll-off" effect: voters who are attracted to the polls by the presidential race will leave blank some of the state and local contests. Turnout is higher in states with competitive party systems, and when races are perceived as close. Approached from another perspective, we find that turnout is higher in states described by Elazar as moralistic, and lower in states termed traditional. Turnout is high in the South for primary elections. Primaries are the crucial elections in one-party areas.[11] (These are areas in which one party dominates; see the section "Party Competition" in this chapter.) In the South, it is not uncommon to have a *runoff primary*. If there are several popular candidates in the initial primary, and no candidate wins a majority, a runoff is then held between the top two or three candidates. The winner of the runoff is the party's nominee. In one-party areas, getting the nomination amounts to winning the office.

Voter unhappiness with their party appears to be more of a problem at the national level than at the state level. State elections show stable voting patterns, evidence of voter loyalty to state parties.[12] The clearest example of this is in the South, where many vote for Republican presidential candidates, but return to the Democratic party for state and local contests. Further evidence of party loyalty was shown when, in 1982, about four-fifths of those identifying with a party voted for the gubernatorial candidate of that party. (Independents split their vote about fifty-fifty.)[13] One-party domination in an area helps to foster party loyalty.

Some states organize ballots according to party, some according to office. Party column ballots make it easy to vote a straight party ticket. With the office ballot, voters must search out their party's candidate for each office and mark the correct spot in order to vote a straight ticket.

Since voter turnout is higher in presidential elections than in state and local elections, a different pool of voters is involved at each level. In general, voters at the state and local level share the same characteristics as voters at the presidential level. Voters are better educated, are strong partisans, have higher status occupations, are older, have more knowledge about politics and more interest in elections than nonvoters. Voters in primaries exhibit even higher levels of these characteristics.[14] In a study of Toledo, Ohio, municipal elections, Howard D. Hamilton found that the gap in social status between voters and nonvoters was greater in municipal elections than in presidential elections.[15] Also, persons who identify with the dominant party in states where one party is dominant are more likely to vote in primaries than those identifying with the weaker party.[16]

The type of electoral system also can affect voter turnout. Local electoral systems can be identified as reformed or unreformed. *Reformed electoral systems* usually have nonpartisan, at-large elections that are held at different times than state and presidential elections. *At-large elections* refer to city councils where all the members are elected from the entire city. The alternative is the *ward or district election,* where council members are elected from separate areas in the city. Reformed systems take great precautions against voter fraud (by using strict registration rules, voting machines, election judges, and safeguards in counting the ballots), and these systems are generally found in suburbs and in the West. Reformed election systems are associated with reduced voter turnout.[17] *Unreformed election systems* usually have partisan, ward elections held at the same time as statewide elections. They generally lack strict precautions against voter fraud, and they usually are found in urban areas, and in the East, Midwest, and South.

A final factor affecting state and local voter turnout is the Voting Rights Act of 1965. Representing landmark civil rights legislation, the Act authorized the federal government to send registrars into areas that had histories of discriminating against groups. Most of these federal registrars went into the rural South, and the number of blacks registered to vote in that region skyrocketed as a result of the law. Table 8–2 documents the increased registration in selected southern states.

One result of black registration and voting was an increase in the number of black elected officials. Only 1,185 blacks were elected to office in 1969; in 1981, there were 5,014.[18] The black vote in the South was critical in the election of Jimmy Carter in 1976. Table 8–3 presents the number of black elected officials in the United States from 1970 through 1986. As one would expect, there have been increases across the board. Hispanic participation also has increased, as has the number of Hispanics holding office. There were 115 Hispanic state legislators in 1985, and twelve mayors.[19]

Gubernatorial Elections

Gubernatorial elections appear to be insulated from national trends. The number of states electing governors in presidential years fell from thirty-four to twelve between 1932 and 1984; thirty-six states elect governors in congressional

TABLE 8–2   Registration Before and After the Voting Rights Act of 1965

| | PERCENT REGISTERED | |
STATE	BEFORE (1960)	AFTER (1975)
Alabama	White 63.6%	76.2%
	Black 13.7	55.8
Arkansas	White 60.9	62.0
	Black 38.0	92.2
Georgia	White 56.8	59.6
	Black 29.3	69.5
Louisiana	White 76.9	71.8
	Black 31.1	58.8
Mississippi	White 63.9	80.7
	Black 5.2	60.7
North Carolina	White 92.1	61.4
	Black 39.1	49.2
South Carolina	White 57.1	46.2
	Black 13.7	44.0
Virginia	White 46.1	59.8
	Black 23.1	49.8

SOURCE: *Statistical Abstract of the United States, 1976*, 97th ed. (Washington, DC: U.S. Bureau of the Census, 1976), p. 466. Reprinted with permission.

election years; and five states elect governors in years different from both the presidential and congressional contests. Neither the Democratic gubernatorial candidates in 1964 nor the Republican gubernatorial candidates in 1980 and 1984 benefited greatly from their party's presidential victories. According to Malcolm E. Jewell and David M. Olson, "partisan gains and losses in governors' races usually follow the direction, but not often the magnitude, of the presidential and congressional trends."[20]

Malcolm E. Jewell and David M. Olson also examined the safety of

TABLE 8–3   Black Elected Officials, by Office

YEAR	TOTAL	U.S. AND STATE LEGISLATURES	CITY AND COUNTY OFFICES	LAW ENFORCEMENT	EDUCATION
1970	1,479	179	719	213	368
1972	2,275	224	1,112	263	676
1974	3,007	256	1,607	340	804
1976	4,006	299	2,284	415	1,008
1978	4,544	316	2,616	458	1,154
1980	4,963	326	2,871	534	1,232
1982	5,241	342	3,017	573	1,309
1984	5,865	396	3,367	657	1,445
1986	6,384	410	3,800	676	1,498

SOURCE: *Statistical Abstract of the United States, 1987*, 107th ed. (Washington, DC: U.S. Bureau of the Census, 1986), p. 240. Reprinted with permission.

incumbent governors. (By 1987, only two states still barred second consecutive terms for governors.) They examined races for all states from 1963 through 1986, and found that, on average, only one-fourth of incumbents seeking reelection were defeated. (They also discovered that, when no incumbent was running, the party in power was twice as likely to be defeated.) On the whole, though, party identification was found to be more important in explaining these votes than incumbency.[21]

As is true of presidential campaigns, candidate personality, campaign organization, and funding are important in gubernatorial campaigns. Issues, especially the issue of tax hikes, also play an important role, but it is difficult to generalize about their impact. Jewell and Olson studied gubernatorial races from 1962 through 1984 in which incumbents were defeated, and came to three conclusions:

> In over 40 percent of the elections the traditional party strength of one party and/or the extent of unity in one or both parties help to explain the outcome. In over 40 percent of the elections the personality or experience of one or both candidates assumed particular importance. In three-quarters of the races some aspects of the incumbent governor's record were credited by the media with playing a substantial part in his defeat, with taxes being the issue in almost half of these cases.[22]

Not all political scientists accept this conclusion. Gerald M. Pomper and Susan S. Lederman found that voters are not always the ones who wish to limit state taxation, and that high spending can be politically advantageous for governors. They studied gubernatorial elections from 1948 through 1964 and found no association between the vote and gubernatorial taxing and spending programs.[23] Governors who concentrate tax increases and spending programs in their first year do themselves a favor. Early spending can be beneficial in that it gives voters time either to forget about gubernatorial extravagance, or to see the fruits of the spending.

Jewell and Olson suggest that several factors affect the success or failure of tax increases by incumbents in gubernatorial campaigns. They cite the state's political climate, the mood of the voters, the skill of the opponent in using the issue, and the governor's ability to defend the tax increase. Governors who can show that the tax was necessary, show what the money accomplished, and rally interest group support will be in good shape.[24]

Do state voters hold governors responsible for the condition of the state's economy in the way voters hold presidents responsible for the condition of the national economy? Jewell and Olson studied elections in 1982 and found, first, that party identification was the most important predictor of votes for governor, and, second, that prospective and retrospective judgments about the success of the *president's* economic policies were also important, more so than any judgment about economic conditions caused by the governor. In other words, the state of the economy affects the vote for governor, but it is the *president's* policies that count, not the governor's! These judgments were also more important than the voter's personal financial or employment condition.[25]

A final note on gubernatorial elections. Unlike presidents and vice presidents, governors and lieutenant governors do not always run as a team. In some states they are elected separately, and the result can be a governor from one party and a lieutenant governor from a different party. This can cause many problems for the governor, especially if the state constitution grants the lieutenant governor significant power when the governor is out of the state.

State Legislative Races

Just as the president's party in the U.S. Congress loses seats in midterm elections, so does the president's party in state legislatures. James E. Campbell found that the president's party gains seats in presidential elections in proportion to the presidential vote in the state, and that midterm losses also are in proportion to the prior presidential vote.[26]

According to Gregory A. Caldeira and Samuel C. Patterson, in state legislative races in competitive states, incumbents are not routinely returned to office. In competitive states, party support and campaign efforts are important variables in determining the outcome.[27] However, Susan E. Howell found that campaign activities had no relationship to the percentage of votes state legislative candidates received in Louisiana. Incumbency and past elective office were more important in these Louisiana contests. Howell found that it was important for candidates to gain access to a network of elites—other officials, their staff members, business people, and members of political organizations—who could help their campaign, and incumbents were more likely to have such access. Expenditures were also related to mobilizing these elites.[28]

Turnover in state legislatures is relatively high, for several reasons. Some people run for the state legislature to get publicity that will be useful when they return to private life; they have no intention of making a career out of legislative service (lawyers and real estate brokers, for example, often use this strategy). Incumbent legislators often attract lucrative job offers. Some find legislative service boring or frustrating. Some find the demands of constituents too great, considering the relatively low compensation they receive.[29] And many, of course, go on to other offices. Both national parties invested money in the 1988 state legislative races in preparation for the redistricting that will take place after the 1990 Census.[30] Each party wants to control as many governorships and state legislatures as possible in order to control the design of the new congressional districts.

Judicial Selection

States handle the selection of judges in a variety of ways. Some hold partisan elections; some nonpartisan elections; some select judges through appointment; and some use a combination of appointment and election. Partisan elections bring the highest voter turnout and the greatest participation by the public. It can be argued, however, that citizens are not experts on judicial matters, that they are not equipped to judge the qualifications of would-be judges, that partisanship introduces elements into judicial selection that should not be there. It also can be argued that judges should be protected from political influences, that they should arrive at their decisions without concern for popular sentiment. Appointment resolves some of these problems, and puts power into the hands of the governor as well. Governors can be expected to have the knowledge necessary for making informed choices, and to pay attention to bar association recommendations. But governors might want to reward campaign supporters, or loyal party members, at the expense of other possible nominees. There is hesitation about putting so much power in the hands of one person.

A compromise method of judicial selection has been adopted by many states, including California and Missouri. With this method, often called the Missouri Plan, the governor appoints a commission that includes lawyers, named by the state bar association, and lay people. When a judicial vacancy occurs, the commission nominates three candidates. The governor chooses one name from the list, and this person serves as judge for at least a year. At the next election, voters are asked to retain or remove this judge. (No opposing candidate is listed on the ballot, and the incumbent judges are almost always returned.) The judge then serves an extended term before facing the voters again.

This combination form of selection attempts to ensure that judges meet the two requirements that the public demands of judges: that they be qualified, and that they be responsive. While it is rare for judges to lose their elections under this plan, they know the possibility is there. But the political pressure involved in this process might be less than in partisan elections. However, Peverill Squire and Eric R. A. N. Smith found that voters commonly approach such elections in a partisan fashion. In a study of the 1982 California state supreme court confirmation elections, they discovered that voters with partisan knowledge based their judicial votes on their party identification and their opinion of the governor who originally appointed the justice.[31] Voters who do this are, of course, defeating the purpose of nonpartisan elections. Suffice to say that there is no perfect way to select judges.

INITIATIVES, REFERENDA, AND RECALLS

In addition to voting for candidates, voters at the state and local level are often asked to vote on issues and the tenure of public officials. The initiative, the referendum, and the recall are the mechanisms for doing so; they are lasting reforms that rose out of the Progressive Era. These reforms stem from a mistrust of legislatures, political parties, and politicians. They are popular in western states, and are examples of direct legislation, or direct democracy. *Initiatives* are mechanisms that allow voters to propose legislation and, once the proper number of petition signatures is gathered, put these proposals on a ballot. With a direct initiative, people write a proposal and put it on a ballot. With an indirect initiative, people write a proposal, but first give the legislature an opportunity to make it law. If the legislature does not do so by the end of its session, then the proposal goes on a ballot. There has been a dramatic increase in the use of initiatives in the 1980s.[32] *Referenda* are somewhat similar. Here, the legislature makes the proposal, but puts it on a ballot to ensure popular support. Some states have compulsory referenda, requiring that specific measures, such as state constitutional amendments or tax increases be put before the public.

In the 1987 elections, by using initiatives and referenda, voters dealt with proposals to close nuclear plants, to put deposits on beverage containers, to control resort development, to legalize lotteries and racetrack betting, to outlaw discrimination against homosexuals, and to spend money for the construction of new baseball stadiums.[33] Initiatives and referenda have been popular methods for making nuclear freeze statements, dealing with toxic waste issues, ensuring civil rights protections (such as fair housing laws), and controlling public finance measures.

Direct legislation can wreak havoc with government finances. Voting on these proposals usually is low, with those feeling the most strongly participating. When the issue is a proposal to increase school budgets, those with the strongest feelings are usually those who are opposed to tax increases. Sometimes tax increases are necessary, though, and governments can be in effect held hostage by the minority voting on the issue. The best example of this is California's Proposition Thirteen, adopted in 1978. Proposition Thirteen was a reaction to skyrocketing property values and property taxes in that state. Even though government, business, and labor were opposed to this initiative, it passed overwhelmingly. It reduced all property taxes by 60 percent, and the state was forced to cut back some services and to develop special funding for others. To a certain extent, power shifted from localities to the state, since state aid was now given out with more strings attached. Police and fire expenditures could not be reduced; salaries for local government workers were frozen; and counties were not allowed to disproportionately cut health services.[34]

A *recall* is a special election to determine whether or not an elected official should be removed from office prior to the expiration of his or her term. Again, a set number of signatures on petitions is required before the election can be called. Most recall states require gathering signatures that amount to 25 percent of the votes in the last election—not an easy task. The states differ in whether the vote count used is the total vote (the number of votes cast for all offices in the election), or the total votes tallied for the office in question. To use recall successfully it is necessary to have a well-financed campaign and a large number of unhappy voters.[35]

The officials who are subject to recall are specified by statute or in the state constitution. In most states with recall, the ballot includes the name of the official who is being challenged, and the names of those who wish to take over the position. In some states, a separate election is necessary to determine who will succeed the recalled official. Gubernatorial recall has been rare: Only Lynn J. Frazier of North Dakota in 1921 has been recalled. A recall was set in motion in 1988 against Evan Mecham of Arizona. Mecham was in the interesting position of facing a recall and an impeachment at the same time. He was removed from office by the state senate as a result of the impeachment charges, and the recall election was canceled.

But a recall election does not have to succeed in order to influence the actions of the official involved; the threat of a recall, or even a failed recall, can

SOURCE: Jack Higgins, Chicago Sun-Times. Copyright 1983. Reprinted with permission.

make the official more responsive to the opinions of those who are unhappy. Recalls can have serious consequences. A recall of two Democratic state senators in Michigan in 1983 resulted in giving the other party control over the state senate when the two Democrats were replaced by Republicans.[36]

Such actions may make government more responsive to the voters, but they violate the principle of representative government and intrude on legislative authority. The wording of initiatives and referenda is occasionally so confusing that people do not know what a yes or no vote means. State courts can remove ballot issues for a variety of reasons, including using inaccurate words in titles and descriptions or addressing more than one issue at a time. Initiatives were removed from ballots in seven states in 1984.[37]

Interest groups are active on many proposals, with business groups sometimes spending huge sums to support or to oppose referenda. The U.S. Supreme Court has ruled that corporations are protected by the First Amendment to the U.S. Constitution, and that they can spend money to publicize their views on issues. The relevant case is *First National Bank* versus *Bellotti* (435 U.S. 765, 1978), which invalidated a Massachusetts law that restricted corporate contributions to referenda campaigns.[38] Some groups pay people to collect signatures; many spend their money on advertising aimed at voters. In 1982, the California ballot included a measure that would have instituted controls on handguns. Approximately $10.0 million was spent by interest groups on both sides of the issue. The largest contribution, $2.5 million, came from the National Rifle Association.[39] As with campaigns for political office, however, the side spending the most money does not always win the battle.

Direct legislation is an important method for people to use to cut through red tape and bureaucracy, and its use can reduce feelings of political impotence. Direct legislation does not favor a particular ideology; both liberals and conservatives have won using it. A suggestion has been made to allow for a national initiative for proposing federal legislation. But not everyone has the time, money, or political skills necessary to be involved in direct democracy. Some initiatives have threatened the rights of minorities. A 1964 initiative in California overturned an open housing law that had been enacted by the state legislature. Other proposals have suggested quarantining AIDS victims.[40] It is worth remembering, however, that ours is a representative, not a direct, democracy. According to Thomas E. Cronin, many political scientists feel that asking voters to judge the substantive merits of major issues is "to strain their information and interest."[41]

STATE POLITICAL PARTIES

Party Organization

Parties in the United States are built from the ground up, allowing decentralization and diversity. Parties of the same label can vary in organization and ideology across the states, and face varying levels of competition from the opposition. The base unit of the party organization is at the precinct level. From the precinct level the party organization moves upward to the ward committee, the county central committee (or legislative district committee), the state central committee, and finally to the national committee. Some of the lower-level party positions will be vacant, since party members sometimes look on these positions as involving tedious chores. The higher levels do not exert much influence over the lower levels; the national committee's impact is confined to the rules it enforces over the selection and seating of delegates to the national convention.

State and county chairs are the most visible and significant party officials, and they are the administrators and publicizers of the party organization. County organizations are often the strongest, largely because there are so many officials elected at the county level. (Party organizations are naturally most concerned with contests that match their geopolitical level.) Wards are smaller than counties and contain precincts. They are headed by ward leaders. Precinct chairs keep lists of voters in the precinct, identify the party affiliation of these voters, and help the voters get to the polls on election day. Precinct chairs are either elected at precinct caucuses or, in strong-party cities, appointed by ward leaders.[42]

Charles Press and Kenneth VerBurg point out that party organizations differ in how their units are organized, the names they give them, the number of officers they have, the size of the party committees, how the party selects officers and committee members, and how local affiliates are organized.[43] They also differ in how well financed they are. In 1984 over 60 percent of the state Democratic parties had budgets of under $250,000 per year, whereas only one-fourth of the Republican parties were in the same boat.[44]

Some state parties are allowed to endorse candidates in primary elections, and this can greatly increase party influence over nominations in areas where the voters take such endorsements seriously. Where allowed, formal endorsements are usually made in a convention prior to the primary. Some states make such endorsements a matter of law, while in other states they simply come under party rules. Where the law is involved, endorsed candidates reap certain benefits, such as ease in getting on the ballot or in gaining the top position on the ballot. While endorsed candidates do not always win nomination and election, endorsements usually carry electoral advantages, facilitating fund-raising and attracting volunteers who will help the campaign.[45]

Party organizations are not usually as neat as this chapter has suggested. Parties can be cohesive (rare), bifactional (party reformers may oppose the party organization, for example), or multifactional (influenced by community and interest groups). In some states, professional politicians have control; in others, average citizens do. And in some states it is a mixture of both. Party organizations that are strong at the state level might be weak at the local level. Thus parties cannot be thought of in monolithic terms. There are officeholders and office seekers (in terms of both public office and party office), activists, contributors, loyal voters who support the party in primary and general elections, and occasional supporters. The priorities and goals of these groups are not always the same. Also keep in mind that Republicans in a given state may operate differently from Democrats in the same state.

While each party level is autonomous, there are some joint activities. There is some sharing of services. There is also some financial backing from the national party. The Republican national party, having more resources to begin with, is better able to help out state parties than is the Democratic national party. Party resources are, of course, used mainly for electoral purposes; party activity dies down in nonelection years.

State parties make wide use of primary elections to nominate candidates and, to the extent that primaries are relied on, they weaken parties by robbing them of the power to choose who will represent the organization. Some states (Massachusetts, Rhode Island, Colorado, and New Mexico, among others) have offset some of the problems of primaries by using *preprimary conventions*. With this system, candidates must first compete in the party convention. The convention delegates eliminate the weakest candidates, and then decide who will be placed on the primary ballot. Delegates favor and reward party loyalty. Primary voters still cast the ballots, but some of their choices will have been made for them by the party.

The level of party competition, campaign finance regulations, and nonpartisan elections will be examined in an effort to illustrate the similarities and differences among the state parties.

Party Competition

Jewell and Olson have studied levels of party competition in the states, examining the number of years that each party controlled the governorship and the state legislatures from 1965 to 1988. They developed four categories for the states: Democratic dominant, Democratic majority, competitive two-party, and Republican majority. The Democratic dominant states are in the South, where Republicans rarely win governorships or control legislatures. Democratic majority and Republican majority states are ones where both parties contest the governorship and both normally win at least 40 percent of the vote. Only two states—New Hampshire and South Dakota—are Republican majority states. There are no Republican dominant states. Competitive two-party states include states where one party usually controls the legislature and the other party controls the governor's office; states where one party controls the legislature and where gubernatorial control is shared; and states where partisan control is balanced among the three branches.[46] States with diverse populations (large populations, with small percentages of the population living in metropolitan areas), with higher levels of education, with strong local party organizations, and with more owner-occupied homes tend to be competitive.[47] (It is important to keep a caveat in mind: measures of party competition are imperfect, especially in areas where the political climate is quickly changing.)

The South still may be classified a Democratic dominant area, but that is gradually changing. Southerners supported Republican presidential candidates in five of the eight contests since 1956, but until recently conservative Democratic officials at the state and local level were able to keep party members happy. Lately, the Republican party has succeeded in electing some governors (in Virginia in 1969, 1973, and 1977; in Tennessee in 1978 and 1982; in Texas in 1978 and 1986; and in Arkansas in 1980). Some voters are switching their affiliation from Democratic to Republican, and the South is gradually becoming more like the rest of the country.

Outside of the South, most states have substantial two-party competition. During the 1970s there was a Democratic trend (spurred in part by the Watergate scandal in 1974), but since then Republicans have shown some success in winning gubernatorial and legislative offices. Jewell and Olson say the increase in competitiveness is due to a variety of factors. Population migration helps weaken traditional party ties and encourages competition where little previously existed. The erosion of the New Deal Democratic coalition also leads to more competition. The increasing numbers of people calling themselves independents and the increasing numbers of ticket-splitters have had an impact as well.[48]

The degree of competitiveness in state party systems is important. Democracies rest, in part, on the notion that parties will be responsive to their members. Competition is one way of ensuring that responsiveness. Lack of competition can damage the legitimacy of a state electoral system. And research has shown that competitiveness has an impact on policies; competitive states tend to spend more on education and welfare benefits.[49]

Campaign Finance Regulation

Presidential elections are not the only ones where costs have skyrocketed in the past twenty years. In 1982, gubernatorial candidates in California and New York each spent more than $23 million.[50] Frank J. Sorauf found similarities in the patterns of growth for congressional candidate expenditures and for state election expenditures. Size and population help to explain the increase in costs, but Sorauf also attributes the increase to political culture: areas that are affluent, that have a voluntaristic fund-raising culture, that have a communication-centered culture, and that have a tolerance for long and expensive campaigns are the places where the increases have occurred.[51]

Campaign finance reform has not been confined to national elections; most states also changed their elections laws in the 1970s. States are required to comply with *Buckley* versus *Valeo,* which is to say that they cannot impose spending limitations on candidates unless those candidates receive public funding. Beyond this, there is a great deal of variation in how states regulate campaign finances. Herbert E. Alexander has been a pioneer in this area, and his work is greatly (but not exclusively) relied on here.[52]

All the states have disclosure laws that require reporting of contributions and expenditures. There is some variation in these rules; generally required are the names, addresses, occupations, and principal places of business of the contributors, and the amounts and dates of the contributions. States have different threshold amounts at which reporting is required. (For example, Colorado has a threshold of $25, while Louisiana's is $1,000.)[53]

Candidates are required to disclose their personal finances in thirty states.[54] While such laws can provide useful information to voters, they pose a serious problem for minor parties such as the Socialist Workers Party. Contributors to such parties fear that the information required in disclosure reports might be used to harass them. In some states lawsuits have arisen over this issue, and some exceptions have been granted to minor parties. *Buckley* versus *Valeo* provides justification for such decisions. It states that exemptions may be granted, on a case-by-case basis, if there is a reasonable probability that harassment or reprisals might result from the disclosure. Such reasoning is important in democracies that cherish competitive elections.

Contribution limits vary by state and by level of candidacy. About twenty-five states have no limits on donations. Eighteen states have relatively simple restrictions, while seven have relatively complex restrictions. States may limit contributions in terms of calendar years, in terms of two-year periods, or in terms of election periods. Some have single contribution limits that apply to campaigns for all state offices, while others have different limits for the different state offices, for party committees, and for PACs. In some states, only individuals are limited; in other states party committees and PACs are limited as well. Florida, Kansas, North Carolina, and Wyoming encourage the strengthening of parties by allowing unlimited contributions to and by party committees and by limiting contributions by individuals and PACs.[55]

Twenty-four states restrict at least some direct corporate contributions, but only ten states limit direct labor union contributions. Most states allow corporations and unions to form political action committees, which have increased at the state level as well as at the federal level.[56]

Thirty states have independent, bipartisan commissions that oversee the implementation of elections rules. Members are appointed by the governor in most of these states. The commissions receive, tabulate, and audit the required reports on campaign contributions and expenditures. Some of these commissions have the power to issue subpoenas and assess penalties. Obviously, the effectiveness of the campaign regulations depends on these agencies. The state commissions are faced with the same problem as the Federal Election Commission: With the amount of paperwork to be processed and with underfunding, they rely on filed complaints and newspaper reporting to uncover violations.[57] California, Connecticut, Florida, and New Jersey have strong enforcement records.[58]

Public funding of state elections is provided by sixteen states. Their methods for collecting and distributing the money vary. Income tax checkoffs or income tax surcharges are used to collect money. Participation is relatively low in states with a tax checkoff, even though it does not increase the amount of tax owed or decrease any refund.[59] The money is then given either to the parties or to the candidates or to both. Nine states give the money to parties. In Idaho, the parties can use this money only in the general election, not in the primaries.[60] In seven states public funding is tied to expenditure limits.[61] According to Sorauf, evidence is mixed on whether or not public funding encourages new candidates or benefits incumbents. He points out that the availability of the public funds may encourage competition, whereas the spending limits make it harder for challengers to defeat incumbents.[62]

Ruth S. Jones came to several important conclusions in her study of state public financing. Public funding does bring new money into campaigns, with Democrats receiving more public money than Republicans, since they outnumber Republicans. According to Jones, the majority party receives more than its fair share of the funds only when they are collected and allocated on the basis of party. As with other reforms, the consequences of public funding mechanisms may surprise those who initiated them.[63]

Judicial elections and their funding come under special scrutiny because of concern over judicial ethics. Judicial campaigns tend to cost less than other campaigns, with expenditures generally running to five figures, that is, not over $100,000. Funds are raised largely from the candidates and from other attorneys and law firms, with individual contributors a secondary source of funds. Some areas exhibit what Sorauf calls nonpublic regulation of campaign finance in judicial elections. The example he provides is Dade County, Florida, where the bar association raises money for a single fund, and direct contributions by lawyers to individual candidates are discouraged. The bar association then distributes funds to judicial candidates in amounts based on the association's assessment of their qualifications.[64]

As previously noted, money also is raised to support or oppose initiatives and referenda. Organized groups, particularly PACs, dominate the funding for these campaigns, some of which are quite expensive. Over $23 million was spent in campaigns for twenty-two ballot issues in California in 1980. Large expenditures are usually associated with campaigns in opposition to the suggested law.[65]

There appears to be little independent spending by individuals or groups in state and local elections. Since the states have different reporting rules, and not all require the reporting of independent expenditures, it is difficult to know for sure.[66]

Only a small amount of systematic data has been collected about local campaign financing. It appears that campaign costs have not increased at this level as much as they have for higher levels, largely because local campaigns (except in large cities) make less use of expensive technology and television ads. Hawaii, Seattle, and Tucson provide some public funding for local races. Local funding is covered, of course, by state rules and constitutions. Some states allow communities leeway in regulating local campaign financing; others do not. Sorauf describes the local fund-raising environment:

> Without very much specific regulation, attention to enforcement, or even ordinary media publicity, campaign finance in the localities probably relies to an unusual extent on very interested money. All observers seem agreed on that point. Real estate owners and developers, contractors with the city or county, downtown

commercial interests, and organized labor (especially unions of teachers and public employees) have become the classic municipal "fat cats."[67]

Thus the states as well as the national government are concerned about controlling campaign costs, about contribution disclosures and limitations, about public funding, and about PACs. A reminder: Do not let the preceding paragraphs make you forget that there is tremendous variation among the states. Generalizations here are extremely risky.

Nonpartisan Elections

Americans have a love-hate relationship with political parties. Many of us identify with and are loyal to parties, and we enjoy following partisan campaigns. At the same time, many of us view partisan politics suspiciously, fearing corruption and power elites. Our regard for "rugged individualism" leads many of us to argue that we should vote for the person, not for the party. We dislike the notion that we might take marching orders from any organization. Antiparty sentiments were prevalent during the Progressive Era, and one of the reforms inspired by that time is the use of nonpartisan elections. It was felt that nonpartisan elections (mostly used at the local level) would clean up politics, taking vested interests out of it. More than half of the 78,000 governmental units in this country are filled with persons elected in nonpartisan elections.[68]

Some of these areas have truly nonpartisan elections, while in others voters are quite aware of the party affiliations of the candidates (even though these party affiliations do not appear on the ballot). In some places, organized groups formally or informally put candidates forward for office, strengthening the role of interest groups in local politics. The use of nonpartisan elections raises a host of questions in relation to democratic theory: Do nonpartisan elections encourage participation? Do they promote a full discussion of issues? Is there a partisan or class bias in nonpartisan elections? Do they result in responsive officials? Do they provide adequate representation for the voters? All of these questions cannot be fully answered here, but an overview of these issues is provided.

Willis D. Hawley studied nonpartisan elections, and the title of his book, *Nonpartisan Elections and the Case for Party Politics,* gives his conclusion away.[69] Hawley first discusses the history of the reform movement, and shows that a middle-class and upper-middle-class bias existed among those who wanted change. The reformers were concerned about the corruption that existed in party machine city governments at the turn of the century. Hawley points out that the Progressive movement was not monolithic; he argues that municipal reformers were more conservative and elitist than were the Progressives who gave their attention to state and federal issues (and who supported child labor laws and minimum wage laws). The reformers believed that metropolitan problems were apolitical, that they could be solved with good business practices. Their focus was on efficiency in government.

In addition, many reformers believed that certain kinds of people (professionals and experts) were better suited to govern than others. These reformers were not trying to destroy one elite (those controlling the party machines) in order to supplant it with grass-roots power; they were trying to supplant the old elite with a new one. Indeed, voter turnout in nonpartisan elections is lower than turnout in partisan ones.

Elections in which the names of candidates, but not their party affiliations, are listed on the ballot—formally nonpartisan elections—gained popularity in this country in the 1920s and 1930s. Hawley found that today nonpartisan elections are most prevalent in city elections in the West and in the southern and border states, and least prevalent in the mid-Atlantic area. He also discovered that suburban areas were no more likely to have nonpartisan elections than central cities. In some states, elections for certain offices (such as city council) are partisan, while elections for other offices (school board membership or judgeships) are nonpartisan.

Hawley found that there is indeed at least a small partisan bias to nonpartisan elections:

> It has been argued that by eliminating the candidates' party affiliations from the ballot and reducing the likelihood of party activity, nonpartisan elections (a) make it more difficult for the voter to identify candidates who reflect their interests and (b) demand higher levels of interest and motivation to participate in local politics. Although these "burdens" are distributed equally throughout the population, Republicans are more likely than Democrats to deal with them successfully.[70]

Under such a system, it is the better-educated people, the upper-middle-class citizens who are more likely to participate, and these people have a tendency to be Republicans. Hawley's research showed that the degree to which Republicans benefited from nonpartisan elections varied depending on the size of the community, with the Republican bias greater in larger cities. It is interesting to note that the Democrats who win nonpartisan elections are more conservative than the Democrats in partisan elections.

There are policy consequences to this, which one would expect, given the policy differences between Democrats and Republicans. Cities with nonpartisan elections, according to Hawley, do not place the solution of social problems high on their agendas. Another interesting finding—Republicans who win partisan elections are more willing to attack social problems than Republicans who win in nonpartisan elections. Hawley argued that a partisan election encourages less conservative policies because it

> (a) facilitates political action in the face of conflict, (b) reduces the voters' vulnerability to demagoguery and enhances the political opportunities of ethnic minorities, and (c) encourages the resolution of community issues in the political arena by elected public officials.[71]

From all this, Hawley concludes that partisan politics tend to encourage the redistribution of power and resources, especially when the parties are strong and democratic. He joins other political scientists in calling for the rejuvenation of political parties.

The nonpartisan approach to government attempts to take politics out of government; this is not possible. Even in places where the parties truly take a back seat, politics is involved. It is politics of a different sort than party politics, but it is politics all the same. It can be clean or dirty, just as can partisan politics.

STATE ELECTIONS AND THE MASS MEDIA

In some ways the media environment for state and local politicians is similar to that for national politicians. Comments and actions are scrutinized by the local and regional press; candidates spend large sums to hire media consultants and design ad campaigns; many state and some local candidates even stand the expense of advertising on television. In general, new campaign techniques such as direct mail fund-raising and the use of computers have filtered down to state and local candidates, going first to those who can afford them and then gradually spreading to others as the cost of the technology has declined. That said, there is still a great deal of variation found across states and offices. For many offices at the local level, television is not an efficient means for communicating with voters; it reaches too many people who cannot vote for a particular office. Nonetheless, well-heeled candidates for such offices have been known to use television.

State government is a low-visibility topic. Readers and viewers are not terribly interested, and editors respond by letting other stories crowd state government stories out. Ambitious politicians may be stingy with the local press, while granting special interviews with *The New York Times* or other national media that take an interest. State politicians are often working with ambitious journalists as well, journalists who see state and local politics as minor league stuff. Much statehouse coverage, therefore, results from press releases.[72]

It would be logical to presume that, with the professionalization of state legislatures, with the increasing quality in governors, and with the increasing importance of the issues handled at the state level, the media would respond by improving and expanding their coverage. This has not been the case. Increased legislative activity gives reporters less time for analytical pieces or investigative stories; they are busy simply trying to keep up with legislative output. And according to Tom Littlewood, state officials are better at managing the news than they used to be. State and local politicians now know how to stage news as well as do national political figures.[73]

The problem has not been ignored. Senator Paul Simon, in his days before Congress, started a statehouse journalism internship program at Sangamon

State in Illinois. In this program, selected college graduates receive stipends of $440 a month in a postgraduate training program. Their first semester involves academic preparation, the second an internship with a statehouse bureau.[74] Such programs, unfortunately, are not the norm. As long as newspapers and news broadcasts have limited amounts of space and time, and as long as readers and viewers lack interest in state politics, stories about the subject will be few and far between.

Campaign coverage of state and local elections reflects the local political environment. Where political parties are strong, events such as endorsement meetings will receive heavy coverage. Where parties are weak, individual candidates will get a lot of play. Where the elections are nonpartisan, issues will play a special role.

The quality of local newspapers varies; there are crusading weeklies, but there are also weeklies that serve essentially as advertising forums. There are high-quality newspaper chains and low-quality chains. The quality of local television news shows also varies widely; in general they fall well below the standards of the network shows. (After all, it is at local stations where people start, where they get the experience that wins them spots at the network.) The audience for local television news, however, is huge.

SUMMARY

It remains ironic that the levels of government that affect their lives most directly receive so little of the public's attention. Incredible growth has been taking place at the gubernatorial and state legislative levels, but the public is not well informed about these changes. Interest in state and local elections is low, as is voter turnout. Low turnout takes on a special dimension in states that allow initiatives or referenda; significant issues are being decided by a minority of the citizens. Political parties exist at various levels of strength and competition, and they face the fact of nonpartisan elections in many localities. As is true for national candidates, campaigns are run in an environment involving the influences of campaign finance laws and the mass media, but the impact of these elements varies tremendously among states and campaigns.

SUGGESTED READINGS

BEYLE, THAD L., ed., *State Government: CQ's Guide to Current Issues and Activities*. Washington, DC: Congressional Quarterly. Published biennially.

CASSEL, CAROL A., "The Nonpartisan Ballot in the United States," in Bernard Grofman and Arend Lijphart, eds., *Electoral Laws and Their Consequences*. New York: Agathon Press, 1986.

CRONIN, THOMAS E., *Direct Democracy: The Politics of the Initiative, Referendum and Recall*. Cambridge, MA: Harvard University Press, 1989.

ELAZAR, DANIEL J., *American Federalism, A View From the States.* New York: Harper & Row, 1984.

HAWLEY, WILLIS D., *Nonpartisan Elections and the Case for Party Politics.* New York: John Wiley, 1973.

JEWELL, MALCOLM E., and OLSON, DAVID M., *Political Parties and Elections in American States* (3rd ed.). Chicago: The Dorsey Press, 1988.

JONES, RUTH S., "Financing State Elections," in Michael J. Malbin, ed., *Money and Politics in the United States.* Chatham, NJ: Chatham House, 1984, pp. 172–213.

———, "State Public Campaign Finance: Implications for Partisan Politics," *American Journal of Political Science* 25 (May 1981), pp. 342–361.

KENNEY, PATRICK J., and RICE, TOM W., "Party Composition in the American States: Clarifying Concepts and Explaining Changes in Partisanship Since the 1950s," *Political Behavior* 7 (1985), pp. 335–351.

KING, JAMES D., "Comparing Local and Presidential Elections," *American Politics Quarterly* 9 (July 1981), pp. 277–290.

NORAGON, JACK L., "Political Finance and Political Reform: The Experience with State Income Tax Checkoffs," *American Political Science Review* 75 (September 1981), pp. 667–687.

POMPER, GERALD M., with Susan Lederman, *Elections in America* (2nd ed.). New York: Longman, 1980, see especially Chapter 6.

SABATO, LARRY, *Goodbye to Good-time Charlie* (2nd ed.). Washington, DC: Congressional Quarterly Press, 1983.

SCHUCK, PETER H., "What Went Wrong With the Voting Rights Act," *Washington Monthly* 19 (November 1987), pp. 51–55.

DISCUSSION QUESTIONS

1. What impact do the national government and national politics have on state electoral systems?

2. Which is better, a partisan or a nonpartisan election? Why? What criteria are important in answering this question?

3. What difference does the level of party competition make in state elections?

4. Should candidates for governor and lieutenant governor run as a team?

5. Which method is best for selecting judges: election, appointment, or the Missouri Plan? Why?

6. Of the campaign finance regulations discussed, which are most necessary at the state and local level?

7. Choose a significant recent political event or personality in your state and discuss the media's performance in covering that event or personality. Be sure to point out the differences between print coverage and electronic coverage.

8. How would you describe the political culture in your state? (Include an assessment of your state's level of party competition.)

NOTES

1. Thad L. Beyle, ed., *State Government: CQ's Guide to Current Issues and Actitities, 1987–88* (Washington, DC: Congressional Quarterly, 1987), p. xvii.

2. Larry Sabato, *Goodbye to Goodtime Charlie,* 2nd ed. (Washington, DC: Congressional Quarterly Press, 1983).

3. William K. Stevens, "Governors Are Emerging as a New Political Elite," *The New York Times,* March 22, 1988, p. 8.

4. Alan Ehrenhalt, "Power Shifts in State Capitols As Professional Lawmakers Take Over Leadership Spots," *Congressional Quarterly Weekly Report* 41 (September 3, 1983), p. 1767.

5. Daniel J. Elazar, *American Federalism: A View From the States,* 3rd ed. (New York: Harper & Row, 1984), p. 110.

6. Ibid., p. 117.

7. Ibid., p. 118.

8. Robert S. Erikson, John P. McIver, and Gerald C. Wright, Jr., "State Political Culture and Public Opinion," *American Political Science Review* 81 (September 1987), pp. 797–813.

9. Material in this section draws heavily on Malcolm E. Jewell and David M. Olson, *Political Parties and Elections In American States,* 3rd ed. (Chicago: The Dorsey Press, 1988), Chapter 1.

10. Charles Press and Kenneth VerBurg, *State and Community Governments in the Federal System,* 2nd ed. (New York: John Wiley, 1983), p. 428.

11. Jewell and Olson, *Political Parties and Elections,* p. 209.

12. Ibid., p. 182.

13. Ibid., p. 183.

14. Ibid., p. 113.

15. Howard D. Hamilton, "The Municipal Voter: Voting and Nonvoting in City Elections," *American Political Science Review* 65 (December 1971), pp. 1135–1140.

16. Jewell and Olson, *Political Parties and Elections,* p. 114.

17. John J. Harrigan, *Politics and Policy in States and Communities,* 2nd ed. (Boston: Little, Brown, 1984), p. 127.

18. *Statistical Abstract of the United States, 1982–1983* (Washington, DC: U.S. Bureau of the Census, 1982), p. 488.

19. *Statistical Abstract of the United States, 1987,* 107th ed. (Washington, DC: U.S. Bureau of the Census, 1986), p. 241.

20. Jewell and Olson, *Political Parties and Elections,* p. 186.

21. Ibid., pp. 188, 190.

22. Ibid., p. 195.

23. Gerald M. Pomper with Susan S. Lederman, *Elections in America,* 2nd ed. (New York: Longman, 1980), pp. 115, 125.

24. Jewell and Olson, *Political Parties and Elections,* p. 200.

25. Ibid., p. 207.

26. James E. Campbell, "Presidential Coattails and Midterm Losses in State Legislative Elections," *American Political Science Review* 80 (March 1986), pp. 45–63.

27. Gregory A. Caldeira and Samuel C. Patterson, "Bringing Home the Votes: Electoral Outcomes in State Legislative Races," *Political Behavior* 4 (1982), p. 63.

28. Susan E. Howell, "Campaign Activities and State Election Outcomes," *Political Behavior* 4 (1982), p. 414.

29. Robert S. Lorch, *State and Local Politics: The Great Entanglement* (Englewood Cliffs, NJ: Prentice-Hall, 1983), pp. 173, 174.

30. Steven V. Roberts, "Two Parties Spend Heavily in States, With an Eye to 1991 Redistricting," *The New York Times,* October 29, 1988, p. 1. See also Tom Watson, "Drawing the Line(s) in 1990: A High-Stakes Game to Control the Legislatures," *Governing* 1 (May 1988), pp. 19–23.

31. Peverill Squire and Eric R. A. N. Smith, "The Effect of Partisan Information on Voters in Nonpartisan Elections," *Journal of Politics* 50 (February 1988), pp. 169–179.

32. David B. Magleby, "Taking the Initiative: Direct Legislation and Direct Democracy in the 1980s," *PS: Political Science & Politics* 21 (Summer 1988), pp. 600–611.

33. Michael Oreskes, "Voters in Referendums Protect the Pocketbook," *The New York Times,* November 5, 1987, p. 15.

34. "States Tackle Tough Fiscal Issues," *Intergovernmental Perspective* 5 (Winter 1979), p. 7.

35. "Recalls of Elected Officials," in Thad L. Beyle, ed., *State Government: CQ's Guide to Current Issues and Activities, 1985–86,* (Washington, DC: Congressional Quarterly, 1985), p. 28.

36. Joseph F. Zimmerman, "Populism Revived," in Thad L. Beyle, ed., *State Government: CQ's Guide to Current Issues and Activities, 1986–87* (Washington, DC: Congressional Quarterly, 1986), p. 27.

37. Andra Armstrong, "Ballot Initiatives in 1984," in Thad L. Beyle, ed., *State Government: CQ's Guide to Current Issues and Activities, 1985–86* (Washington, DC: Congressional Quarterly, 1985), p. 26.

38. Zimmerman, "Populism Revived," p. 25.

39. Ibid.

40. Magleby, "Taking the Initiative," p. 608.

41. Thomas E. Cronin, "Public Opinion and Direct Democracy," *PS: Political Science & Politics* 21 (Summer 1988) p. 613.

42. John J. Harrigan, *Politics and Policy in States and Communities,* 2nd ed. (Boston: Little, Brown, 1984), p. 134.

43. Charles Press and Kenneth VerBurg, *State and Community Governments in the Federal System,* 2nd ed. (New York: John Wiley, 1983), p. 504.

44. Jewell and Olson, *Political Parties and Elections,* p. 49.

45. Ibid., pp. 94–100.

46. Ibid., pp. 29, 30.

47. Samuel C. Patterson and Gregory A. Caldeira, "The Etiology of Partisan Competition," *American Political Science Review* 78 (September 1984), pp. 691–707.

48. Jewell and Olson, *Political Parties and Elections,* pp. 44, 45.

49. Harrigan, *Politics and Policy,* p. 139.

50. "States Strengthen Campaign Finance Laws," in Thad L. Beyle, ed., *State Government: CQ's Guide to Current Issues and Activities, 1985–86* (Washington, DC: Congressional Quarterly, 1985), p. 53.

51. Frank J. Sorauf, *Money in American Elections* (Glenview, IL: Scott, Foresman, 1988), pp. 262–264.

52. Herbert E. Alexander, *Financing Politics,* 3rd ed. (Washington, DC: Congressional Quarterly Press, 1984), Chapter 7.

53. Ibid., pp. 163, 164.

54. Ibid., p. 173.

55. Ibid., p. 165.

56. Ibid., p. 169.

57. Ibid., p. 172.

58. Sorauf, *Money in American Elections,* p. 290.

59. Alexander, *Financing Politics,* pp. 173–176.

60. Ibid., p. 176.

61. Sorauf, *Money in American Elections,* p. 275.

62. Ibid., p. 283.

63. Ruth S. Jones, "State Public Campaign Finance: Implications for Partisan Politics," *American Journal of Political Science* 25 (May 1981), pp. 342–361.

64. Sorauf, *Money in American Elections,* p. 273.

65. Ruth S. Jones, "Financing State Elections," in Michael J. Malbin, ed., *Money and Politics in the United States* (Chatham, NJ: Chatham House, 1984), pp. 209, 205.

66. Sorauf, *Money in American Elections,* p. 274.

67. Ibid., pp. 293, 294.

68. William O. Winter, *State and Local Government in a Decentralized Republic* (New York: MacMillan, 1981), p. 154.

69. Willis D. Hawley, *Nonpartisan Elections and the Case for Party Politics* (New York: John Wiley, 1973).

70. Ibid., p. 64.

71. Ibid., p. 132.

72. Charles Press and Kenneth VerBurg, *American Politicians and Journalists* (Glenview, IL: Scott, Foresman, 1988), Appendix.

73. Tom Littlewood, "Awaiting the Renaissance in Statehouse Journalism," in Thad L. Beyle, ed., *State Government: CQ's Guide to Current Issues and Activities, 1986–87* (Washington, DC: Congressional Quarterly, 1986), pp. 75–78.

74. Ibid., p. 77.

Into the
Twenty-First
Century

REALIGNMENT

Elections are the key components of democracy. Their results have important consequences in terms of both political culture and government policies. The term *party system* is used to describe an era when one party dominates national politics and policies, and when it possesses allegiance from a majority of voters. (Such a party is termed the *majority party* since it has the loyalty of a majority of Americans.) The existence of these party systems and the process by which we change from one party system to another are the subjects of this chapter. We begin with more definitions.

The notion of a party system is very much tied to party identification in the electorate. Recall from Chapter 7 that political scientists developed a concept known as the *normal vote* to describe the situation that would exist if all Democrats in a presidential election voted for the Democratic nominee, and all Republicans voted for the Republican nominee.[1] For example, if Democrats outnumbered Republicans 55 percent to 45 percent in party identification, then the Democrats would win the election by a fifty-five to forty-five margin if there were a "normal vote." In reality, this never happens. Some Democrats will vote for the Republican nominee, and vice versa. (And some party identifiers will not vote at all.) The major way of classifying elections is by comparing the actual vote results with the "normal vote." The party with the most identifiers during a party system is called the majority party. (This is a bit confusing. Ours is essentially a two-party system, and we call the Democratic and Republican parties "major parties" to distinguish them from the various minor parties that attract little support. But of the two major parties, one has more support than the other at any given time and is called the "majority party.")

A *maintaining election* is one where actual vote results closely resemble the normal vote, an election where the reigning party in power retains its status (the election of 1940, for example, when the Democrats and Franklin D. Roosevelt were returned to the White House). A *deviating election* is one where voters abandon the majority party at the presidential level, but support it in terms of state and local offices and party identification. (The elections of 1952 and 1956 are examples, when Republican Dwight Eisenhower was elected.) This abandonment of the majority party is temporary, with voters returning to the fold after one or two elections. (As voters did in 1960, electing Democrat John Kennedy.) An election that returns the majority party to the White House after a deviating election (such as the elections of 1960 and 1976) is called a *reinstating election*. Maintaining, deviating, and reinstating elections take place within a single party system. In the examples above, the party system is that of the Democratic New Deal coalition.

When one party system is replaced with another, it is called a *realigning election,* or a realignment. In 1932, for example, a Republican party system was brought to an end when Franklin Roosevelt defeated Republican incumbent Herbert Hoover. The Republican party went from being the majority party to being the minority party, and the Democratic party did the opposite. The resulting realignment brought major changes to our political way of life. Our political culture, spurred by the Great Depression, changed from one that avoided government involvement in matters of social welfare to one that encouraged it. From this realignment came policy results including the Social Security program for retirement and the regulation of the stock market through the Securities and Exchange Commission—activities that before had been private matters became matters of government policy.

Realignments correspond to the party systems described in Chapter 1. The first party system lasted until 1824. During this period American political parties were created, and a two-party pattern was established. Parties were made up of politicians who saw themselves as political amateurs who were happy to serve a term in office and then go back to their private lives.[2] However, the party in power, the Federalist party, was unresponsive to public opinion, and was dead by the 1820s. In the second party system, Andrew Jackson's Democrats fought with the Whigs, a loose coalition united largely by their opposition to Jackson.[3] The second party system collapsed in 1860, in part because of its failure to come to grips with the slavery issue. During the third party system, Democrats were strong in the South, while Republicans controlled the East and the West. Midwestern farmers began to feel their interests were not being represented adequately by the political parties, and formed organizations including the Granger movement, the Farmers' Alliance, and eventually the Populist party to argue their case.[4] These developments, and an economic panic in 1893, encouraged a breakdown of the third party system in 1896. Republicans and Democrats remained the major parties, but the important issues, and the groups supporting each party, changed. The Republican party dominated politics during this period, except in the South. The fourth party system lasted until the Great Depression and the election of 1932. Franklin Roosevelt was elected president, and the Democratic party gained majority status, which it has retained more or less until today.

What causes realigning elections? Scholars are not in total agreement. Generally speaking, realignments occur when a new *issue* arises, or an old issue is redefined, in such a way as to cut across existing party lines. The parties respond by polarizing, taking opposing, clear-cut positions on the issue. This results in changes in the images of the parties as perceived by the voters. Another way to put this is to say that a new issue cuts across the issue that dominated the old party system. In 1896, the issue was the silver standard versus the gold standard; it had surpassed the slavery issue, which had been the dominant concern in electoral politics in 1860.

Voter turnout in realigning elections is high, and another cause of realignment is *mobilization,* the participation of citizens who heretofore had not voted in elections.[5] There is evidence that many such nonparticipants were brought into the system in 1932, and they voted for the Democratic party. A possible contribution to realignment is *conversion,* Republicans changing their party identification and their votes to Democratic, or vice versa. But there is little evidence that conversion takes place on a scale large enough to produce realignment.[6]

A possible factor in some realignments is *generational change.* The generation that comes of political age during a realignment is likely to remain quite loyal to the majority party. Their children will be somewhat loyal; their grandchildren will be much less so. By the time the grandchildren reach political age, the issues that defined the realignment are likely to have faded, to have less salience. Also, the values of the grandchildren may be different from those of their grandparents. In such cases, the weakness in party loyalties makes it easier for one party to supplant the other.[7]

Still another factor associated with realignments is the presence of *leadership* able to steer the political system through the turbulence. The 1932 realignment would not have been so significant without Roosevelt. A related factor is the ability of the status quo leaders to resist change.

One of the hallmarks of realignment is the presence of *minor-party activity* preceding the critical election. Voters unhappy with the major parties seek leadership elsewhere, as they did, for example, with the Populist party in the third party system. The major parties co-opted many Populist principles, and the Populist party died.

We have seen that realignments have occurred about once every 35 years. According to this pattern, we were due for a realignment in the late 1960s. Most political scientists agree that this realignment did not occur. One explanation for the lack of dramatic change has to do with changes in party identification. Recall that more and more people called themselves independents in the 1970s and 1980s. The entire scheme of classifying elections according to party systems is meaningful only when party identification matters to most voters. The greater the number of independents, the less useful is the normal vote concept. Independents now make up almost one-third of the electorate. Not all of these independents vote, but enough of them do to throw off predictions of election outcomes that are based on Democratic and Republican identifiers. And the independent vote can be crucial in close elections.

Political scientists have coined the term *dealignment* to describe an era where parties are not very meaningful, where issue voting and ticket-splitting are high, where one party does not retain the White House very long. During these times the parties are not polarized around crucial issues (or at least are not polarized in a way that is meaningful to voters). In a period of dealignment, the electorate is volatile, splitting tickets and bouncing from one party to the other in its presidential vote. Many political scientists believe that the current era is a period of dealignment.[8] Remember that many voters now cast retrospective votes; that is, in making their voting decisions, they examine the past record of the candidates and decide on that basis whom to support. If they approve of a nominee's past record, they vote for that candidate, regardless of party affiliation. If retrospective judgments are important, and party identification unimportant, then the concept of the normal vote is next to useless, and realignment unlikely.

But there is a great deal of controversy over these terms and definitions, particularly the definition of realignment. In the next section, we examine the different approaches taken by political scientists who attempt to explain the current volatility that exists in the American electorate.

REALIGNMENT CONTROVERSIES

Some scholars stress the importance of which groups support each party.[9] In this sense, realignment occurs when core groups that support one party switch to the other party. If the changes balance each other out, no realignment occurs. But if the changes are lopsided, favoring the out party over the majority party, realignment does occur. (Group support also is important in distinguishing deviating elections from realignments. If groups happen to vote against their party in a given election, but retain allegiance to their party in the long run, it is a deviating election. If groups vote against their party, and remain against their party in the long run, it is a realignment.) To other scholars, the influx of new voters, a "surge," could also count as a realignment, even if all the new voters support the same party, even if the party they support is the continuing majority party.

The notion of realigning elections first arose in the writings of political scientist V. O. Key, who called them "critical elections." He used the term *secular realignment* to describe important changes that took place over time, over a series of years instead of in one presidential election.[10] A gradual drift of groups from one party to another occurs in a secular realignment. Some political scientists argued that a realignment is something that takes place relatively suddenly; the big change occurs and then it is over, a new party system is in power. Such realignments are easy to identify. But secular realignments bring up all sorts of complex questions. When do they begin? When do they end? How can you tell if you happen to be in the middle of one? Research indicates that the 1932 critical election is more accurately described as a secular realignment.[11] The electorate quickly switched to Democrats at the presidential level, but changes in party identification at the state and local level were years in arriving, in part because the state and local Democratic parties were different from, and less attractive than, the national Roosevelt-led Democratic party.[12]

The idea of secular realignments presents the notion that it is best to think of party systems in terms of phases. A realignment occurs, a new party system begins, goes through adjustments, and finally enters a period of decline or decay before the next realignment.[13] It makes sense that during a secular realignment certain elections would signal the coming change in the electorate. Gerald M. Pomper has added to the lexicon of elections by naming those elections where the nature of party support changes but the majority party remains in power *converting elections*. Pomper cites 1836, 1896, 1960, and 1964 as converting elections.[14] Realignments did not occur in these years, but election results showed that the party system was not running smoothly.

Finally, there is a great deal of controversy as to why the political system did not experience a realignment in the late 1960s. Whether or not we are in the midst of a secular realignment favoring the Republicans is another question. Or are we entrenched in dealignment? The next section addresses these issues.

ARE WE EXPERIENCING DEALIGNMENT?

Issues

Have new issues arisen that divide the groups supporting the Democrats and Republicans in new ways? Have the parties polarized on these issues? According to James L. Sundquist, three major issues dominated the 1960s and 1970s: racial strife, the Vietnam War, and crime. In addition, many young people rebelled against their elders, and women and homosexuals became aware of the need to organize to protect their rights. Social issues that formed around these interests became increasingly important in politics. Did the parties polarize around these issues? According to Sundquist, they did not.[15]

Sundquist points out that until late 1967, both parties supported the war in Vietnam, and by the time the Democrats started moving against the war, the Republicans were going in the same direction. Thus the parties did not stake out opposite positions on the war; they did not polarize. The problems relating to civil rights, ghetto crime, antiwar protests, and welfare were tangled together, all fitting under the rubric of the "law and order" issue. But voters were not of a single mind on these problems. One could be in favor of a crackdown on ghetto crime but also strongly in favor of protests against the Vietnam War, for example. As Sundquist put it, "Not all of the elements of the [law and order] issue cut across the electorate on the same axis."[16] The issue was too diffuse to allow polarized political groupings. While these issues were of great import, and shook up the New Deal coalition, they did not facilitate realignment.

The Watergate scandal brought down President Nixon, and made things difficult for Republican candidates temporarily, but the scandal was more damaging to Nixon personally than to his party. The ability of the Republicans to bounce back and win the presidency by large margins in 1980, 1984, and 1988 certainly proves that the Watergate scandal was not a realigning issue favoring the Democrats.[17] It is possible that the Watergate scandal disrupted an ongoing secular realignment that will eventually benefit the Republicans, but it was not a realigning issue. Neither is the abortion issue. While Republican platforms support the right-to-life position, and while Democratic platforms support the pro-choice stance, pro-choice and right-to-life advocates are found in both parties. In order for this issue to have a polarizing effect, pro-choice advocates would have to support one party, and right-to-life advocates the other. As Sundquist writes,

> Potent as the crosscutting issues have proved to be, they appear to lack the power to supplant the New Deal party system with a new one organized on a different rationale, along a new line of cleavage, and with a new definition of the party conflict. Separately, no one of the crosscutting issues is sufficient; none is of the magnitude of the great issues that brought about the major realignments of the past—slavery in the 1850s, free silver in the 1890s, or response to the hardships of the Great Depression in the 1930s.[18]

Did the popularity of Ronald Reagan signal a shift in attitudes that could lead to realignment? In the 1980s, the Republican party began stressing moral issues: prayer in the schools and an anti-abortion amendment. It also promoted supply-side economics. Again, the answer is no. Studies show that, while Reagan himself was quite popular, support for the Reagan agenda was not high. In 1980 most voters favored slightly more conservative economic policies than those under the Carter administration, but people voted for Reagan in spite of their doubts about supply-side economics, not because of their faith in it. According to Kathleen A. Frankovich,

> The voters supported Reagan on two issues and disagreed with him on two others. They agreed that the United States should be more forceful in its dealings with the Soviet Union, even at the risk of war, and agreed, as Republicans traditionally have argued, that inflation was more important than unemployment. But, unlike Reagan, the electorate supported the Equal Rights Amendment, and disagreed with him about the Reagan-Kemp-Roth 30 percent tax cut.[19]

Nearly two-fifths of the Reagan voters said that their main reason for choosing Reagan was that "it was time for a change," hardly an ideological validation of Reagan's proposals.[20] Not only was there little support for a conservative agenda, enthusiasm for the services provided by big government remained high.

Economic issues were more important to the electorate than social issues; in 1980 more than three-fourths of those polled mentioned economic issues as the most important problems facing the country.[21] The Republicans suffered in the 1982 midterm elections because of a recession. By 1984, the economy had recovered from its 1982 slump, and the vote for Reagan was in large part a positive retrospective judgment on his handling of the economy. On most of the social or moral issues, a majority of voters still were more liberal than Reagan. For example, exit polls taken on election day 1984 showed that two-thirds favored continued legalization of abortion, and a *Los Angeles Times* survey found that only 23 percent of those polled supported a constitutional amendment to ban abortion.[22] In addition, Reagan (and, to some extent, the Republican party) suffered from what became known as the "fairness issue" because of a sense that Reagan was unconcerned about the elderly, the poor, and the handicapped.

At least one political scientist, Walter Dean Burnham, believes that it is

SOURCE: Wasserman, Los Angeles Times Syndicate. Copyright 1988. Reprinted with permission.

possible that the policies of the Reagan years, if continued by his successors, might have the polarizing effect other issues have not had. Burnham argues that Reagan's policies—"from numerous Supreme Court appointments, to regressive consumption taxes, to a budget-balancing amendment, and beyond"— amounted to a declaration of "class, racial, and gender warfare," the effect of which is "inevitably polarizing."[23] Not all political scientists agree.[24]

Thus we see that the issues of the last twenty-eight years have not yet polarized the electorate or the parties. The 1988 presidential election certainly did not produce such polarization; it was marked by an avoidance of the discussion of serious issues. For the most part, both parties have maintained positions in the middle of the political spectrum. Issues are important to voters, and there is more and more congruence between the positions on the issues of the voters and the positions on the issues of the candidates they support. But voters have been fickle as to which party they want to trust. Answers to the question of which party is best able to handle the most important problem facing the country have gone back and forth between the Republican party and the Democratic party during recent elections.[25] As far as issues go, dealignment describes this period.

Party Identification and Voting Behavior

Return to Chapter 3 and reexamine Table 3-1, "Party Identification in the Nation." If one combines weak partisans with strong partisans, one sees that in 1986 the Democrats outnumbered the Republicans 40 percent to 25 percent in party identification. While the percentage of independents has leveled off since 1976, party loyalties have not exhibited the kind of shift necessary to say that the nation has undergone a realignment. The Democrats still are the majority party in terms of party identification. The high percentage of independents, especially among the young (see Table 3-2), indicates that change certainly *could* occur. Should these independents be mobilized to become Democrats, Republicans, or some new party, it could be the beginning of realignment. So far that has not happened.[26] In 1988, voter turnout went down, not up. Approximately 27 percent of those eligible voted for Bush, the lowest percentage to elect a president in this century (in a two-man race).[27]

But the New Deal coalition has been weakened, as a reexamination of Table 4-1, "Change in Support for Democratic Party, 1964–1980," illustrates. Except for blacks and union members, the groups in the coalition show unsteady, often declining levels of support for the party in terms of votes cast. Many of the people in these groups still consider themselves Democrats, but they do not always vote for Democratic candidates, especially at the presidential level. Thus while the New Deal coalition has not fallen apart, it is unstable and ripe for realignment, should other factors (such as polarizing issues and a strong Republican leadership) fall into place. The discussion in Chapter 4 of the *Times-Mirror* study, which suggests that the electorate is fragmenting into at least eleven groups, also shows that the old Republican-Democrat division of the electorate is less meaningful than in the past.

While some of the New Deal groups are supporting the Democrats less fervently, one group is stronger than ever. For the Democratic nominee in 1984, the black vote was 90 percent.[28] Black support fell in 1988, but was still high at 86 percent.[29] But another way of looking at the strong support Democrats get from blacks (and from women) is to argue that it illustrates the loss of white male support the party has experienced. And there are some indications that young blacks are less committed to the Democratic party than older blacks.[30]

The election of 1984 also shows that the change the Republicans have been waiting for may be on the way. During the fall of 1984, polls began showing that the GOP was closing the gap in party identification.[31] The only groups that did not experience a loss of Democratic identifiers were blacks and the unemployed. Also, the percentage of independents voting Democratic declined to 27 percent among whites in general, and to 27 percent for whites under thirty years of age. For those aged eighteen to twenty-nine, 30 percent identified with the Democrats, but 42 percent identified with Republicans.[32] It is possible that this trend will be temporary, reflecting the personal popularity of President Reagan. If it is permanent, then the Republicans will have made important gains. Such gains could feed a generational secular realignment. A series of surveys commissioned by the CBS/*New York Times* in 1980, 1984, and 1988 provide data that address this question. The conclusion reached by E. J. Dionne, Jr., is that

> young people have decidedly shifted their allegiances to the Republicans' benefit. In 1980, Democrats outnumbered Republicans among voters under thirty years old by a margin of two-to-one. Now, the parties are virtually even.[33]

While Republicans have been gaining identifiers, though, the percentage of people describing themselves as *strong* Republicans has not increased in the 1980s. In fact, in 1986 this percentage dropped to 10 percent, the lowest level in decades.[34] And the Republicans' relative weakness among women voters continued in 1988. While 54 percent of male voters chose Bush, only 47 percent of female voters made the same choice.[35]

The Republican party has suffered from the Iran-contra scandal. In October 1986, a CBS/*New York Times* poll showed that 33 percent of the respondents said they probably would vote for the Republican nominee in 1988, and that 32 percent would vote for the Democratic nominee. By January 1987, after people had time to absorb the facts of the arms-for-hostages trade, only 27 percent said they would vote for the Republican nominee, and 39 percent said they would vote for the Democrat.[36] This Democratic lead was, of course, wiped out during the presidential campaign.

In the South, realignment has occurred. The old "Solid South," the solidly Democratic South, is no more. As has been well documented, the South is far more competitive now than in 1960.[37] A 1984 Gallup poll showed that 40 percent of whites in the South identified with the Republican party, and an ABC News exit poll found that 61 percent of all southern voters believed the GOP would better handle the nation's problems. Half of Republican gains in the U.S. House of Representatives came from the South. In 1984, Republicans added four seats in Texas, three in North Carolina, and one in Georgia. They gained a governorship in North Carolina as well. In Texas, the Republicans were also successful at the state legislature level, going from thirty-seven to fifty-three seats in the 150-member body.[38]

With increased education and readily available information about politics, fewer voters are blindly following their party and voting straight tickets. The ability of the Republican party to win five out of the past seven presidential elections has fostered what some call a *"split-level" realignment;* that is to say, at the presidential level, we have experienced a realignment favoring the Republican party, while at the congressional, state, and local levels we have not.[39] In 1984 the number of states with split partisan control (the governor being of one party, the legislature controlled by the other party) reached the highest level since the 1850s, twenty-seven states out of forty-nine.[40] (Nebraska's legislature is nonpartisan.)

This split-level pattern is so secure that some pundits speak of the Republican party having a "lock" on the Electoral College. Republican support in the West (including California), the South (including Texas), and the Midwest is strong enough that, with an attractive Republican candidate, it is difficult for the Democrats to collect enough electoral votes for victory. In each of the elections from 1972 through 1984, the Republicans carried twenty-three states each time, with electoral votes totaling 202 out of the 270 needed to win.[41] According to the *National Journal,* from 1964 through 1984, the Democratic nominee averaged more than 55 percent of the vote in only Massachusetts, Rhode Island, and the District of Columbia. The electoral votes of these states add up to twenty, hardly impressive. New York, Hawaii, Minnesota, and West Virginia averaged over 50 percent for Democratic candidates in these elections, and were won by the Democrats in four. These states control fifty-six electoral votes. Assuming that all these states will continue to support the Democratic party, the Democrats have a base of only seventy-six electoral votes.[42]

Post-1984 election studies show that, in comparison with 1980, the Democrats gained slightly in the West, among non-southern whites, and among Catholics. The Democrats made a leap in increased support among Jews, who had been uneasy with the Carter administration's approach to Israel. The party also gained a little with the thirty to fifty-nine age group.[43]

Rhodes Cook, writing in *Congressional Quarterly Weekly Report,* pointed out that to win in 1988 the Democrats would have to carry some states where Democratic candidates have not been popular for a generation.[44] He noted that the large electoral vote states of California, Illinois, and New Jersey have not voted Democratic since the days of Lyndon Johnson. This pattern continued in 1988.

But matters are not completely bleak for the Democrats. They still are strong in the Northeast; the party carried Maryland and Pennsylvania five and four times, respectively, between 1964 and 1984.[45] (They lost these states in 1988.) And Republican strength in the Midwest has suffered as farmers met with hard times. There also are signs of a Democratic upsurge in the West. In 1988, Dukakis won Oregon and Washington, and received 47 percent of the vote or more in California, New Mexico, and Montana.[46] Many of the states captured by Republicans in recent elections were won by slim margins: In 1976 Gerald Ford won California by 1.7 percentage points, Illinois by 2 percentage points, and Oregon by two-tenths of 1 percent.[47] Such close elections, and the Dukakis victory in Oregon, suggest it would not take much for the Democrats to win these states again.

A *New York Times* editorial put the math of the Electoral College into perspective, reminding us that the "lock" theory overlooks political realities.[48] Good candidates and economic conditions have helped the Republicans. Changes in the economy and good candidates can help the Democrats. The Democratic party experienced a surge in identification after Lyndon Johnson's 1964 landslide, but the Republicans won the White House four years later. Given retrospective voting habits, and the desire of many in the electorate to vote for the person and not for the party, there is no reason why states which have voted Republican in the past must continue to do so.

This examination of party identification and voting behavior leaves us with a mixed message. The Democratic party is still the majority party, but it is vulnerable. The Republicans can be heartened by their popularity with the young, and by their gains in the South. The picture is blurred because there is a growth in the proportion of people who change their party identification as their candidate preferences change.[49] ("If I support Reagan this year, I must be a Republican.") The picture might be clearer if voter turnout in presidential elections was high.

Minor-Party Activity

Since 1960 there has been a tremendous variety of minor parties, parties which have nominated candidates for president. These include a Peace and Freedom party, a Right to Life party, a Consumer party, a Libertarian party, and others. George C. Wallace's American Independent party had some success, especially in the South in 1968. And John Anderson's independent candidacy in 1980 illustrated the frustration that many felt with the major parties and their candidates. These efforts faded quickly when Wallace and Anderson were no longer candidates for president. None of these minor parties yet has had the kind of appeal that truly threatens the major parties.

Leadership

It is safe to argue that most of the presidential leadership provided since 1960 has not been of the quality to spark or to encourage realignment.[50] Our leaders have failed to deal with current issues in a way facilitating polarization.

Reagan successfully imposed his budgetary agenda on the country, and his personal popularity drew many voters into the Republican fold. This can lead to realignment if (1) the voters Reagan attracted to the GOP decide to remain with the party now that Reagan is no longer president, and (2) Republican presidents who share his forceful leadership follow Reagan. The 1980 election was largely a rejection of Carter; the 1984 election showed support for Reagan in his own right. But with many voters disagreeing with the Republican positions on issues other than the economy, it will take more than just a popular president to bring about a realignment favorable to the Republicans.

Conclusion

It appears that the answer is yes; dealignment describes what has been going on in our political system better than realignment. This does not mean that the Republican party will never again be the majority party. It simply has not happened yet. A number of possibilities exist. The electorate could continue to lose faith in parties; many could continue to not vote; the volatility in the electorate could remain. In other words, we could continue to experience dealignment for some time. It may be that the New Deal party system has become so institutionalized that it resists realignment.[51] New Deal policies such as Social Security offer rewards to voters that they do not wish to give up. Recall the high reelection rates for Senators and House members. It is extremely difficult to vote out congressional incumbents, more so than in past party systems. Such an entrenchment could mean that prolonged dealignment is necessary before we can change to a new system.

Or, the Democratic party could go through a resurgence. An issue might come along that polarizes the Democrats and Republicans, and those Democrats who have been voting for Republican candidates for president could decide to come back to the Democratic fold. Or, the issue could favor the Republicans and make them the majority. One possible such polarizing issue is race. The Reverend Jesse Jackson's campaigns in 1984 and 1988, and the 1988 Willie Horton ads, serve to remind the electorate that the United States has unfinished business where race is concerned.[52] Or, a new party could rise to prominence. But the drift we have been experiencing need not last forever. Indeed, it might be merely a phase in a secular realignment.

THE FUTURE OF THE TWO-PARTY SYSTEM

Sidney Blumenthal calls the new style of presidential politics the "permanent campaign."[53] His thesis is that political consultants have replaced party bosses as the connection between politicians and voters. As parties have declined, consultants have taken over, and the result is a never-ending campaign; each political task becomes an opportunity to mold an image, to produce the right "sound bite," to incur favor with a fickle electorate. Blumenthal argues that the permanent campaign "remakes government into an instrument designed to sustain an elected official's public popularity. It is the engineering of consent with a vengeance."[54] It depends heavily on the mass media and polling for its existence. But the popularity of particular candidates or presidents cannot sustain a party system.

Burnham sees the permanent campaign as transitional. He wrote:

> The "permanent campaign" can and does elect people, but it cannot and does not give them the power to govern with the kind of coherence and cross-institutional will that effective state action will come to require. Accordingly, something must happen to the elections themselves, and to the role of the citizenry. Either both will have to be practically eliminated, insofar as any major influence on "serious politics" at the center is concerned, or they will have to be revitalized. The first will require some form of dictatorship, naked or more probably veiled with a strong demogogic, Bonapartist flavor. The second would require not only a vast revitalization of party, but the development of sharply focused political alternatives and the reinvolvement of the public at large in deciding what the fundamental business of American society is to be all about.[55]

But the future looks bright for parties in the United States. As Burnham notes, the parties *are* being revitalized. Undeniably, they went through a rough period, but then so did the country. Few institutions were left unmarked by the upheavals of the 1960s and 1970s. Some people lost faith in parties; some wanted more control over the presidential nomination system; some refused to participate in electoral politics; some revised our system of campaign finance; and some have worked hard to revive and rebuild the parties as organizations.

As we have seen, the Republican party was the first to start the rebuilding, out of necessity. After the resignations of President Nixon and Vice President Agnew, the party hit an all-time low in terms of popularity. It is a tribute to the two-party system that the GOP did not wither away. Instead, it fought, it organized, it raised and spent money, it pioneered new campaign techniques, and it came back strong.

There is no reason to believe that the Democrats cannot respond in a similar fashion to their own post-Reagan predicament; indeed they are well on their way.[56] In 1988, the Democrats were able to overcome some of their past fund-raising problems. Nominee Michael Dukakis was well funded almost from the beginning of his campaign, and the party collected $4.8 million in donations in June and July of 1988 alone.[57]

The percentage of persons seeing significant differences between the two major parties had increased from 46 to 50 percent in the 1952–1976 period. This figure had further increased to 63 percent in 1984.[58] The major parties are exhibiting greater ideological differences than they have in years.[59] Strong conservatives control the Republican party. The Democrats nominated an old-fashioned liberal in 1984, and, although some elements of the Democratic party argued for a move toward the center in 1988 and while nominee Michael

Dukakis was not the most liberal of the contenders, the influence of Jesse Jackson's liberal agenda on the party was pervasive. Increased ideological voting could break up old regional or ethnic cleavages in the electorate; it might revive interest in campaigns and increase voter turnout. Warren E. Miller discovered that, among younger, college-educated voters, there is a realignment along ideological lines, with liberals joining the Democratic party and conservatives the Republican party.[60]

Political parties in the United States have always been adaptable, and they are finding ways to adjust to new conditions. The use of computers, professional consultants, and the mass media have reduced the need for volunteers in campaigns. This is unfortunate in that it reduces the connection between parties and citizens at the most basic level. But it is inevitable, given that both spouses work in most families today. The pool of people available to volunteer is thus smaller than it once was. Door-to-door canvassing does not always make sense; fewer people are at home to talk to the canvassers. Whether we like it or not, the media are a good way to reach voters. Xandra Kayden and Eddie Mahe, Jr. predict that both major parties will have their own cable networks.[61] (Each party produced convention programs for cable in 1988.) Such a development would surely improve the ability of the parties to communicate with and to educate the electorate. It might even help them balance out the influence of the major network and print media.

Parties may never be as popular with the public as they were in their heyday, but the two-party system will survive. It is intertwined with our political institutions and our political culture. It is inextricably interwoven with our definition of democracy.

SUGGESTED READINGS

ABRAMSON, PAUL R., *Generational Change in American Politics*. Lexington, MA: D.C. Heath, 1975.
ABRAMSON, PAUL R., JOHN H. ALDRICH, and DAVID W. ROHDE, *Change and Continuity in the 1984 Elections* (revised ed.). Washington, DC: Congressional Quarterly Press, 1987.
BARNES, JAMES A., "Tuned-Out Turnout," *National Journal* 20 (July 2, 1988), pp. 1743–1747.
BURNHAM, WALTER DEAN, *Critical Elections and the Mainspring of American Politics*. New York: W.W. Norton, 1970.
———, *The Current Crisis in American Politics*. New York: Oxford University Press, 1982.
———, "The Eclipse of the Democratic Party," *Society* 21 (July/August 1984), pp. 5–11.
CAMPBELL, BRUCE A., and RICHARD J. TRILLING, eds., *Realignment in American Politics: Toward a Theory*. Austin, TX: University of Texas Press, 1980.
CHUBB, JOHN E., and PAUL E. PETERSON, eds., *The New Direction in American Politics*. Washington, DC: The Brookings Institution, 1985.
CLUBB, JEROME M., WILLIAM H. FLANIGAN, and NANCY H. ZINGALE, *Partisan Realignment: Voters, Parties, and Government in American History*. Beverly Hills, CA: Sage, 1980.
COOK, RHODES, "Despite Gains in Some Groups, Democrats Still Have Far to Go," *Congressional Quarterly Weekly Report* 46 (December 3, 1988), pp. 3442–3443.
FERGUSON, THOMAS, and JOEL ROGERS, *Right Turn: The Decline of the Democrats and the Future of American Politics*. New York: Hill and Wang, 1986.
KAYDEN, XANDRA, and EDDIE MAHE, JR., *The Party Goes On*. New York: Basic Books, 1985.

Ladd, Everett Carll, "The Brittle Mandate: Electoral Dealignment and the 1980 Presidential Election," *Political Science Quarterly* 96 (Spring 1981), pp. 1–25.

———, "On Mandates, Realignments, and the 1984 Election," *Political Science Quarterly* 100 (Spring 1985), pp. 1–25.

———, *Where Have All the Voters Gone?* (2nd ed.). New York: W.W. Norton, 1982.

Lawrence, David G., and Richard Fleisher, "Puzzles and Confusions: Political Realignment in the 1980s," *Political Science Quarterly* 102 (Spring 1987), pp. 79–92.

Lipset, Seymour Martin, *Party Coalitions in the 1980s*. San Francisco: Institute for Contemporary Studies, 1981.

Maisel, Louis, and Joseph Cooper, eds., *The Impact of the Electoral Process*. Beverly Hills, CA: Sage, 1977.

Pomper, Gerald M., "The Decline of the Party in American Elections," *Political Science Quarterly* 92 (Spring 1977), pp. 21–41.

Sabato, Larry J., *The Party's Just Begun*. Glenview, IL: Scott, Foresman, 1988.

Sundquist, James L., *Dynamics of the Party System* (revised ed.). Washington, DC: The Brookings Institution, 1983.

Wattenberg, Martin P., "The Hollow Realignment, Partisan Change in a Candidate-Centered Era," *Public Opinion Quarterly* 51 (Spring 1987), pp. 58–74.

———, *The Decline of American Political Parties, 1952–1984*. Cambridge, MA: Harvard University Press, 1986.

DISCUSSION QUESTIONS

1. Check the *Gallup Report, Public Opinion* magazine, *Public Opinion Quarterly* or a newspaper for stories on party identification. What is the current balance between Republicans and Democrats, and how does it compare with the voting returns for the presidential election of 1988?

2. What is the division of Democrats and Republicans in your county? (Check with your local board of elections.)

3. What situation do you feel describes the current state of affairs:

   a) Pro-Republican realignment (regular or secular)

   b) Dealignment

   c) Continuing Democratic party system

4. Do you believe that an issue (or issues) will emerge in the next few years that will provide a catalyst for realignment? If so, what issue do you think might accomplish this?

5. What are the strengths and the weaknesses of the Republican and the Democratic parties?

6. What are the prospects for the emergence of a new major party?

NOTES

1. Angus Campbell, Philip Converse, Warren Miller, and Donald Stokes, *The American Voter* (New York: John Wiley, 1960).

2. L. Sandy Maisel, *Parties and Elections in America: The Electoral Process* (New York: Random House, 1987), p. 31.

3. Ibid., pp. 32, 33.

4. Ibid., p. 39.

5. Kristi Andersen, *The Creation of a Democratic Majority: 1928–1936* (Chicago: University of Chicago Press, 1979).

6. Helmut Norpoth, "Under Way and Here to Stay, Party Realignment in the 1980s?" *Public Opinion Quarterly* 51 (Fall 1987), pp. 376–391.

7. See Paul R. Abramson, *Generational Change in American Politics* (Lexington, MA: Lexington Books, 1975); Paul Allen Beck, "A Socialization Theory of Partisan Realignment," in Richard G. Niemi, ed., *The Politics of Future Citizens* (San Francisco: Jossey-Bass, 1974), pp. 199–219; M. Kent Jennings and Richard G. Niemi, *The Political Character of Adolescence* (Princeton, NJ: Princeton University Press, 1974); Jennings and Niemi, *Generations and Politics* (Princeton, NJ: Princeton University Press, 1981); and Norpoth, "Under Way and Here to Stay."

8. See Norman H. Nie, Sidney Verba, and John R. Petrocik, *The Changing American Voter* (Cambridge, MA: Harvard University Press, 1976); Helmut Norpoth and Jerrold Rusk, "Partisan Dealignment in the American Electorate: Itemizing the Deductions Since 1964," *American Political Science Review* 76 (September 1982), pp. 522–537; Everett Carll Ladd, *Where Have All the Voters Gone?* 2nd ed. (New York: W.W. Norton, 1982).

9. See John R. Petrocik, *Party Coalitions: Realignments and the Decline of the New Deal Party System* (Chicago: University of Chicago Press, 1981).

10. V. O. Key, Jr., "A Theory of Critical Elections," *Journal of Politics* 17 (February 1955), pp. 3–18.

11. Andersen, *The Creation of a Democratic Majority*.

12. James L. Sundquist, *Dynamics of the Party System*, revised ed. (Washington, DC: The Brookings Institution, 1983), Chapter 11.

13. Jerome M. Clubb, William H. Flanigan, and Nancy H. Zingale, *Partisan Realignment: Voters, Parties and Government in American History* (Beverly Hills, CA: Sage, 1980), Chapter 1.

14. Gerald M. Pomper with Susan S. Lederman, *Elections in America,* 2nd ed. (New York: Longman, 1980), p. 92.

15. Sundquist, *Dynamics of the Party System,* Chapter 17. See also Richard J. Trilling, *Party Image and Electoral Behavior* (New York: John Wiley, 1976).

16. Ibid., p. 384.

17. See Robert G. Lehnen, "Realignment and Short-Term Crisis: A Case Study of Public Opinion during the Watergate Era," in Bruce A. Campbell and Richard J. Trilling, eds., *Realignment in American Politics* (Austin, TX: University of Texas Press, 1980), pp. 110–131.

18. James L. Sundquist, "Whither the American Party System?—Revisited," *Political Science Quarterly* 98 (Winter 1983-84), p. 591.

19. Kathleen A. Frankovich, "Public Opinion Trends," in Gerald Pomper, et al., eds., *The Election of 1980, Reports and Interpretations* (Chatham, NJ: Chatham House, 1981), p. 115. Warren E. Miller argues that in 1980 voters *were* moving to the right. See "The Election of 1984 and the Future of American Politics," in Kay Lehman Schlozman, ed., *Elections in America* (Boston: Allen & Unwin, 1987), pp. 293–320.

20. Ibid., p. 103. See also John P. Robinson and John A. Fleishman, "Ideological Trends in American Public Opinion," *Annals of the American Academy of Political and Social Sciences* 472 (March 1984), pp. 50–71.

21. Douglas A. Hibbs, Jr., "President Reagan's Mandate From the 1980 Elections," *American Politics Quarterly* 10 (October 1982), p. 398.

22. Seymour Martin Lipset, "The Elections, the Economy and Public Opinion: 1984," *PS: Political Science & Politics* 18 (Winter 1985), p. 30.

23. Walter Dean Burnham, "The Eclipse of the Democratic Party—Revisited," *Society* 21 (July/August 1984), p. 41.

24. See John E. Chubb and Paul E. Peterson, "Realignment and Institutionalization," in Chubb and Peterson, eds., *The New Direction in American Politics* (Washington, DC: The Brookings Institution, 1985) for a discussion of Reagan and "institutional" realignment.

25. Thomas Ferguson and Joel Rogers, *Right Turn: The Decline of the Democrats and the Future of American Politics* (New York: Hill and Wang, 1986), p. 31.

26. A recent CBS/*New York Times* survey provides a timely measure of party identification. In *"Some Subtle Problems Undermine G.O.P. Victory,"* The New York Times, November 14, 1988, p. 9, Adam Clymer reports that 34 percent of those polled called themselves Republicans, while 37 percent called themselves Democrats.

27. Richard L. Berke, "Experts Say Low 1988 Turnout May Be Repeated," *The New York Times,* November 13, 1988, p. 17.

28. Walter Dean Burnham, "The Future of American Politics," in Ellis Sandoz and Cecil V

Crabb, Jr., eds., *Election '84* (New York: Mentor, 1985), p. 219.

29. E. J. Dionne, Jr., "'Solid South' Again, but Republican," *The New York Times,* November 12, 1988, Section 1, p. 17.

30. Michael Oreskes, "New Generation of Blacks Drawn Less to Democrats," *The New York Times,* October 27, 1988, p. 1.

31. Thomas E. Cavanagh and James L. Sundquist, "The New Two-Party System," in John E. Chubb and Paul E. Peterson, eds., *The New Direction in American Politics* (Washington, DC: The Brookings Institution, 1985), p. 43.

32. Ibid., p. 46.

33. E. J. Dionne, Jr., "Lure of the Young to Reagan Turns Into Capital for Party," *The New York Times,* October 31, 1988, pp. 1, 8.

34. Larry J. Sabato, *The Party's Just Begun* (Glenview, IL: Scott, Foresman, 1988), p. 118. Again, Warren E. Miller disagrees. He cites figures showing that the percentage of strong Republicans was 8 percent in 1978, 9 percent in 1980, 10 percent in 1982, and 12 percent in 1984. See "The Election of 1984 and the Future of American Politics," pp. 293–320.

35. "Exit Poll: Men, Middle Class Boost Bush," *USA Today,* November 9, 1988, p. 3A.

36. E. J. Dionne, Jr., "G.O.P. Losing Control of the National Debate," *The New York Times,* February 1, 1987, Section 4, p. 4.

37. See Everett Carll Ladd and Charles D. Hadley, *Transformations of the American Party System,* 2nd ed. (New York: W.W. Norton, 1978), and Sundquist, *Dynamics of the Party System,* revised ed.

38. Cavanagh and Sundquist, "The New Two-Party System," pp. 54, 55.

39. Everett Carll Ladd, "On Mandates, Realignments, and the 1984 Election," *Political Science Quarterly* 100 (Spring 1985), pp. 23–24.

40. Walter Dean Burnham, "The Future of American Politics," in Ellis Sandoz and Cecil V. Crabb, Jr., *Election '84* (New York: Mentor, 1985), p. 230.

41. E. J. Dionne, Jr., "Democrats, Upbeat After Atlanta, Emerge With Ambitious Strategy," *The New York Times,* July 27, 1988, p. 12.

42. James A. Barnes, "Democrats' Huge Electoral Hurdle," *National Journal* 20 (Convention Preview, June 20, 1988), p. 12.

43. Lipset, "The Elections, the Economy," p. 36.

44. Rhodes Cook, "Map Leaves Democrats Little Room for Error," *Congressional Quarterly Weekly Report* 46 (July 23, 1988), p. 2014.

45. Barnes, "Democrats' Huge Electoral," p. 12.

46. Dionne, Jr., "'Solid South' Again, but Republican," p. 17.

47. Dionne, Jr., "Democrats, Upbeat After," p. 12. See also Jack W. Germond and Jules Witcover, "Bush Has No Sure Lock on Electoral College," *National Journal* 20 (July 9, 1988), p. 1818.

48. "The Electoral College's Cold Calculus," *The New York Times,* July 8, 1988, p. 20.

49. Lipset, "The Election, the Economy," p. 34.

50. See Warren E. Miller, "The Scar of a Turbulent Decade," *Society* 21 (July/August 1984), pp. 28–29.

51. John E. Chubb and Paul E. Peterson, "Realignment and Institutionalization," in Chubb and Peterson, eds., *The New Direction in American Politics* (Washington, DC: The Brookings Institution, 1985), pp. 1–30.

52. See Thomas B. Edsall, "Race Continues to Be a Wild Card in American Politics," *The Washington Post National Weekly Edition* 5 (August 8-14, 1988), p. 12; Harry MacPherson, "How Race Destroyed the Democrats' Coalition," *The New York Times,* October 28, 1988, p. 27; Michael Oreskes, "In Racial Politics, Democrats Losing More Than Elections," *The New York Times,* November 20, 1988, Section 4, p. 5.

53. Sidney Blumenthal, *The Permanent Campaign* (Boston: Beacon Press, 1980).

54. Ibid., p. 7.

55. Walter Dean Burnham, "Elections as Democratic Institutions," in Kay Lehman Schlozman, ed., *Elections in America* (Boston: Allen & Unwin, 1987), p. 58.

56. See A. James Reichley, "The Rise of National Parties," in John E. Chubb and Paul E. Peterson, eds., *The New Direction in American Politics* (Washington, DC: The Brookings Institution, 1985), pp. 175–200.

57. Richard L. Berke, "Democrats Raise $4.8 Million in 2 Months; Party Lists the Donors," *The New York Times,* August 17, 1988, p. 14.

58. Martin P. Wattenberg, *The Decline of American Political Parties 1952-1984* (Cambridge, MA: Harvard University Press, 1986), p. 141.

59. See Sundquist, *Dynamics of the Party System,* p. 447; and David G. Lawrence and Richard Fleisher, "Puzzles and Confusions: Political Realignment in the 1980s," *Political Science Quarterly* 102 (Spring 1987), pp. 79–92. See also Reichley, "The Rise of National Parties."

60. Miller, "The Election of 1984 and the Future of American Politics," p. 308.

61. See Xandra Kayden and Eddie Mahe, Jr., *The Party Goes On* (New York: Basic Books, 1985), Chapter 7.

Afterword

The presidential election of 1988 was the latest in a series of elections that have disappointed the American people. The candidates, the level and tone of debate, the role played by the mass media—all were criticized. This state of affairs should not surprise us. It is a result of the natural progression of events since 1960.

In 1960, Democrats nominated a candidate about whom many party leaders were doubtful because of his youth and inexperience. Kennedy used primary elections to prove his mettle to party leaders. A wealthy man, Kennedy was able to finance his campaign without much help from his party. There were few serious distinctions between the two candidates on the issues. Media impressions, particularly televised impressions, were important to voters because of the heavy use of television ads and the televised debates.

These characteristics continued and intensified with the elections that followed. With the dominance of primary elections for selecting convention delegates, party leaders have lost control over presidential nominations. Relatively obscure politicians, inspired by the openness of the nomination process, seek the presidential nomination and sometimes win it (McGovern, Carter, and Dukakis, for example). Thus the public is sometimes presented with a major-party nominee about whom they know little. Voters, no longer close to parties, continue to rely heavily on the media for information on candidates and issues. With public funding of presidential elections, parties play a muted role in campaign financing. Issues play a more important role in some elections than in others. When candidates stress issues, the media tend to follow. The reverse is also true.

In Chapter 1, the distinction was made between procedural democracy and substantive democracy. Since 1960, the procedures involving presidential elections have become more open and democratic. But the substantive impact of these changes is another question. In popularizing presidential nominations and elections, we have trivialized them. We are a society heavily imbued with the mass media. Our catch phrases, our jokes, our fashions, our lifestyles, and our politics are affected by what is presented on television. Presidential elections are now TV shows. Lacking the guidance of experienced party leaders, these elections float on whatever current is fashionable. Lacking a grounding in party loyalty, voters float among candidates and issues, attaching to some in one election and to others in the next. The public, thirsting for substantive information about candidates and issues, is frustrated with the superficiality of network television coverage, but so busy that the public finds it hard to go beyond this coverage.

It is likely that we will continue to be unhappy with the process until we learn to put elections back into perspective. That perspective is best provided by strong political parties. Parties provide people with something in which they can believe, a philosophy that puts day-to-day concerns and televised images into focus. Campaigns divorced from parties are bound to be trivial.

The distaste left by the 1988 election may provide what it takes to begin the revival of political parties in the electorate of the United States. If so, then that sad campaign will have been worth it.

Index

Jones, Ruth S., 219
Jordan, Hamilton, 18
Joslyn, Richard, 6, 18, 64, 66
Judicial selection, 210–11
 campaign financing, 219
 compromise method of, 211

Kagay, Michael R., 24
Kalmbach, Herbert, 136
Kaplan, Dave, 159
Karnow, Stanley, 127
Katz, Daniel, 12
Kayden, Xandra, 240
Kean, Governor Thomas H., 202
Keefe, William, J., 99, 100, 103
Keeter, Scott, 157
Kefauver, Estes, 121
Kennedy, Edward M., 14, 139, 146–48
 Chappaquiddick accident, 146
Kennedy, John F., 6, 106, 120–25, 228
 assassination, 126
 1960 presidential election, 120–25
  Catholicism issue, 121–22, 125
  Kennedy-Nixon televised de-
   bates, 123–24
Kennedy, Robert, 86, 103, 121, 136
 1968 presidential election, 130–31
Kernell, Samuel, 194
Key, V. O., Jr., 50, 231
Kiewiet, D. Roderick, 60
Kinder, Donald R., 60, 61–62, 65, 66
King, Wayne E., 19
Kissinger, Henry, 134
Klorman, Ricardo, 60
Kritzer, Herbert, 91

Ladd, Everett Carll, 80, 102, 230, 235,
 236
Landon, Alfred M., 24
Lang, Gladys Engel, 21
Lang, Kurt, 21
Laundering money, 136
Lautenberg, Frank, 182
Lawrence, David, 122
Lawrence, Jill, 166
Lazarsfeld, Paul, 16, 59
Leach, Jim, 187
Leadership, realignment and, 229,
 237–38
Lederman, Susan S., 67–68, 108, 209
Lehnen, Robert G., 232
LeMay, General Curtis, 132
Lengle, James I., 91
Leone, Richard, 168

Levy, Mark R., 20
Lipset, Seymour Martin, 27, 29, 30,
 167, 233, 236, 237
Literacy tests, 45
Littlewood, Tom, 222–23
Local elections, 201–23
 campaign financing, 219–20
 candidates, 202
Locke, John, 1
Lock theory, Electoral College,
 236–37
Lodge, Henry Cabot, 122
 1964 presidential election, 126
Loftus, Thomas A., 203
Lorch, Robert S., 225
Luttbeg, Norman R., 53, 169
Lynch, Dotty, 19

McCafferty, Patrick, 63
McCarthy, Eugene, 19, 86, 92
 1968 presidential election, 130–31,
  133
McClelland, David C., 50
McCloskey, Herbert, 35
McClure, Robert D., 67
McConnell, Mitch, 180
McGinniss, Joe, 63, 131, 133
McGovern-Fraser Commission, 86
McGovern, George, 86, 87, 95, 102,
 107, 136, 149, 155
 1972 presidential election, 134–38
  direct-mail fund-raising, 136–37
  voter evaluation, 135–36
  voting results, 138
McIver, John P., 204
MacPherson, Harry, 238
Maddox, William S., 79
Magleby, David B., 212
Mahe, Eddie, Jr., 240
Mail registration, 46
Maintaining election, 228
Maisei, L. Sandy, 79, 87, 88, 89, 98,
 102, 228, 229
Majority party, definition of, 227–28
Making of the President 1960, The
 (White), 124
Manatt, Charles, 103
Manheim, Jarol, 11, 12, 14, 61
Mann, Thomas E., 195
Marin, Richard, 160
Markus, Gregory B., 33–34, 169
Married people, voter turnout and, 52
Maslow, Abraham, 50–51